Sacred World

Drala

In order to join heaven and earth,
May the ultimate, unchanging warrior
Always protect you.
May you have long life, freedom from sickness,
  and glory.
May your primordial confidence flourish.
May the virtuous mark of excellent windhorse
Always be uplifted.

Sacred World

The Shambhala Way to Gentleness, Bravery, and Power

SECOND EDITION

Jeremy Hayward
AND *Karen Hayward*

SHAMBHALA
Boston & London
1998

SHAMBHALA PUBLICATIONS, INC.
Horticultural Hall
300 Massachusetts Avenue
Boston, Massachusetts 02115
http://www.shambhala.com

9 8 7 6 5 4 3 2 1

FIRST SHAMBHALA EDITION
Printed in the United States of America

♾ This edition is printed on acid-free paper that meets the
American National Standards Institute z39.48 Standard.
Distributed in the United States by Random House, Inc.,
and in Canada by Random House of Canada Ltd.

Library of Congress Cataloging-in-Publication Data
Hayward, Jeremy W.
Sacred world: the Shambhala way to gentleness, bravery,
and power/Jeremy Hayward and Karen Hayward.—2nd ed.
p. cm.
Includes bibliographical references and index.
ISBN 1-57062-361-9 (pbk.)
1. Spiritual life. I. Hayward, Karen. II. Title.
BL624.H378 1998   98-19286
294.3'444—dc21   CIP

To

Chögyam Trungpa,
Dorje Dradül of Mukpo Dong,

and to

Sakyong Mipham Jampal Thrinley Dradül,
his son and successor in the ancient lineage
of Shambhala warriorship

Contents

PREFACE TO THE SECOND EDITION

THIS SECOND EDITION OF *Sacred World* has been completely revised throughout. We have altered the order of presenting the material to reflect an emphasis on simplicity and clarity. We have tightened considerably the overall presentation, while new material has been added, especially in chapters 14 through 19. As a result, we feel that the essential principles of the Shambhala teachings—how to put a spiritual but nonreligious outlook into action in the modern world—stand forth more clearly and effectively in this edition.

The need for a universal spirituality beyond particular religions has become quite well known in recent years. Especially clear is the need for training and nourishing the human heart's tremendous potential for kindness and for appreciating ordinary sacredness. Many religious teachers have begun to think and talk about this. His Holiness the Dalai Lama has begun to suggest a "secular ethics" along these lines. Yet it was in the midseventies that Chögyam Trungpa, one of the great pioneers of Buddhism in the West, first brought this idea forward as a practical possibility in his Shambhala teachings, on which this book is based. When, in 1976, he first introduced to the world the sacred path of spiritual warriorship, it was revolutionary. And these ideas have had a major, if often unacknowledged, influence on the spiritual life of the West in the past twenty years.

We wish wholeheartedly to express our appreciation to everyone who read the various manuscripts at various stages and gave us their honest responses. We especially thank our friend and editor, Emily Hilburn Sell. Finally, we would like to express our gratitude to Shambhala Publications for bringing this edition of *Sacred World* into print.

Jeremy Hayward and Karen Hayward
January 1, 1998

Sacred World

CHAPTER I

Discovering Basic Goodness

WOMEN AND MEN EVERYWHERE, at all times and in all cultures, have the capacity to wake up and live fully, passionately—to *enjoy* their lives in the deepest sense. We all have the capacity to be aware of depth and meaning in a sacred world and to live our lives with heart no matter what twists and turns they may take. And we have the capacity to care for others as well as ourselves. Yet as one Native American elder and healer, Vernon Cooper, points out: "Everybody's hurrying, but nobody's going anywhere. People aren't living, they're only existing. They're growing away from spiritual realities. These days people seek knowledge, not wisdom. Knowledge is of the past; wisdom is of the future. We're in an age now when people are slumbering. They think they're awake, yet they're really sleeping. But this is a dangerous age, the most dangerous in human history. People need to wake up."

What does it mean to "wake up," and how do we do this? Perhaps we start to wake up by rediscovering the ordinary sacredness of our life. We sometimes catch a glimpse of ordinary sacredness when we come across our familiar world freshly, as if for the first time. A sudden sound, a flash of color, a bitter smell, a gentle gesture, can penetrate our thoughts and call us from our daily rush. Photographer Freeman Patterson describes this beautifully:

> Have you ever noticed, on returning home from a holiday your increased sensitivity to the details of your home? You glance around when you step in the door, and some things in the house may actually seem unfamiliar for a few minutes. You notice that the English ivy looks spectacular in the west window, that the living room walls are more cream than ivory. You notice the light of the evening spilling across the little rug at the foot of the stairs, something you can't recall seeing before. But these moments pass quickly, familiarity is restored, everything is in its place, and you stop seeing once more.

The sun peeks through an overcast sky and momentarily cheers you up; you see a brightly colored bird, hear strange music, suddenly get a whiff of fresh manure; you are shocked by the power and energy of a thunderstorm; someone touches you affectionately. The unexpected and penetrating quality of such perceptions captures your attention and, like a fresh breeze, can wake you up to what is happening *at that very moment*—the *only* moment in which you actually live and experience your life. And these glimpses of our ordinary but sacred world, as we will see, can lead us into a deeper reality beyond the surface of our perception.

Such moments have varying degrees of intensity, from the merest flash to the deeply affecting. They happen frequently throughout our daily lives, though we usually ignore them in our rush to achieve goals that seem more important. In childhood, people often have experiences that appear simple and ordinary but that they remember as powerful and profound. They remember their perception shifting suddenly and the world opening up and becoming alive, almost as though a black-and-white sketch had turned into a van Gogh painting.

Frederick Franck, painter and Zen drawing teacher, tells about such an experience:

> On the dark afternoon—I was ten or eleven—I was walking on a country road; on my left a patch of curly kale, on my right some yellowed Brussels sprouts. I felt a snowflake on my cheek, and from far away in the charcoal-gray sky I saw the slow approach of a snowstorm. I stood still. Some flakes were now falling around my feet. A few melted as they hit the ground. Others stayed intact. Then I heard the falling of the snow, with the softest hissing sound.
>
> I stood transfixed, listening . . . and knew what can never be expressed: that the natural is supernatural . . . that what is outside happens in me, that outside and inside are inseparable.

Young children are less caught up in thinking *about* their world. More often than adults, they are able to perceive their world *directly,* without the barrier of language, and to feel the basic goodness of that world. And sometimes as adults we can recall that way of being. Jeremy remembers the period in his life—he was about seven years old—when he actually felt the transition between the awareness of the world's sacredness and the loss of that awareness. On one occasion, he was lying in bed having recovered from the flu.

I woke up that morning feeling better. The fever had broken, but I was to stay in bed for at least one more day. My mother propped me up on some pillows and gave me a puzzle to do, but I was not interested in it and pushed it aside. I lay quietly, relaxed and at ease, nothing on my mind, looking around the room. I glanced down at the blanket on my bed—it was made of soft orange wool, hand-knitted in a kind of honeycomb pattern. The blanket seemed to glow and to stand out in 3-D. I felt a wave of love for the blanket that extended out to the whole room. Looking around, I realized that the whole room was glowing in the same way and seemed, too, to be soft and alive, and radiating love back to me. I remember thinking that this is how the world *really* is. As soon as I noticed this "perception of the heart," it began to fade and was replaced by a sense of sadness and loss. By again relaxing and deliberately trying not to think about it, I could bring it back, but soon I lost it completely. During this period of my life, I often found myself in situations in which I noticed this way of perceiving the world and its sacredness and could feel the sadness of its fading.

Perhaps, even now, you can recall such moments of awareness of basic goodness, or "perception of the heart." But as we grow up, almost all of us, in modern society, lose the ability to perceive the world directly, and we forget that this ability even exists. This loss is tragic, but it is *not* a natural and necessary stage of growing up, as much child development theory suggests. The rational intellect, which begins to awaken at about the age of eight, does not *need* to displace perception of the heart but can complement it so that the two modes of awareness—rational thought and intuitive perception—can enrich each other. And one of the purposes of this book is to show you how you may recover your perception of the heart.

The world can penetrate us if we let it. If we relax our habitual anxieties for a moment and all our ideas about the world, all our interpretations, and just let ourselves see and hear it as it is, then we can feel the living energy of the world. We connect ourselves directly to it. This experience of direct connection might seem extremely simple, but it can affect us profoundly. Yet as Freeman Patterson says, "these moments pass quickly, familiarity is restored, everything is in its place, and you stop seeing once more." To restore our sense of sacredness in the world, we need to learn how to open to these moments beyond the familiar.

Basic Goodness Is the Inherent Nature of the Sacred World

All humans, no matter what their racial or cultural background, are capable of knowing and living within sacredness. This is our birthright, beyond all dogma. It is an expression of the *basic goodness* of the world. At the most basic level of our being, we have everything we need to celebrate our lives on this planet. The world supports us. When we stand on the earth, we are held upright—usually, we don't sink in quicksand. When we breathe, we breathe oxygen, which gives life—usually, we don't breathe noxious gases. When we eat, we nourish our bodies with good food grown in the earth—usually, if we pay attention, we don't eat poison. When we bathe, we clean ourselves with water, fresh and pure—

usually, we don't bathe in a chemical dump. The earth cares for us. And *if we care for it,* it will continue to care for us.

The world is multilayered and rich. It has unfathomable depth and vastness and wisdom. Everything in the world is alive and connected to everything else in a way that is vital to the world's existence. This harmony is basic goodness. Our earth hangs in the sky and turns and moves. The sky rains on the earth, and trees grow. Trees help make air, and animals breathe. Birds fly in the air, flowers attract bees. Bodies have livers and hearts, brains and nerves and muscles, teeth and claws, and all the rest. Hurricanes have their own power and energy, as do tulips and mosquitoes, and maybe even the gods.

We have perceptions and awareness, so that all of this beautiful and powerful world comes within our experience. Everything works together. This is basic goodness. It is very basic, yet utterly *real* beyond all politics, mythologies, or religious theorizing. It is healthy, direct, and so ordinary that we usually don't think twice about it. If we actually allow ourselves to trust this world, we can start to relax and welcome it into our lives rather than tightening ourselves against unknown hostilities. We can feel it, see it, hear it, open all our senses to its profundity.

The basic goodness of our world is not the "good" side of a world divided into good and bad. When we divide the world in that way—even in our minds—we automatically put conditions on everything around us so that it is good if it fulfills our conditions and bad if it does not. Basic goodness is unconditioned because it does not depend on any limitations or boundaries, or on conditions of any kind at all. It is like a rock over which a stream is flowing. The rock is there whether the stream is warm or cold, whether it flows quickly or slowly or not at all. Basic goodness is just there—like the rock—no matter what is happening, how we are feeling, or how we are judging our situation as "good" or "bad." Basic goodness has nothing to do with "feeling good." Nevertheless, in order to relax and connect directly with this world, we need a deep trust in its basic goodness.

The world's basic goodness is even more basic than the forms we experience with our senses. It is felt in the open, creative space that permeates and illuminates everything. Without this space, you couldn't see or hear or move or even exist. It is the most basic of any goodness you can think of. It is before thought or the birth of anything. Everything is created from this and exists in this. Each one of us is permeated by this creative living space. In it, we live and move and have our existence. Living space is not an abstract idea; it is as close and intimate to us as water to a fish.

This sense of basic goodness is hard to think about, but you can feel it. You can discover it by allowing space to be in and around the details of your perceptions. When people are crowded together, you usually don't see space or details—you see a crowd. When sounds are crowded together, you hear a noise. When your thoughts are crowded together, you get a headache. Your world closes in on you. You feel claustrophobic, which is basic fear. But when you see the physical space around an object, then you can *see* the object clearly and brightly. You can see the details. When there's the space of silence around sound, you can actually *hear* each word. When you allow space into your mind, your thoughts become illuminated—as if you turned on the light in a dim room. If you can feel the space in and around your perceptions, suddenly, magically, the world *is there* in all its reality, as it is—genuine and good and sacred. Experiencing this space of basic goodness can change your perceptions.

Even small glimpses of the ordinary sacred world, if we pay attention to them, quickly show us that the world has fathomless depth that extends vastly beyond the surface of ordinary human perception. Renowned Buddhist teacher Chögyam Trungpa speaks of it in this way:

> The realm of perception is limitless, so limitless that perception itself is primordial, unthinkable, beyond thought. There are so many perceptions that they are beyond imagination. There are a vast number of sounds. There are sounds that you have never heard. There are sights and colors that you have never seen. There are feelings that you have never experienced before. There are endless fields of perception.
>
> Because of the extraordinary vastness of perception, you have the possibilities of communicating with the depth of the world—the world of sight, the world of sound—the greater world. In other words, your sense faculties give you access to possibilities of deeper perception. Beyond ordinary perception, there is super-sound, super-smell and super-feeling existing in your state of being. These can be experienced only by training yourself in the depth of meditation, which clarifies any confusion or cloudiness and brings out the precision, sharpness, and wisdom of perception—the nowness of your world.

Basic Goodness Is the Inherent Nature of All Beings

Since we are all part of the sacred world, we also possess basic goodness, hidden deep within our conditioned, rigid, narrow ways of believing and acting—like a jewel hidden in a heap of garbage, as a traditional analogy goes. Our basic goodness also does not exist in contrast with something "bad" in us. It is not something that would dawn on us if only we finally weeded out all of our undesirable habits; or figured out just how our parents went wrong in raising us; or became thin, beautiful, and rich; or attained our ideal of a spiritual person. Basic goodness is, *already,* our inherent nature.

The unconditioned basic goodness of humans is recognized at the inner heart of almost all spiritual traditions. This profound vision of human nature is summed up succinctly by the sixteenth-century Confucian Wang Yangming: "Every person has a sage within his breast. It is just that people do not fully believe in this sage and bury it away." And the eighteenth-century Taoist sage Liu I-Ming says, "At first, human nature is basically good. There is originally no distinction between the sage and the ordinary person. It is because of the energy of accumulated habits that there comes to be a difference between sages and ordinary people."

In the Buddhist teaching, our basic goodness is known as our buddha nature. The word *buddha* literally means "awake." As the great contemporary Tibetan yogi and teacher Ugyen Tulku Rinpoche says:

> Buddha nature is present in ourselves as well as in everyone else, without any exception whatsoever. . . . Our buddha nature . . . is called empty . . . wakefulness. The empty aspect, the essence, is like space that pervades everywhere. But inseparable from this empty quality is a natural capacity to cognize and perceive, which is basic wakefulness. Buddha nature is called self-existing because it is not made out of any-

thing or created by anyone. . . . This self-existing wakefulness is present in all beings without a single exception.

All humans have the potential to wake up in the moment, to discover the basic goodness or buddha nature of themselves and the sacred world, but there are obstacles to doing this. Buddhists acknowledge the exertion and commitment to being genuine that are necessary in order for our basic goodness to blossom. They acknowledge the dross, the tendency to dualistic thinking in terms of "good" and "bad," "me" and "you," that covers our buddha nature. To Buddhists, however, the dross, the garbage, is like manure, which can be transformed into food for a beautiful flower bed, rather than something that forever keeps us from our basic goodness. Ugyen Tulku Rinpoche continues:

> The buddha nature is already present as the nature of our own mind, just like the unchanging brilliance of the sun shining in the sky. But due to our dualistic thinking, this sun of the buddha nature is not evident; we don't see it. . . . The conceptual thoughts we have day and night obscure our buddha nature, just like the sun in the sky is momentarily covered by clouds and seems to be obscured. Due to the passing clouds of ignorance we do not recognize buddha nature.

Our basic goodness, then, is usually obscured by the clouds of our confusion, the "passing clouds of ignorance." But we can use those clouds to help wake ourselves up and allow the depth and wisdom of the world to penetrate our awareness. We'll be talking more specifically in later chapters about how we can begin to do this.

Basic Goodness Brings Cooperation and Compassion

There is yet a further aspect to basic goodness. We all want to find meaning in our lives, to find value and depth. We yearn to find something real—to feel and experience intensely and wholly. When the yearning for genuineness is strong enough, we want to do something about it—to seek a different way of living. This is the essence of spiritual training. Yet however precisely we try to define what we want *personally,* another unspoken longing nonetheless remains. The longing is for something deeper than the dogmas of the numerous spiritual, healing, and religious traditions. It touches a commonalty in people's actual experience that goes beyond mere personal development. It is a search for community—community with other humans as well as community with all species that share the earth as home. Many of us long to build a good human society that cherishes the earth and all that live on it—a society that acknowledges and nourishes sacredness and basic human goodness.

Basic goodness is expressed in the fundamental ability of all humans to cooperate—that is, in their ability to join together to build a good human society. Because we all share the same earth and the same living and creative space of basic goodness, our lives are intertwined and connected at a profound level. The feeling of unselfishness that can guide us at times to simple, or even extreme, acts of generosity or altruism stems from this interweaving of our existence. We usually take an immediate interest in the happiness of only a small circle of family, friends, and others, but our interest in the well-being of others *can* extend far beyond. Our circle of caring naturally extends to total strangers, for example, when we see reports of wars or disasters on television. People are frequently willing to risk their lives when they see that the life of a complete stranger is in danger. This fundamental caring and intelligence has guided us to cooperate with each other, to build houses and highways, to grow and eat wholesome food, and to create and sustain good human societies. Without the decency and courtesy that spring from our basic goodness, ordinary human community would be impossible.

Personal spiritual training means nothing if it is not intimately concerned with caring for others. And this means that, in our modern world, spiritual maturity must include caring for our society and for the planet we share; it must be deeply concerned with creating a good human society. Such a society is a real, practical possibility. A growing number of people in the world now see the urgent need for such a society and are working individually and in groups toward bringing it about, each in their own way.

Shambhala Teachings of Warriorship

To live a life founded on the understanding and direct experience of basic goodness, and to build a society on that foundation, is to be truly human. But to be truly human in ordinary life requires a sense of bravery, daring to live genuinely, even in the face of obstacles like fear, doubt, depression, or external aggression. That is, to live genuinely, you have to be a warrior, to have the courage to know who you are, through and through. Whether you are happy or depressed, young or old, neurotic or sane, you can recognize the inherent nature of goodness that is more profound and enduring than all these ephemeral ups and downs. When you are authentic, genuinely being just who you are, you can be open to that basic goodness in yourself and others, even when it seems obscure or buried. Being a warrior means never giving up on anyone, including yourself.

This ideal of spiritual warriorship is the basis of the Shambhala teachings of Chögyam Trungpa, who was widely known as one of the first and most senior Tibetan teachers to bring Tibetan Buddhist practice to the West. Born and trained in Tibet, he was forced by the Chinese communist invasion to escape over the Himalaya Mountains in 1959. He led friends and followers in an extraordinary adventure of danger and companionship, described in his autobiography, *Born in Tibet.* He traveled to England in 1963 and studied Western philosophy and comparative religion at Oxford University. There, he learned to speak English as fluently as a native and developed a firsthand understanding of Western culture. In 1970, he settled in the United States, with his English wife, and taught throughout North America and Europe until his death in 1987.

Chögyam Trungpa saw that many people in North America and Europe had a great hunger to discover an inner path of development in their lives but were cut off from that possibility because of their experiences of "religion" or their belief that the modern scientific worldview no longer accommodated religious insights. In response, in 1977, he began to teach the Shambhala path of sacred warriorship—how to live one's life in a profound and enriching way.

This book is based on those teachings of sacred warriorship. We will take a journey through ordinary experience into the sacred world. We will try to uncover the obstacles to "waking up" and living in sacredness. And we will explore specific practices of how to work with those obstacles and claim our fundamental human birthright.

CHAPTER 2

Trust

Trust in Reality

*T*HE SACRED WORLD is always already present, calling for our attention and interest. We can learn to trust it and relax into its wisdom. Basic trust is not trusting *in* some belief or some idea that the world will help us. It is simply trusting the world, as it is. It is very much like breathing, which is your very nature. When you breathe out, you trust that the next breath will come in. You don't think about it or wonder about it; you trust. When you take a step, you trust that the earth will support you. When you eat, you trust that your stomach will digest the food. When you go to sleep at night, you trust that you'll wake up in the morning. You also trust that at some point in your life you will die, which need not be so frightening if you trust the basic goodness of the world. This is basic trust.

To be trusting *is* your basic goodness, trusting not only the basic functions of breathing, eating, and walking but the sacredness of your whole world. Such trust grows as you discover that the world beyond your basic fear is intelligent and living. There is wisdom in the world that is there beyond our control or attempts to figure it out. There is energy and awareness in the environment that we can tune in to, a natural order that we can see directly and appreciate. We are part of this wisdom, this energy, and this order. Standing back, looking at it, trying to figure out how to control it doesn't help much. Being immersed in, connected to, and permeated by this world leads us further.

Trust is making a connection with this reality, with the rocks and trees and birds, with our bodies and minds, with the sky and the earth and all the elements. We stand on the earth, but we are also standing in the sky, walking, eating, breathing in it. This sky is full and vibrating. We are not immersed in an unfeeling, void, stupid universe but in one that is deep and rich. We can trust this. We don't have to make up this world or invent anything or cook up situations to feel real. We can afford to take delight and relax into the world, to let ourselves feel at ease.

Learning to Be

Your basic trust relaxes you and lets you *be*. It is simple, unremarkable, ordinary experience, but at the same time, it is very powerful; it has a quality of fulfillment. Like the vast, profound, blue sky that is itself free from clouds yet accommodates everything, from the small white fluffy clouds of a summer's afternoon to the violent cumulus of a thunderstorm, you can let yourself be with whatever you are feeling.

Trusting in this way makes it possible to stop gritting our teeth and steeling ourselves to live through the pain, whether it be imaginary or real. We don't have to crawl back into our stale, dead, "safe" shell. When we relax, it is possible to enter "no-man's-land" without grasping or holding on, to diffuse the aggression we feel toward ourselves, and to feel the moisture and nourishment that gentleness brings. The entire panorama of our mind—our shakiness, uncertainty, fear, hope, excitement—can *be* there and play itself out without our constant interpretation, guesswork, and judgments. This is such a relief.

Because we are part of the wisdom of the world, our moods—elation, depression, boredom, whatever—are all trustworthy. They are part of our being and our journey and give us feedback about how to go on. We can listen to their messages to us. You don't need to regard some as healthy and good and others as bad and unworthy. Depression, or a dull, numb state of mind, is just as trustworthy and intelligent as elation. Our constant level of stress, tension, and struggle comes from lack of trust, but even these states are trustworthy.

To trust is to be free from the doubt of "being in two minds." Fundamentally, you *are* of only one mind, so you can be fundamentally free from doubt. Basic trust is unconditional: there is no polarizing distrust. When you trust, you drop the good-versus-bad, perfect-versus-imperfect tug-of-war that conditions your view of yourself and the world. You don't look to a belief system for confirmation or condemnation. You trust whatever occurs at any given moment because you have discovered that you yourself are profoundly trustworthy.

It is hard to trust our moods because we so rarely allow ourselves to experience them fully. Usually, when we are happy, we want it never to end, and we are simultaneously afraid of losing it. So we try to hold on to our happiness, which keeps us from experiencing it fully. When we are bored, we usually try to entertain ourselves because boredom feels empty and threatening. When we are depressed, we don't accept that it may be an intelligent response to the situation at hand but instead consider it unpleasant, something to get out of.

These moods tend to become threatening because we *perceive* them as threatening. If we try to deny or get rid of a mood, it only becomes stronger. But if we give up our resistance and doubt, by realizing that the mood is trustworthy, then we truly make friends with it. We can allow ourselves actually to feel fully.

We don't need to check constantly on whether we are feeling the right thing or not. Constantly checking up on yourself implies that you lack trust in your genuine being. It cuts you off from the world. To develop basic trust, you have to give up wondering how far you have come and how far you can go. It means giving up measuring yourself against your own expectations or others' achievements. It means giving up assessing yourself against any standard at all, even your own.

We do not know the depth and breadth of our world, and we cannot know all the answers, or even all the questions. When we open our minds beyond our cultural myths and theories, we realize that the universe is mysterious; we have no idea what is really true. We can only trust our basic goodness and the sacredness of the world. This can bring a sense of great joy and relief: we don't have to pretend to know all the answers anymore. We feel the boundary of our familiar world, and we do not shrink back from that which is outside of it—that which is strange to us.

As Seng-ts'an says in "On Trust in the Heart":

Clinging to this or to that beyond measure
The heart trusts to by-paths that lead it astray.
Let things take their own course; know that the Essence
Will neither go nor stay;

Let your nature blend with the Way and wander in it
free from care.

Instead of working so hard to get everything in your life
just right, when you learn to trust, you can let the intelligence
of basic goodness determine the course of your life. It brings
great relief and joy to be able to relax in this way. People
familiar with the Australian Aboriginals have said that, on a
walkabout in the Australian outback, each morning they
wake up at dawn and dance and sing with delight and
humor, like young children. Even when there is no food or
water to be seen for miles around, they will sing, "Oh, what
a wonderful day it is today! What shall we do?" as if they
had never seen the sunrise before and had not a care in the
world. Because they are able to trust, they have an intimate
love for every plant and insect that lives in that desert and an
intimate relationship with the gods of the land. They never
go without sufficient food and water to sustain themselves,
though they may often be hungry and thirsty, and when they
find enough for the day, they spend the rest of the day playing
together, having ceremonies, and celebrating the beautiful sacred world they love so much.

Even when your body is not working according to your
idea of "health," you can still trust your fundamental well-
being, wisdom, and steadiness. A true doctor knows that *she*
does not heal you. She can only help your body tune in to its
own wisdom and heal itself. When we are free from doubt,
we, too, can trust our body to heal itself. We often experience
this level of trust in life-threatening situations, but it is a basic
state of mind that is always there for us.

The story of the scientist Ivan Pavlov, founder of behavior-
ism, illustrates this level of basic trust. Early in the century,

before the time of antibiotics, Pavlov was dying of a massive systemic infection. He lay in the hospital close to death, and the doctors could do nothing for him. He quietly asked his assistant to go to the riverbank where he used to play as a boy, fill a pail with warm mud, and bring it to him. The assistant discreetly brought the mud to Pavlov, who spent a long time kneading it as he had done as a child. The fever broke, and he recovered. Pavlov trusted his intuition that he needed to play with the mud; he trusted his memory of being contented by the riverbank as a child; he trusted his body as he lay there kneading the mud, being with the mud. Simply put, Pavlov trusted his world.

Physician and author Larry Dossey reports another story of basic trust. In July 1989, six men made a trek across Antarctica. One of the men, Keizo Funatsu, became separated from the others in a blinding snowstorm. His only chance for survival, he knew, was to bury himself in the snow and wait to be found. He dug a pit and settled in. "Very few people have that kind of experience, lost in the blizzard," he later recounted. "I said to myself, 'Settle down, try and enjoy this.' In my snow ditch I truly felt Antarctica. With the snow and quiet covering me, I felt like I was in my mother's womb. I could hear my heart beat—boom, boom, boom—like a small baby's. My life seemed very small compared to nature, to Antarctica." The next morning, Keizo heard his teammates calling his name, and he stood up, unhurt, joyfully shouting, "I am alive!"

Dossey comments, "Completely covered with snow, Keizo Funatsu had realized that to do anything would have meant almost certain death. He had simply to be, not do." He didn't resist the situation he was in by giving in to fear or panic. You may not find yourself in this extreme situation, but the fact is that whenever we are in any difficult situation, whether it be grief over losing someone or our own general unhappiness, the advice we usually hear is to "Keep busy. Do something." Dossey continues:

> There is an aspect of experiences such as [this] that runs counter to the modern belief that real change requires robust effort. . . . [It] was an attitude of watching, waiting, silence, and emptiness—ways of being, not doing. . . . Many people who experience sudden breakthroughs in health frequently speak of an inner attitude of accepting the universe on its own terms—not dictating what ought or should happen—in spite of the dreadful circumstances they are enduring at the time. . . . This is not a self-effacing, passive, giving-up stance; it is one of attunement and alignment with what they perceive to be the inherent rightness of all that is.

When we trust profoundly, we relax our iron grip on ourselves and our own viewpoint. We see other sides of issues. We see conflicts and successes from other people's point of view as well as our own, and we see our own lives within the larger scope of society. In turn, we see our society within the context of the global community and feel the place of humans on earth in the context of all of life and of the life of earth itself.

This change of viewpoint is very similar to the experience that many astronauts have reported. Soaring way above, they see the whole planet earth, alone and fragile. They see the continents, the major mountain ranges, the oceans and weather patterns. They see no lines or colored patches delineating nations, as appear on globes and maps. Rather, they report a profound sense of the unity of life on earth and of their interconnectedness with all beings on the earth. For many astronauts, this new vision has transformed their lives.

Trusting Whatever Occurs

Trusting the basic functions of breathing, eating, and walking is natural. But trust is also recognizing that the entire world is sacred and whole and feeling that you're part of this harmony. This *should* be natural, but we've been taught to be wary and suspicious—to look at the world as wild and hostile, uncaring, mindless, and dangerous. If we experience it this way, it's because we haven't made a real connection to it in all its details. We don't know how it looks or smells or functions. If we do anything blindly, without awareness, it could be dangerous. We can slip on a stair in our own home, for example, and break a leg.

Allowing ourselves the space to relax and *be,* to stay open and be present without struggle, does take exertion, however. Even being present while you are just sitting and looking out the window takes exertion. Lack of exertion, or laziness, means not paying attention but running around speedily and mindlessly. Nor does trust mean just sitting around believing that the world will support us. When we put out energy by paying attention to our world, being curious about it, and responding to it, then we begin to find that the world responds to us. When we put out, something comes back, but *only* if we put out.

Suppose we decide to go canoeing. If we just jump into a canoe on a windy day, with heavy shoes and no life jacket on, not knowing how to swim properly or even paddle properly, the canoe may tip over, and we may be in a heap of trouble. But if we respect the power of the water and the wind, we can wear our life jacket and learn how to be present in that situation safely and mindfully, paying attention to all the details. Then we can expand our awareness to really making a connection with that world. The waves lift the boat, and you can relax with the rhythm as the wind pushes you faster than you can propel yourself. You can feel the energies of the trees along the shore and see luminous colors in the rocks. The rocks have different personalities, and some feel enlivened with presence. All sorts of animals may appear—beaver, ducks, loons, fish, turtles, deer—but instead of being wild and afraid, they seem gentle and curious.

This doesn't only happen in Disney movies. It is the real world. As you relax into being there quietly and surrender your fear, your perception shifts, and suddenly you connect fully with the energies around you, your mind and body work together, and you feel included. Then you find yourself immersed in a dance. Energy goes out and comes back in a circle, and you can respond with it rather than react against it. Even in a storm, you would know just what to do. You could feel what the wind tells you.

Messages from the World

When we trust the world, relax our tight hold on ourselves, and pay attention to the details of reality in the moment, something magical happens. You start to notice strange occurrences and realize that the world speaks to you; it reflects your trust. You get definite feedback from your environment. Messages come back, sometimes as painful reminders of your lack of awareness and sometimes as joyful confirmation that you are managing to stay open. You start to have an actual exchange with this alive, vibrating world of energy and awareness. Sometimes, this response is direct and fast, with an obvious cause and effect: your mind is speeding along, you don't pay attention, and you cut your finger; or you're angry with your friend and yell at him and he yells back. Maybe you forgot to put gas in the car and it runs out. At other times, the response of the world may seem mysterious, with no obvious cause-and-effect connection to our action, yet it is clear and precise—and obvious if we are awake. Perhaps you forgot to set your alarm and a crow helpfully wakes you up at exactly the right time.

Many years ago, Jeremy was in the middle of a dispute within an organization of which he was a director. He had written a first draft of an angry and outspoken letter that he intended to circulate. When he turned on his computer to write the final draft, the screen flatlined. He says, "I was in too much anguish and speed to wait the week it would take for the computer to be fixed, so I actually bought a new computer. Later it seemed that sending the letter had not been helpful overall. Only much later did I realize with something of a shock that, in the broken computer, I had received a very clear message to wait."

Sometimes we can feel the auspicious quality, the deeper meaning, of coincidences. They are always messages pointing to a bigger picture. We do not mean "messages" in the sense of giving us specific information about what to do next. Rather, they are messages that tell us when we are actually tuning in to reality rather than being lost in a dream world, messages showing us how to go forward harmoniously, sometimes by simply saying "Wake up!" Karen describes a couple of humorous messages:

I was sitting outside thinking about how helpful, but also how difficult, it can be to go toward emotion rather than running from it—about leaning into these "painful points." I looked up and saw a porcupine, full of painful points, casually wander into my yard in the city, totally relaxed and carefree. It wasn't in the slightest bothered by the dog barking at it or by my presence. In fact, it walked *toward me* and settled down to munch on the grass. I had never before seen a porcupine in my yard in the five years I have lived here. I thought that it might be even harder to lean into *those* painful points. A few nights before, I was walking down the hall in my house feeling a lot of confusion. Suddenly, I was struck in the head by a bat, which the cat must have brought in. My first thought was, "Well, I must have 'bats in the belfry'!"

In both cases, the literalness of the coincidences made me laugh and lighten up. The messages weren't serious or profound, particularly. But my mind was very literally reflected, and there was an exchange with the environment. They reminded me to pay more attention to the magic and richness and humor of the world instead of dwelling in my mind when it's little and solemn.

Messages happen all the time and can be quite ordinary. We only think they are strange when we're not used to trusting that such things do happen. Or we might ignore them as nothing much and just say, "So what?" If we ignore a situation, or try to manipulate it to our advantage, then we violate our relationship of trust with the world, and we lose the ability to hear those messages from reality. But when we do trust in those messages, the world is responsive and can be surprising. It was just such a message that first guided Jeremy to America from England, in 1965. He recalls:

> I was trying to decide whether to make a career change from physics, the subject of the doctorate I was just finishing, to molecular biology, which was all the rage then. I felt an urgent need for change, more out of a longing for a larger world than from a driving interest in biology. After speaking to the director of the molecular biology laboratory in Cambridge, I hesitated for weeks. One day, I was wandering along the street, wondering what to do and trying to find *some* way to resolve the decision, when I came upon a traffic jam. Right there, stopped in front of me, was the bus to the molecular biology laboratory. Without further thought, I stepped on the bus, rode to the laboratory, and told the director I wanted to make the change. A year later, I was on my way to America with a research fellowship in molecular biology. I had planned to return to England in two years but was kept in America by a series of smaller coincidences until, in 1970, I met Chögyam Trungpa and stayed.

Often the stories of how people come across the spiritual teaching that really touches their heart are about coincidences, or messages, like this one. Often, too, we hear such stories in relation to changes of career or how someone met a partner who brings deep meaning to his life. And it is not just in the large moments of our lives that we can connect, or not connect, with our world. Some days, everything we do seems to work out, and everything we say seems appropriate.

We are in tune with our environment, with people, with our world. Other days, nothing seems to go right, and the world gives us feedback that we are missing the point. If we pay attention to these small details of our lives, we will find that they are tiny cracks opening into a living and meaningful world. Of course, trusting your world doesn't mean that you will get everything you want or be taken care of without effort on your part. It is not trusting that you will always find pleasure and avoid pain. It is trusting the wisdom of *reality*. You discover how to make connections with the sacredness of the real world. And the point is that the real world is alive and well and *responds* to your openness.

CHAPTER 3
—————

Opening to Intuitive Wisdom

W HEN WE TRUST THE WORLD and relax into it, we begin to see that our world is rich and vivid. It may not necessarily be nice or pleasant, but it is a living world, and it *wakes us up*. And as we wake up, we feel the detailed textures and energies of our thoughts, our emotions, our perceptions, and our environment. Our thoughts, emotions, perceptions of color, sound, and so on change every moment. Every thought appears to our mind and then goes, and likewise every emotion, though some may stick around longer than others. And the world around us—the world of color, sound, taste, smell, and sensation—that, too, is constantly changing. No matter how hard we try to hold on to a good feeling of being in love, or the sight of a beautiful sunset or a forest, or the companionship of an animal, all these change.

Those thoughts, colors, sounds, and so on are all filled and surrounded with living space. If there were no space, there could be no change, and it would be a dead world. The space within our thoughts and perceptions is so obvious that we usually take it completely for granted. If a group of people is asked to make a list of all that they are experiencing at that moment, very few people mention space. Yet there is space outside us, and space within our minds, and eventually we may discover that the space outside and the space inside are not two different spaces.

The open space of experience is neither purely subjective, within our own minds, nor purely objective, within the external world. It transcends even these distinctions. The sixteenth-century Confucian sage Wang Shihuai—who, like all Chinese scholar-sages, was also strongly influenced by Taoism—writes:

> The name "mind" is imposed on the essence of phenomena. The name "phenomena" is imposed on the functioning of mind. In reality there is just one single thing, without any distinctions of inside and outside and this and that. What fills the universe is both all mind and all phenomena.
>
> Students wrongly accept as mind the petty, compartmentalized mind that is vaguely located within them and wrongly accept as phenomena the multiplicity of things and events mixing together outside of their bodies. Therefore they pursue the outer or they concentrate on the inner and do not integrate the two. This will never be sufficient for entering the Path.

That living space that pervades all experience is the basic goodness of the world, of which we spoke in chapter 1. The complete openness of basic goodness is pervasive in all phenomena, like space. That space can be experienced directly because, as we said, it is an intimate part of every moment of our life. Yet it is very hard to grasp it by conceptual thinking. It is the totality of our experience, felt directly, before we divide that experience into little bits through our conceptual

thinking. All the spiritual, philosophical, and religious traditions have been able only to point to it and suggest it. As
Buddhist master Seng-ts'an said, "The more you talk about
it, the more you think about it, the further from it you go."

Physical and Mental Are the Same Energy

If we are to overcome the split between sacredness and the
ordinary world we experience with our senses, it is important
to understand that the physical world arises, no less than the
mental, within the open space of unconditioned goodness. All
that we experience—thoughts, sights, sounds, and so on—
appears and disappears within the space of unconditioned
goodness. As an analogy, we could think of the way salt appears as crystals in a rock pool when the seawater evaporates,
and dissolves back again when the pool is replenished by rain.
The entire physical and mental universes—energy and
awareness—arise together within basic goodness, like two
different kinds of crystals in the rock pool, and only *appear* to
be separate. At the most subtle level of experience, physical
and mental *are the same energy*. As it says in *Zen Dust:* "The
entire world is your eyes; the entire universe is your complete
body; the entire universe is your luminance; the entire universe is within your own luminance."

In modern society, we act as if our minds and bodies were
separate. The modern belief that mind is somehow localized
in the head is very deep-rooted. Most people have no idea
that their mind fills their body and radiates out beyond its
surface. Awareness and feeling are in our bodies, which include our brain but are obviously more than *just* our brain.
In *Healing and the Mind,* TV host Bill Moyers interviewed
neuroscientist Candace Pert. One exchange went like this:

> MOYERS: You're saying that our emotions are stored in our body?
>
> PERT: Absolutely. Didn't you realize that?
>
> MOYERS: No, I didn't realize that. I'm not even sure what I mean by that. What's *down* there?
>
> PERT: You're still thinking it's your brain, but it's the wisdom of the body. Intelligence is in every cell of your body. The mind is not confined to the space above the neck. The mind is throughout the brain and body.

Like many modern men and women, Moyers so identified his mind as being in his head that he thought his body is "down there." He seemed to have no idea that the body could be the location of anything having to do with mind or that it could be a source of feeling and joy—so long as we *can* feel it. There is in reality no fundamental split between mind and body, between the physical and the mental.

Masters of Chi Gong, T'ai Chi Ch'uan, Zen swordsmanship, and Aikido, among others, have demonstrated physical effects of the spiritual energy, *ki* or *chi*, as it is called. For example, in a scene from *Ring of Fire,* a documentary video by two British brothers, Lawrence Blair and Lorne Blair, who spent ten years traveling and filming in the volcanic island chain of Indonesia, one of the brothers went for treatment of an eye infection to an acupuncturist in Djakarta, the capital of Java. After successfully treating him, the acupuncturist demonstrated his chi. First, he touched the hand of one of the brothers, and after a brief pause, the brother pulled his hand away quickly after feeling a sudden burst of intense heat. The doctor repeated the effect with one of the camerawomen who was especially skeptical. After a pause, she, too, pulled her hand away with a look of shock and delight on her face. The doctor explains that anyone can generate this energy if they practice "meditation every day."

The demonstration ended when the doctor crumpled a newspaper supplied by the film crew and held his outstretched arm with the hand several inches from the newspaper. The arm became rigid, there was a pause, and one could see the concentration on the face of the doctor. There was a sudden jerk in his body, and the paper burst into flames, merely through the energy of the chi projected from his arm. The astonished look on the faces of the Blair brothers and the film crew, quite apart from the humbleness and almost childlike candidness of the doctor, leaves little doubt about the authenticity of this scene. The doctor emphasized that it is important in working with this energy not to have negative emotions and aggression because this energy is neutral and could be harmful to others rather than beneficial if it is misused.

Interactions between Consciousness and the Physical World

Interactions between consciousness and the physical world have been investigated as well, for more than fifteen years, at the Aeronautical Engineering Laboratories of Princeton University. A special laboratory has been studying "anomalous" phenomena—that is, phenomena that do not fit into the current scientific view of the world. The researchers have found evidence that suggests a pervasive quality of consciousness throughout space and the ability of this consciousness to affect physical reality. Robert Jahn, the professor of aeronautical engineering who set up the laboratory, conducted the experiments under the strictest scientific controls. The book *Margins of Reality,* which Jahn wrote with Brenda Dunne, the laboratory manager, demonstrates incontrovertible evidence for the ability of participants, simply by their intention, to affect the outcome of a physical event, such as the pattern of Ping-Pong balls falling through a set of pins or the sequence of numbers shown on the display of a random-number generator. Jahn and Dunne found that the most successful participants were those who reported some kind of empathetic feeling of identification with the machines, who in some strange way felt interconnected with the machines.

So chi manifests as both spiritual and physical power, and some scientists are beginning to accept that such a field of power may exist. Scientists have long known, theoretically, that what we normally think of as vacuum—completely empty space—is actually not an empty, passive container but is full and dynamic and interacting with all that is within it. Physicists tell us that within a thimbleful of "empty" space, there is enough energy to boil away all the world's oceans! And this "empty-space" energy—"zero-point energy," as physicists call it—has profound implications for our world of appearance: without this energetic aspect to space, atoms would be unstable, and our entire world would collapse. Physicist Harold Puthoff, director of the Institute for Advanced Studies at Austin, Texas, suggests that chi may be a manifestation of this vacuum energy and is conducting experiments to demonstrate the physical reality of chi. Again, Wang Shihuai writes, "The great ultimate [the Tao] is our true nature; it is the primordial. When it moves it gives birth to the creative force [chi] which from then on belongs to material energy, to the temporal. True nature can give birth to material energy: true nature is not outside of material energy."

The most obvious manifestation of this very subtle physical-mental energy, which some call chi or ki, is the phenomenal world that all sane, ordinary people experience—what we could call the outer level of being. This, however, is a very coarse level of experience. It takes some training of mind and perception to discover the richness and depth of more subtle energies, which nevertheless still lie within quite ordinary experience if we only look for them, listen for them, feel them, sense them.

Tuning in to See *the Subtle Patterns of Energy*

The world that we usually perceive and know with all its boundaries and distinctions is the surface of reality. It is an elaborate play, like a holographic sound-and-light show. The sacred world is full of powerful energy, ki, that has unlimited potential for new patterns and meanings to arise constantly in a kind of self-created cosmic display. This is happening everywhere, and you can find it at every level from the infinitesimally small to the infinitely large. "The very small is as the very large when boundaries are forgotten; the very large is as the very small when its outline is not seen," said Seng-ts'an. You can see the play of energy in a swarm of gnats flitting back and forth in the last rays of the evening sun, in the force of a hurricane as it sweeps the coast, or in the majestic appearance of a comet in the night sky. You can see the cosmic dance in the smallest thought flitting repetitively through your mind, in the movement of a herd of animals or a flock of migrating birds, or in the compassionate action of a great leader. Our bodies and thoughts and the "things" that make up our world are all part of that surface display—patterns of color, sound, smell, and so on., as well as of mental and emotional energy.

There are also energy patterns that are more subtle, not so obvious, but that you can feel when you are willing to open to the unexpected in your world. We can experience the deeper patterns of energy and power in the *qualities* of things. When we see only surface appearances, the mere thingness of separate things, we deaden them. The world becomes flat and meaningless. But if we are open to the qualities of things, to the isness or beingness of things—the blue quality of the sky, the solid quality of the rock, the swirling quality of the wind, the haunting quality of the cry of the loon—and to the connections between things, the meaning of things, then we can feel their energy. We can feel the energy running through us so that we can respond to it and, as well, it can respond to us.

We can tune in to the patterns and qualities of our world when we *see* rather than merely look-at. This distinction between *see* and *look-at* is made by Frederick Franck in *Zen Seeing, Zen Drawing*. He says, "Merely looking-*at* the world around us is immensely different from *seeing* it. . . . Although many of us, under the ceaseless bombardment of photographic and electronic imagery that we experience daily have lost that gift of seeing, we can learn it anew, and learn to retrieve again and again the act of seeing things for the first time, each time we look at them." Franck quotes art historian Rudolf Arnheim as saying, "Every child entering grade school in this country embarks on a twelve-to-twenty-year apprenticeship in aesthetic alienation. Eyes they still have, but see they do no more." Hui Neng, the Zen sage, Franck tells us, said, "The Meaning of Life is to See." Franck adds, "Not to look-at, mind you, but to see!"

And Chögyam Trungpa makes a similar distinction:

> Looking is your first projection, and if you have any
> doubt, then it might have a quality of tremor or shak-
> iness. You begin to look, and then you feel shaky or
> anxious because you don't trust your vision. So some-
> times you want to close your eyes. You don't want to
> look any more. But the point is to look properly. See
> the colors: white, black, blue, yellow, red, green, pur-
> ple. Look. This is your world! You can't not look.
> There is no other world. This is your world. This
> is your feast. You inherited this; you inherited these
> eyeballs, you inherited this world of color. Look at
> the greatness of the whole thing. Look! Don't hesi-
> tate—look! Open your eyes. Don't blink, and look,
> look—look further. Then you might see something.

Usually, we perceive and respond to our world, not directly, but through the medium of words. When we hear a
sound there is a very rapid process: first we have a feeling
toward it—positive or negative—and then we wonder what
to name the sound. We recognize the sound, we put a name
to it, and only then do we respond to it. Sight and the other
senses work the same way, so that we perceive our world
through a filter of words. We walk in the woods and wonder
immediately what type of tree we're seeing or what to call
the wildflower in front of us. This process is usually so fast
that we are not conscious of it, but it happens with everything
we perceive: we live in a world of words and labels. If you
watch your mind in action, you can sometimes catch this la-
beling process happening even with the simplest sounds or
sights.

Sometimes, though, we perceive our world directly and we act directly, without the barrier of words, when, for example, something abrupt or sudden penetrates our perception, as we talked about in chapter 1. When a child cries out, her mother runs to her, without having to say or think anything. That comes after. The mother responds from an inner sense deeper than words. At such times, you can become aware of levels of perception and communication with your world to which you are normally deaf, blind, and numb. We participate fully in our world at those times and can communicate at a deeper level than speech.

By participating physically and emotionally in the world of another being, we communicate with that being. While listening to the troubled story of a friend, you can feel the sorrow he communicates through his body and his environment, perhaps more deeply than through his words. If you stand next to a large oak tree with an open heart, you can feel the life in that tree resonating in your own body. Often you can feel a person's presence as she moves close to you even when your back is turned or when you are in a darkened room. Sometimes you can feel aggression in the atmosphere when you enter a room where there has been a bad fight, and you can feel the peace in the atmosphere of a house of healing. Standing at a particular point on a cliff, you may feel disturbed—not because of a strong wind but just because of the lay of the land. Sitting quietly and without anxiety by the bedside of a dying person, you can bring them peace. But you can feel these things only if you are receptive to the sensations of your own body and beyond your body at that very moment. When we relax and give up keeping track, there is no limit to how far we can extend our openness and participation in the world.

We are not talking about any dramatic revelations here—no sudden flashes of cosmic light or visitors from outer space. We are talking about sensing subtle energies. We can begin to feel these energies in the elemental world—for example, in the pattern of the wind, in the pattern of the bark on a one-hundred-year-old pine tree, in the cries of loons and the squawk of crows, in the way a rock sits majestically atop a bare hill, in a sudden change in the weather. Tuning in to this inner sense is becoming aware of the richness and subtlety of the sacred world.

The English author D. H. Lawrence, who had an extraordinary understanding of the old spirituality of the native peoples of Mexico, writes about experiencing these elemental energies:

> The Indian does not consider himself as created and therefore external to God, or the creature of God. To the Indian there is no defined God. Creation is a great flood, forever flowing, in lovely and terrible waves. In everything the shimmer of creation, and never the finality of the created. Never the distinction between God and God's creation, or between Spirit and Matter. Everything, everything is the wonderful shimmer of creation, it may be a deadly shimmer like lightning or the anger in the little eyes of the bear, it may be the beautiful shimmer of the moving deer, or the pine boughs softly swaying under snow. . . .
>
> There is, in our sense of the word, no God. But all is godly. There is no Great Mind directing the universe. Yet the mystery of creation, the wonder and fascination of creation shimmers in every leaf and stone, in every thorn and bud, in the fangs of the rat-

tlesnake, and in the soft eyes of a fawn. Things utterly opposite are still pure. . . .

It is a vast, old religion, greater than anything we know, more starkly and nakedly religious. . . . In the oldest religion everything was alive, not supernaturally but naturally alive. There were only deeper and deeper streams of life, vibrations of life, more and more vast. So rocks were alive, but a mountain had a deeper, vaster life than a rock, and it was much harder for a man to bring his spirit, or his energy into contact with the life of the mountain, and so draw strength from the mountain, as from a great standing well of life, than it was to come in contact with the rock. And he had to put forth great religious effort. For the whole life effort of man was to get his life into direct contact with the elemental life of the cosmos, mountain-life, cloud-life, thunder-life, air-life, earth-life, sun-life. To come into immediate felt contact and so derive energy, power, and a dark sort of joy.

A modern spokesman for one of the Native American traditions, Wallace Black Elk, a Lakota, describes tuning in to the living qualities of the sacred world in this way:

I learned from the spirit how to find those rocks that contain the sacred powdered paints. . . . We go [to the Badlands] and pray . . . and you can see those special rocks glow in the dark. They look like little colored lights in the dark. You can see the colors that are on the inside. So we go there and take the colors we need. . . . I learned their songs, but there are many songs out there. There are countless songs. Like the fire, it has a song. That fire shapes and forms all life, and each shape has a song. And the rocks, the rocks have songs. Like this rock I wear around my neck, it has a song. All the stones that are around here, each one has a language of its own. Even the Earth has a song. We call it Mother Earth. We call her Grandmother, and she has a song. Then the water, it has a song. The water makes beautiful sounds. The water carries the universal sounds. Now the green. This tree, every green has a song. They have a language of their own. There's life there. . . .

If you see a tree, it doesn't move. It doesn't talk or walk. You just see it. You just see a tree. That's all. But the trees talk. They have a language of their own. So all this green that you see, they communicate. . . .

So each one of the winged-people [birds] has a song. It is the same with the four-legged and creeping-crawler creatures. So that's how come we have an eagle song, a buffalo song, and even a serpent song, a serpent language. . . . So I want to tell you that you have a lot to learn. What you know today, it's just a little bit—like the blink of an eye. . . . So that power is immense.

The experience of subtle mind-energy patterns is found in almost all human groups across the earth, in modern times and as far back as we know—known by a thousand names: gods, devas, spirit-helpers, angels, loas, Japanese kami, or Tibetan drala. These living energy patterns communicate between the loud, colorful, smelly world of appearances that we sense and think we "know" and the fathomless space of formless energy and wisdom within which those appearances arise.

It is possible for all of us, even in our modern culture, to reconnect with these presences and bring their energy into our world to heal it and enliven it and to resanctify our lives by connecting us to a larger, richer world. But while there is a great deal of talk these days about "spirit-helpers," "angels," and so on, there is little discussion of how to train ourselves to be open to this dimension of experience in ordinary life— and how to distinguish real experience from fantasy or wishful thinking. The Shambhala teachings not only suggest that it is *possible* to connect with these subtle energy presences, they provide means to connect that are practical and workable in the context of modern life.

This does not mean that we are asked to "believe" blindly in such powerful but subtle energies. But we *can* begin to be open to them in our own experience. Their power is attracted, and in turn empowers us, when we care for ourselves and the world, when we put loving energy out into the world, and when we wholeheartedly participate in it. All this lies within our own experience when we open our feeling and awareness to such possibilities. As we open our awareness, these living energies can empower us on our journey and show us the way to sacredness. And they can help us to bring the unconditioned, open dimension into our outer existence. We will return, in chapter 16, to investigate these principles and energies in more depth—how they manifest in the ordinary world and how we can call on their help. But now we must turn our attention to the question of why we aren't normally aware of experiencing the sacredness, the unconditioned openness and goodness, and the subtle energy and power of our world.

CHAPTER 4

This Is the Cocoon That Fear Builds

OW THAT WE HAVE introduced the basic principles of the sacred world—universal basic goodness and the richness, fullness, and wisdom of the cosmos—very obvious questions arise: If basic goodness is universal and yet so intimate, so close, so genuine, why don't we experience that sacredness all the time and base our activity on it? Why don't we continually abide in our unconditional goodness, experience the sacredness of our world, and live from within that? Why don't we feel the multidimensional quality of our world and let our lives be energized by that? If we did base our activities and relationships, our political structures and cultural norms, on basic goodness and sacredness, then the world of human society would clearly be a quite different place. What keeps us from doing that?

However intense our occasional spontaneous experience of basic goodness may be, it is inevitably brief. Whether we try to hold on to it or let it go, it passes as we return to our same old habits of thought, emotion, and physical posture. The fresh and clear quality of our minds and the warmth of our hearts seem to get covered over quickly by the more familiar cloudy mind. Sometimes these clouds are pink-tinged clouds—we become lost in romantic fantasies of falling in love. At other times, the clouds are dark and threatening, accompanying fantasies of anger. Frequently, the clouds reflect the same memory of hurt or happiness over and over again.

Even the clouds—pink or green, blue or black—are not really separate from basic goodness. However, it certainly feels as if they cover a precious discovery, leaving us with our same old, thoroughly familiar selves. Yet there is a paradox here. The clouds feel as if they were covering a freshness and an openness of heart that we would dearly love to hold on to, but at the same time, they feel cozy and comforting. They're what we know. No matter that they feel neurotic; no matter that we have seen the same clouds over and over again. Still, they are familiar. They are a safe place for us to hide. This is where we feel "real."

In the Shambhala teachings, this stale, familiar place, patched together with habitual thoughts and emotions, is called the *cocoon*. Its staleness is the key to seeing the cocoon—the thoughts we have heard, the mental movies we have seen, the emotions we have felt before. Whenever anything fresh or sharp or unfamiliar threatens our usual way of being, we race back to the cocoon. We spend a great deal of time in that state of mind and heart; it is cozy, closed-in, "safe," and protected.

Nowadays, physical "cocooning" has become a fashionable concept in big cities. It has even been the subject of *Time* magazine articles. Those who can afford it create a cocoon in their apartment so that they don't have to go out at all to face the danger and ugliness of the city. They buy lots of electronic gadgets, CDs, and videos; order in pizza and gourmet foods; and stay home.

Whole cocoon towns have been built, such as those in

Green Valley, Nevada, where subdivisions are growing up that are entirely surrounded by walls. Each house, too, is surrounded by a wall, and homeowners pledge not to make any changes in them. One of the developers explained, "It's safe here, and clean. And nice. The schools are good, and the crime rate is low. It's what buyers are looking for." Signs on corners read: WE IMMEDIATELY REPORT ALL SUSPICIOUS PERSONS AND ACTIVITIES TO OUR POLICE DEPARTMENT. On garages, there are signs reading YOUR NEIGHBORS ARE WATCHING. In spite of all the regulations, a rash of burglaries broke out, and the neighbors discovered that the burglars were living in houses within the walls of the subdivision. For all their efforts, they hadn't managed to keep reality out of their lives. In a similar walled town in Florida, the golf course and beach were outside the walls. Homeowners eventually became afraid to do the very things they enjoyed—play golf and sunbathe on the beach—because they were in an unprotected area. These are true stories and remarkable external manifestations of the cocoon mind!

These physical ways of cocooning are but manifestations of a deeper cocoon of fear. The real cocoon is in our own being, our minds and hearts. All of us have walls around our hearts and minds to ward off anything that disturbs us or doesn't agree with us. These walls have been building themselves since before we can remember, and they are firmly in place by the time we become aware of them.

The cocoon is not just a facade that we wear for others, however. It is a way that we hide from ourselves as well. We don't want to be exposed or hurt or defeated, so we try to keep out anything that threatens to attack us or seduce us away from our familiar states of mind, however extreme they may be. We tell ourselves our life stories over and over again, improving on them each time. We get so caught up in our fantasies about how we are and who we are that we often don't really feel our uncertainties and fears and our longings for a more fulfilling life.

Most of us don't connect in a simple, genuine way with ourselves and with the world around us. We avoid who we are and the world we are in. Some of us feel inadequate and become depressed, while others try to be superhuman and then feel stressed-out. In both cases, we are trying to be somebody other than ourselves. We try to beat our bodies into conforming to a popular image, and we habitually deny what our bodies are actually feeling—hunger, exhaustion, the need to be touched—dragging them along with us as if they were unruly children, drugging them into speed or sleep. We are plagued by a stream of chatter in our heads, and at the same time, we experience a vague—or perhaps full-blown—feeling of frustration, unhappiness, unfulfillment. To others, we may appear to be efficient, successful, and happy, yet in our hearts, we are afraid that we are missing out on our very lives.

We measure ourselves against some imaginary standard rather than paying attention to our own experience. We actually *invent* ourselves and our experience. Although we sometimes see clearly the ways others are doing this, it's hard to believe that we do it as well. But most of us do it all the time. Instead of being a genuine person with genuine experiences, we act like another person whose experience exists only in our own minds. For some reason, pretending to be someone else feels better than being ourselves, and *we believe that our own pretense is truly who we are.*

And this is a not merely an issue of the modern world; it is also an ancient one. As sixteenth-century Confucian-Taoist sage Liu Wenmin says, "If you do not recognize the root source of the myriad transformations, then you submerge yourself in clever artifice and defiled habits. You see everything under Heaven as a welter of countless different appearances. Thus your spirit is blinded and confused, and your whole life is toil and suffering."

Nor is the cocoon merely a "religious" insight, as the great physicist Albert Einstein saw when he wrote:

> A human being is part of the whole, called by us the Universe, a part limited in time and space. He experiences himself, his thoughts and feelings as something separate from the rest—a kind of optical illusion of consciousness. This delusion is a kind of prison for us, restricting us to our personal desires and to affection for a few persons nearest to us. Our task must be to free ourselves from this prison by widening our circle of compassion to embrace all living creatures and the whole of nature in its beauty. Nobody is able to achieve this completely, but the striving for such achievement is in itself a part of the liberation and a foundation for inner security.

The Masks We Wear: Our Many "Me's"

When you look at the cocoon more closely, you see that you do not have just one idea of "me" but many. You have different "me's" for different occasions. The different "me's" are like roles that we play—a different one for each situation—or like masks we put on to cover how we are really feeling. We slip into our roles automatically, without even realizing it. Each role has different thoughts, different feelings, different moods, and even different muscular tensions and bodily postures. The change of role is so smooth, and the roles themselves so familiar, that we don't really even notice the changes happening. We think each role is the same "me" feeling a different way. We don't notice the automatic nature of the whole process. And if we were asked to describe ourselves, we would probably describe only one or another of our various roles, depending on who was asking us.

Particular emotions are part of our self-image in each role, and when we leave one role and enter another, we often disown the former role's emotions and hardly believe that we could have felt them at all. Frequently, men who abuse their wives and children in one role become bitterly remorseful and disown the abuser in another role. But then the abuser reappears later. All of these emotions are part of our conscious self-image of the moment—"I am angry," "I am in love," and so on—the patches that make the cocoon.

Alex, a meditation student, reports:

I had had a wonderful weekend and arrived at work a little late on Monday morning. One moment, I was in the car saying good-bye to my lover. I felt a bit puffed up and very romantic. But I felt generally pleased with my life. I walked into the office and caught one glimpse of my supervisor and started to shrink physically and mentally. I felt a little nervous and quickly began to think whether I had left anything undone. The lover role was gone for the rest of the day. My subordinate role was able to take a break when I went out for lunch with a friend, and we spent the whole hour gossiping about the boss and feeling irritated about him. But we felt very smug with each other. Thinking about it afterwards, I realized that these three roles—the lover, the subordinate, and the conspirator-buddy—are as familiar as my old T-shirt.

Some of the roles are actually very appropriate in particular circumstances, while others make an awful mess of things. Some people have developed very appropriate roles for their professional lives and feel successful and satisfied with them. Meanwhile, their family lives are in chaos. As one successful lawyer said, "The role I often wear at home seems to act like a spoiled brat that still wants something it didn't get when it was four years old." Other people have smooth and joyful family lives, but in their roles at work, they cannot manage and feel depressed and incompetent. Many people have developed roles that function beautifully when they are with other people, but they have depressed and confused roles when alone.

Spiritual traditions have long known of this fragmentation of the personality. The turn-of-the-century Russian teacher G. I. Gurdjieff puts it this way:

> Man is a plural being. When we speak of ourselves ordinarily, we speak of "I." We say, " 'I' did this," " 'I' think this," " 'I' want to do this"—but this is a mistake. There is no such "I" or rather there are hundreds, thousands of little "I"s in every one of us. We are divided in ourselves but we cannot recognize the plurality of our being except by observation and study. At one moment it is one "I" that acts, at the next moment it is another "I." It is because the "I"s in ourselves are contradictory that we do not function harmoniously.

James Moore, Gurdjieff's biographer, gives a more colorful account of Gurdjieff's view of the plurality of human personality:

> All men and women, Gurdjieff warns, play host to scores if not hundreds of different parasitic identities, each with its blinkered repertoire of behavior. A snub, a flattering letter, a no-smoking sign, a slow queue, a come-hither look—and we are strangely altered. We have one personality with subordinates, another with superiors, one with our mother, another with the tax man—each is Caliph for an hour. One scatters promissory notes which others must redeem: "Certainly. See you in the morning. Only too delightful." One despairing humorless personality may even take an overdose or jump off a cliff—crazily destroying the habitat of all the others. To sum up, our professed citadel of individuality is common as a barber's chair. Very few men are strong enough to confront this impression emotionally and to work within the compass of its appalling implications. Confounding confusion, all these personalities share behavioral "norms" which Gurdjieff reveals as tragically abnormal.

Now many psychologists and therapists, too, are recognizing the strangely well kept secret that, in a very real sense, we are all suffering from multiple personality syndrome. Psychologist Roberto Assagioli, founder of psychosynthesis and one of the first to join spiritual understanding with psychotherapy, called these different "I's" *subpersonalities*. "The organization of the subpersonalities is very revealing," he says, "and sometimes surprising, baffling or even frightening—different and often quite antagonistic traits are displayed in the different roles. . . . Ordinary people shift from one to the other without clear awareness and only a thin thread of memory connects them; but for all practical purposes they are different beings."

The point of seeing all these habitual patterns, the roles that make up the cocoon, is not to judge which roles are good and which are bad or to try to get rid of the "bad" ones and foster the "good" ones. The point is simply to see that so much of our psychic energy is taken up by these completely habitual and automatic modes of thinking, feeling, and acting. Most important of all is to see that the cocoon is not a solid, permanent, unified thing but a constantly changing flux of masks and roles. It was patched together higgledy-piggledy as we grew up. This ever-changing hodgepodge is what we now believe we are, and what we need to free ourselves from.

Understanding the multiple roles we play and the multiple "me's" that we identify with is very helpful on a spiritual path. Most of us believe that we are a single and unified, if maybe somewhat neurotic, person. Somehow, we think, to mature means that this not very sane person changes into the *same,* but now wise, person. Conventional psychology as well as many therapies reinforce this belief that we just need to become better versions of the same person. When we understand the patched-together nature of the cocoon, however, and the multiple personalities that make it up, we can see a different approach. We can nourish our awareness of the many roles so that they no longer control us. We no longer believe, each time a different role automatically pops up, that this is the *real* "me." Gradually, the inappropriate roles begin to dissolve when we see them clearly. We begin to realize that we *can* step out of our cocoon, taking along the roles that are helpful and leaving the rest behind.

The attitude toward our cocoon distinguishes a meditative path, such as the Shambhala path of warriorship or a Buddhist path, from systems of therapy that are based on analysis of the cocoon. The idea that you can find an ultimate "cause" of your suffering by going back over and over your personal history is, from this point of view, a very partial solution. It might make a more comfortable cocoon, but it also can make a stronger and more solid cocoon. The important point is that any investigation or analysis of the cocoon should come from the point of view of wanting to *let the whole thing go.* Only what helps us to see our cocoon clearly, as in a mirror, without getting caught in it further, can be helpful.

No matter how much pain we are in, moments of discovery and fresh experience *do* occur. We can cultivate these glimpses of basic goodness, no matter how insignificant they feel, rather than constantly going over and over our pain and delving into its history. The focus of a spiritual path is on opening to the sacred world beyond the cocoon. This is the reason for looking at the cocoon—so that we can step out of it, again and again. But the cocoon is many-layered, and the cocoon-maker—our "me"—is very clever and deceptive. So we have to go slowly and carefully, step by step, looking at the cocoon with clarity and bravery.

CONTEMPLATIONS

At the end of some chapters, we suggest *contemplations.* Please try these contemplations with a light touch, experiment with them, enjoy them. They are our attempts to share with you some of our experience of the path and suggestions about ways you could go about investigating the topics for yourself. We hope they will help you to make the teachings more personal. But take your time; there is no hurry. Some things you may understand in a flash; other things can take years. Progress on a spiritual path evolves gradually over time and in the context of practice. If you don't base your study on the foundation of a spiritual practice, it will be difficult for you to gain more than a superficial experience of all we will be describing.

Please remember the teaching of sages of all time: Don't rely on authority and on hearing the teachings of others; *experience the truth for yourself*. Wang Yangming, one of the most influential and learned thinkers in Chinese history, combined Taoism, Zen Buddhism, and Confucianism in his teaching and was also a highly successful leader both in civil administration and in military campaigns. The school of neo-Confucianism, which brought new life to Confucianism in the great period of the early Ming dynasty in China, arose out of his teaching. Yet Wang Yangming reminded people, "Sincere belief [in the teaching of the sages] is certainly right, but it is not as cogent as verifying the truth within yourself. If at present you have not found the truth in your mind, then how can you dogmatically follow what you have heard in the past, without seeking to find out if it is correct? The great chaos in the world is due to the triumph of empty words and the decline of genuine practice."

Meeting Yourself Each day for a week, have a fifteen-minute meeting with yourself sometime during the day or evening. Choose a different time each day, but make a specific appointment and write it down on your calendar. Maybe Monday it will be at 10:00 AM, Tuesday, at 9:15 PM, and so on. The purpose of this meeting is to stop what you are doing for a while and pay attention to yourself—your body, your thoughts, your feelings and emotions.

Pay attention to the details. Start with your body: How are you sitting? Is your posture straight or slumped? Where are you holding tension—in your shoulders, your jaw? Now move on to your thoughts: What were you thinking just before the appointment? Are you concerned with something that you just can't "get off your mind"? Are your thoughts moving quickly, from subject to subject, or are they quite sluggish? Are you thinking about what else you should be doing? Do you feel you are avoiding something you don't want to relate to? Notice how you're feeling in general: Are you tired, anxious, restless, slow? And pay attention to your emotional state: Do you feel irritated, angry, resentful, passionate, excited, happy? Do you see any patterns or habits in the way you are now that repeat in the way you usually experience yourself? Do you often sit in this posture, think and feel this way?

The point is to be with yourself fully and honestly, but not to be solemn about it. You don't have to try to change anything, although if changes do occur as you pay attention to your present state, notice them. You can do this exercise of "meeting yourself" spontaneously at any time you remember it, but do it at least once a day for a week.

Getting Acquainted with Your Masks   Write down some of the main roles you play in your daily life. For example, you may play the roles of doctor, mother, wife, intimate friend, acquaintance, professional colleague. Think about what circumstances these roles occur in and what masks you wear for each of them. Keep it simple. In your role as doctor, you may wear a mask of efficiency and knowledge (even at times when you may not know what you're doing) or a mask of compassion (even when you may be tired and don't really care). In your role as wife, you may wear a mask of love (even when you feel angry) or one of anger or resentment (even when you feel loving). You may have a mask of love even when you actually do feel loving: the mask may be covering your soft, vulnerable heart. Look at your posture in each of these masks. How do you feel, as you wear it? What are your usual thoughts? Recall what you do when you feel disturbed in your masks. Just look. Don't judge whether the mask is good or bad, and don't try to figure out how to change anything.

Seeing the Wild Mind   Find some time to be home alone. Now turn on the TV, the CD player, the cassette player, and the radio—all at once—everything you have. Vacuum the floor, make a "to do" list, eat, and keep as busy as possible for half an hour. Then turn everything off and sit down in a comfortable place in your favorite room or outside and listen to the silence; listen to your thoughts.

Appreciating Who You Are   How you think about yourself affects deeply how you feel about yourself and your life. Having looked at your cocoon world, spend a little time contemplating your personal feeling of basic goodness. Do you feel that you are basically good in a deep way, beyond the conventional concepts of "good" and "bad"? What are your doubts about the basic goodness of yourself and others? Having acknowledged your doubts, put them aside for a moment and think that you *are* basically good. Contemplate how you feel caring, gentleness, and affection toward other people, animals, or places in your own life; how you feel affection from others; how it affects your life. How does basic goodness show in your life? Have you had moments when you experienced the world in a simple and genuine way? Forget about ideas, concepts, *shoulds,* obligations. What makes you laugh and cry, touches your emotions? Where is your heart?

Have the intention for a whole day to acknowledge moments of freshness and genuineness when they occur in your daily life. These occur all the time, but usually, we don't notice unless the moment is dramatic. Having the intention to recognize these moments is the first step toward seeing the basic goodness and sacredness of the world.

CHAPTER 5

Fear: The Gateway to Fearlessness

*A*S FAR AS IT CAN, our cocoon creates its own comfortable world. It does this by selecting what best fits it from the infinite range of possibilities "outside," in the realms of senses, color, sound, and so on. According to meditation experts, as well as brain-mind scientists, our senses don't passively perceive things that exist in an "objective world," like a camera or tape recorder. On the contrary, we largely perceive the external world not as it actually is but according to our *expectations* of it. We don't live in just any old world but in one tailor-made to keep us as secure and comfortable as possible. The cocoon adapts us to the world and the world to fulfill our expectations of it.

This is illustrated by an old folk parable. An old man is standing at the entrance to a village when a sour-looking young man comes along. He says, "Old man, what are the people like in your village? I am wondering whether to settle here." The old man asks, "What were they like in the village you left?" To this, the young man replies, "Horrible! They were mean-spirited, lazy, and humorless." The old man replies, "Son, you will find the people of this village exactly the same." Later, another young man comes along and asks the same question. When the old man asks about the people in his previous village, he replies, "They were wonderful! They were full of humor and joy, and so generous." The old man replies, "Son, you will find them just the same here."

You may not feel that you are manipulating your world, but if you look closely, you can see that the world actually conforms to your beliefs in very simple ways. If you are feeling down on yourself, everyone seems to be belittling or not appreciating you. If you think of people as friends, they appear to like you. If you believe that the world is out to get you, it appears to be full of sharks. If you are in love, the world constantly reminds you of your lover.

Of course, we can't manipulate the world to be as we want it to be *all* the time. When we cannot remake the world to fit our expectations, when something happens that simply does not fit our idea of how the world should be, then we experience *fear*. Biologically, fear exists as a warning system to alert the organism to the presence of something foreign or unrecognizable, something strange. Psychologically, we twist this basic and valuable biological function into a warning system for our cocoon. Whenever a sudden event occurs that does not immediately find a place in our cocoon world, we feel fear. It may be just a twinge of anxiety or outright terror, but it is the automatic response to unpredictable change. When anything unexpected or unrecognizable comes along, we feel threatened, and we fall back quickly into our habitual roles. While we are in these habitual roles, we hardly feel the underlying fear that maintains them. If something or someone forces us to change or simply to experience something out of the ordinary, fear can manifest itself as laziness—an unwillingness to change due to inertia—or as irritation, sometimes amounting to outright aggression.

When you follow any spiritual practice, sooner or later you

are bound to encounter the deep fear that drives the cocoon. Sometimes fear becomes a reason to give up the practice and to renounce the whole idea of spirituality. As soon as we touch fear, we want to run from it: it can be extremely powerful and threatening. A great deal of our lives is based on avoiding fear. Fundamentally, we are afraid of the great uncertainty of death, and this manifests as fear of uncertainty at all levels. So we surround ourselves with familiar things and people and fill our lives with familiar habits. We are afraid of change because it brings uncertainty, so we try to hold on to the familiar and avoid anything strange or unusual.

That we fear anything even slightly out of the ordinary or strange is beautifully illustrated by a story reported recently in our local newspaper. Ms. Mars, who taught a performance art class, gave her students their final assignment: to walk very slowly through a mall to the shop where they could buy bottled water. During the walk, security guards approached the group and informed them that they were making customers feel uncomfortable. After the group explained that they intended to buy something, they were not asked to leave after all. "As soon as you move outside of the normal tempo or rhythm of what people expect, it's looked upon in a paranoid and suspicious way rather than in a curious one," Ms. Mars said. "Whenever we do something that is unexpected, even if it's not aggressive, it's perceived as aggressive." We react to anything unexpected with fear.

Buddhist teacher and psychologist Jack Kornfield calls the cocoon a "body of fear." He says, "Our fear creates a contracted and false sense of self. This false or 'small' self grasps our limited body, feelings, and thoughts, and tries to hold and protect them. From this limited sense of self arises a deficiency and need, defensive anger, and the barriers we build for our protection. We are afraid to open, to change, to live fully, to feel the whole of life; a contracted identification with this 'body of fear' becomes our habit."

Ironically, by maintaining the cocoon, we are deadening ourselves to our creative energy. By avoiding life, we are starving ourselves to death. We are afraid to die, yet we are afraid to live. When we see an injustice happening at work or at school, right there in front of our eyes, often we just shrug our shoulders and walk away suppressing our outrage. Yet when we feel mistreated, often we explode in anger without pausing to look at what is behind the anger. Or perhaps, when a friend tells us of her affection for us, we shrink back and become polite and distant or make it into an opportunity for an affair. We do not open ourselves to the affection and let it flow through us, responding to it from our own hearts. In so many ways, we avoid fully living.

Our ultimate fear is that we will die and be obliterated from the earth, losing all our connections with family and friends. Death is very frightening, but the reason we feel so afraid of it is that we already feel separated from our world. Our fear has closed us off and separated us from everything we love and care for. We feel utterly isolated and separated because we don't feel our interconnection with the richness and fullness of the sacred world. Naturally, we fear death as ultimate extinction rather than as a transition from one state to another *within* the sacred world.

Tibetan Buddhist Sogyal Rinpoche writes:

> Why do we live in such terror of death? Because our instinctive desire is to live and go on living, and death is a savage end to everything we hold familiar. We feel that when it comes we will be plunged into some-

thing quite unknown, or become totally different. We imagine we will find ourselves lost and bewildered in surroundings that are terrifyingly unfamiliar. We imagine it will be like waking up alone, in a torment of anxiety, in a foreign country; with no knowledge of the land or language, no money, no contacts, no passport, no friends.

Fear Underlies Our Habitual Roles

Everything we do and don't do in our habitual world comes from fear. Fear is covered over by the habitual roles and behavior patterns of the cocoon. The slightest interruption of these habitual patterns brings an immediate response of fear. If we experiment with changing one of our habitual patterns, or if the circumstances of our life force us to change without warning, we will quickly encounter the fear that lies below the surface. Facing our fear begins with becoming mindful of all the ways that create a familiar, habitual, and safe world to close off fear. If we look closely at our habits of body and speech, emotional habits of reaction, and habitual thoughts and beliefs, we can see how these patterns recur in our lives.

Habits of the body include how we walk, how we enter a room, how we sit down, and so on. Some people stride forcefully forward, chest puffed out, nose leading the way, as if they were determined to save the world. Some people, men and women, walk with their shoulders swaggering and hips stiff, as if they imagined themselves to be football players. Some people slouch, their chests caved in, their stomachs loose, as if they would like to melt into the ground. Everyone has a characteristic way of tensing their body against the threat of the world.

We also have habits of speech. Some people speak loud and fast, like a machine gun—to attack before they are attacked. Others speak softly, slurring their words a little, perhaps hoping no one will hear them. Others speak with an excited, speedy optimism that would like to turn the whole world into a party. Still others speak with a soft, musical tone that would seduce the world to their side. Each way of speaking may be appropriate in some circumstances, but when it is our habitual way, it sorely limits our flexibility in relating to the world. Our speech habits are part of the armor that keeps the world away from us and keeps us from feeling our fear.

Emotions, too, can become rigid and stereotypical: we may be habitually angry or resentful or enthusiastic or fawning. We learn to regard certain situations or types of people as threatening and others as friendly. We react according to these habitual ways of seeing others rather than responding appropriately to each fresh situation.

We have habitual ways of thinking about ourselves and the world. We carry around an image of ourselves and a story of who and how we are. We have a visual image of our face, an inwardly felt sense of our bodily shape, an idea of the sound of our voice, a view of how we are coming across to other people. These images are so strong and definite that we are often surprised and shocked when we see a photograph of ourselves or hear our voice on tape. Sometimes when we hear other people's views of what we were like at a meeting or a social gathering, we simply do not recognize the person they are describing. Our response of indignation, or depression, to such a description hides the fear that _we don't really know who we are at all._

Most people find it very difficult to hear, let alone accept, ideas that don't fit into their belief systems. Some people instinctively feel that the ways of foreigners or of people of a different race are somehow inferior to their own. Even if they try to be kind to foreigners, they may not quite regard them as equal. Fundamentally, most of us are afraid of strangers, just because they are strange to us. The mere difference of others has been the cause of many wars.

Anger and fear are stimulated in some people by religious beliefs that differ from their own. Many people actually are more frightened by an open mind than by religious beliefs that differ strongly from theirs. Someone who strongly believes in the existence of an external God is often more disturbed by someone who—when asked if they, too, believe—replies, "Well, yes and no," than by someone who simply says, "No." An atheist who vehemently denies the existence of such a God can be more angered by an agnostic than by someone who affirms belief in God. A contrary belief is something to fight against, by which people can test and strengthen their own views. Openness and uncertainty in others arouse uncertainty in ourselves, and it is this uncertainty that we most truly fear.

The rigid belief that science is the *only* way we can know the truth about the real, vast universe can cover a profound fear of that uncontrollable vastness. Unexamined scientific beliefs are as rigid and restrictive as any other culturally transmitted and automatically accepted beliefs. And they profoundly affect the way we perceive and act in the world. Many people are frightened by the idea that they could have a direct intuitive understanding of the world and their profound connection to it. They dismiss intuitive insight as a way of knowing the world because it goes too much against the modern, scientific, rational, information-based view of knowledge. They turn away in anger—beneath which is fear—from insights of their own that could show them the fullness and interdependence of their world.

Doubt as an Expression of Fear

One of the most habitual expressions of fear is doubt. It is the root of many of the obstacles we encounter. There are, of course, healthy and intelligent forms of doubt. An example is the wholesome skepticism of a sharp mind that does not accept anything on authority alone. A genuine spiritual path does not demand that we blindly follow instructions. It encourages us to question intelligently and test what we are told against our own experience. But other forms of doubt drag us down and steal away our awareness and cheerfulness. In this negative pattern of thinking, we may doubt our own experience of the path.

Doubt can cause us to lose faith in the power of spiritual practice to transform our lives and cause us to collapse back into the cocoon. At any point on your journey, doubt can prevent you from going further. The sham world of masks and false ambitions often seems so vivid that our experience of basic goodness and the dignity of spiritual practice seems more like an escape from reality than a genuine experience of it. Amid so much mindless confidence that the "real world" is harsh and aggressive and that humans are fundamentally selfish, we doubt our own insight and experience. We may feel shameful or guilty and doubt that basic goodness exists within us or that we are able to nourish it and base our lives on it. We may glimpse the power and beauty of the sacred world and feel overwhelmed by it, doubting our ability to go further into it. We can find many very intelligent-sounding reasons to doubt sacredness so that we can hold on to our cocoons.

Doubt in the very idea of the basic goodness of human beings permeates modern society. The belief that humans have a fundamental and ineradicable fault—an "original sin"—has become dominant even among those who have rejected traditional religion. The sense of guilt and shame at having committed some unremembered wrong has been transmitted from generation to generation right down to the present. We feel that we did something very wrong, long, long ago, something that we cannot erase and that makes us undeserving. Because we have this idea, it is very difficult for us to accept or even understand the idea of basic goodness. Lack of self-esteem has become an epidemic in modern society. Belief in our fundamental blameworthiness is so deeply rooted in our upbringing that we accept it without question as the final truth about human nature. Yet the fundamental blameworthiness, or basic badness, of human nature is far from being a universal truth. Is human nature *fundamentally* sinful—or aggressive, in modern terms—or are these qualities simply the obscurations that separate us from our basic goodness? Chögyam Trungpa says of this:

> Coming from a tradition that stresses human goodness, it was something of a shock for me to encounter the western tradition of original sin. . . . It seems that this notion of original sin does not just pervade western religious ideas. It actually seems to run throughout western thought as well, especially psychological thought. Among patients, theoreticians and therapists alike there seems to be great concern with the idea of some original mistake, which causes later suffering—a kind of punishment for that mistake. One finds that a sense of guilt or being wounded is quite

pervasive. Whether or not people actually believe in the idea of original sin, or in God for that matter, they seem to feel that they have done something wrong in the past and are now being punished for it.

There may be some truth to the idea of sin if we understand sin as a pattern of destructive behavior, of self-doubt and self-hate, that has been passed down from parents to children for generations. The idea is helpful when it reminds us of our tendency toward selfishness and egotism. The idea of *original* sin as a fundamental part of our nature, however, from which we can never be free, only breeds more self-doubt and self-hate. This pernicious idea of a flaw in human nature that never can be healed has crept unnoticed into many of the institutions that govern our lives: into the sciences, into our educational system, into economic theory, and into many systems of psychotherapy. It has created a vision for human society based on fear and greed, a vision that the Shambhala teachings call a *setting-sun* vision. Setting-sun vision, which inspires the ignorance of the cocoon, is the attitude of degradation, despair, and meaninglessness that pervades so much of our world today—which could hardly be called a vision at all. The setting-sun society is the cocoon writ large, the "body of fear" of an entire nation.

The Gateway to Fearlessness

There is an alternative to turning away from fear, an alternative approach to fear that can open us up: we can *stay with it and go into it*. Fear itself is not the problem. It is our struggle and resistance to it. It is our *avoidance* of fear, our fear of fear, that closes us off from the world. Far from being a problem, experiencing fear can be a blessing, because without experiencing fear we would be forever stuck in our cocoon and we could never discover fearlessness.

Fear shows us the way out of the cocoon and each time we dare to step across our fear, the cocoon dies a small death. Fear is related to the word *fare*—it is the dues we have to pay to get across to fearlessness. It is the boundary of the cocoon, the boundary that we have to cross to open to a larger world of energy and joy. *The only way to practice with fear is to stay with it and go through it, no matter how intense it may be.*

As you practice seeing and stepping through your fear, you may discover something quite remarkable—that honestly going through fear is enjoyable. It is actually a relief to be able to face fear. You may find that it is all right to be afraid and begin to feel gentle and tender toward your fearful mind and heart. Fear wakes us up. We may be shaking in our boots, but we know that we can go on, and if we are kind to ourselves we *can* go on—into the fear and beyond it— without losing our minds. Karen recalls a powerful experience of going beyond fear:

> I had organized a talk for Chögyam Trungpa Rinpoche at the University of Chicago and before we were to go there he asked me to give an introductory talk about him. Normally this wouldn't have been a big deal, but I was young and he was a formidable person to speak in front of and there were going to be 500 "intellectual" people there. Well, I immediately panicked and tried to get out of it—to no avail. Trungpa Rinpoche sat me down and told me everything I was to say including that he was a "very busy man." He also said that I should speak slowly and

look at everyone in the audience as my friend. I was so panicked he wouldn't let me drive there. And, of course, I couldn't remember a word of what he told me to say.

When the time came, he was seated on the stage behind me and I was handed a microphone. I had to start talking and did but had no idea where the voice was coming from. My first thought was "Oh, I've never talked on a microphone before." I knew I couldn't say *that*, but I determined to go through with the introduction. Then I remembered the instruction to speak slowly and see everyone as my friend. I relaxed and the fear just dissolved. I felt so much appreciation for the audience who had come with their good hearts, so expectantly. When I finished, as well as relief I felt so much heart and compassion.

When we face fear—or situations and thoughts that we are afraid of—and acknowledge it with kindness, the fear does not *necessarily* go away. It may even seem to become deeper and stronger, but nonetheless it changes its quality. As we stay with the fear, no longer covering it over but gently touching it and coming to know it, a new strength develops in us. We find we really are capable of facing fear, without running from it. *This willingness to face fear is itself fearlessness.* Fearlessness is not merely the numb absence of fear. It is the strength and dignity that are nourished each time we face fear directly. The fearlessness that we discover through being willing to experience our fear gently and honestly makes us fully human.

Having discovered the strength that comes from stepping directly into fear, you will know that you need never give up, whatever twists and turns your path may take. The foundation of the entire path of warriorship is the willingness to see, touch, and let go of our cocoon gently by crossing through fear. This practice of fearlessness is always there for you to go back to. Whenever you lose your way, you always know how to begin again. Fearlessness is like the foundation of a house, the solid base on which the rest of the house is built, whether it is a country cottage or a huge mansion. Even if we renovate the house inside and out, we don't change the foundation.

Sometimes your life may seem dark and obscure. You may feel stuck, or you may not know where you are going or if you are really going anywhere at all. Yet you move forward even when you seem stalled. Again and again you will find yourself at the beginning. Yet it can feel like a fresh start from a beginning that you have never known before. You will go through this process over and over again. Each time you go through the gateway of fear, you touch a more profound level of fearlessness and genuine confidence.

At other times your way may seem bright and clear. In a sudden moment you may feel genuine confidence and joy. Such glimpses of unconditioned genuineness may themselves evoke fear, because they can be so different from your habitual image of yourself. But they do give you the bravery and inspiration to go forward. They provide you with a vision for your life and with guidance on your journey of opening to the sacred world.

The vision of human life and society based on goodness and the sacredness of the world is symbolized in the Shambhala teachings by the image of the *great eastern sun* which is contrasted with the vision of the setting sun. Sacredness in the world and human goodness are symbolized by the image of the physical *sun*. Just as the physical sun is a constant source of warmth and brilliance, so sacredness and basic goodness are fathomless sources of creativity that are always available if only we can open our minds and look. Like the physical sun, the sacred world is always *here*. To see it we just have to open our eyes and *see*. This vision is called *great* because it goes far beyond narrow human prejudices and fear. It is a primordial vision found in cultures throughout history. It is not dependent on dogma or moralistic judgments of relative "good" and "bad." And, like the *eastern* sky at dawn, the vision of sacredness and basic goodness inspires wakefulness, freshness, and confidence in our actions. Just as we feel like facing toward the sun when we awaken in the morning, so vision of the *great eastern sun* shows us how to go forward in our life in a fearless, gentle, and wholehearted way.

CONTEMPLATIONS

Uncovering Your Fear   To uncover your underlying fear, you need to discover its hiding places. Look closely at your habits of body speech, emotions, and beliefs. For one week, pay particular attention to when you feel uncomfortable, nervous, irritable, or lazy. What is it that you don't want to do? How do you feel around strangers? How do you feel if you have to do something unfamiliar—give a public talk or a report to a class, go for a job interview, or get up two hours early or stay up two hours beyond your usual bedtime? How does your body feel when you enter a room with everyone watching? How do you feel when someone presents ideas you find unacceptable, stupid, naive, or foolish? Do you usually feel that you are right and get angry when people disagree with you? Perhaps you are at a meeting and you feel something is not right, but are afraid to speak out? Notice when you feel a resistance to change or when you feel pushed.

These are simply suggestions as to where you might look for situations that make you uncomfortable—the sharp points of your life. You can best find your own sharp points. It is easy to know when you are uncomfortable or irritated if you are willing to look and be a little bit honest with yourself.

Working with Fear Choose one of the situations that you discovered in the previous exercise. Notice how you try to avoid uncomfortable feelings and the situations that provoke them. Maybe you've been aware of these habitual patterns for a long time, but you try to ignore them or run away from them. Keep looking at the discomfort in your life. Find the fear in each situation as it arises.

When you do notice the fear underlying your habitual thoughts, emotions, and actions, try to let it be there without pushing it away or reacting to it. When you feel your fear, really feel it. Go toward the situation instead of running away from it (as long as the situation itself is not dangerous or overwhelming), and go toward the fear in your own mind instead of ignoring it. Give in when you feel the fear. Don't struggle or try to build yourself up. Let it make you meek— shy, almost. Feel your soft heart and vulnerable body. See what happens. Remember, it's all right to be afraid. This is just an exercise—if you begin to panic or if the exercise inter- feres with something practical that you need to do, stop and try again another time.

Playing with Fear Play with your fear—as long as it's not life-threatening or hurtful to yourself or others. Begin to see how to go through fear and that there is something delightful about going through it. You may want to go to extremes, such as bungee jumping or parachuting, but that is not necessary. There are plenty of ordinary daily-life fears to play with. Here are a few possibilities:

Talk directly to someone you usually feel nervous around; see if you notice any humor in your nervousness. Take a freezing shower, if the thought of it makes you afraid you'll get pneumonia on the spot. If you do not like to be out in the countryside, spend an evening alone in the woods.

Do you tend to sleep late because you fear that you will be tired if you don't get enough sleep? Try getting up an hour earlier for a few days. Do you always buy the same vegetables at the supermarket? Try a different kind, even if you are afraid you will ruin dinner.

Watch a horror movie, listen to ghost stories, ride a roller coaster, or sit in a dark room. What frightens you? Is there a slight thrill in that? Where is the fun in the fear? Take a playful leap into fear and see what happens.

CHAPTER 6

Opening the Cocoon with Mindfulness

*I*F YOU HAVE BEGUN to understand the nature of the cocoon, its basis in fear, and why we have to go beyond it, you might now be wondering, How do I get out? First, it is important to understand that the cocoon in itself is not a problem. The cocoon is a necessary phase in our growing into human society, and in that sense, it is itself a manifestation of basic goodness. At some point in life, the habits that make up our cocoon were helpful to us and protected us. Later, these same habits came to prevent us from living responsively, from opening to new possibilities. One young woman grew up in a household filled with a great deal of bitterness and unspoken wounds. Her father was usually silent, and whenever she spoke to him with any real feeling, he snapped back at her with a sneering, angry tone. She learned to protect her heart from him. Now, whenever she is with especially quiet men, she feels suspicious and threatened, imagining them to be brooding and quietly putting her down. She realizes that not all quiet men are like her father, but she has great difficulty seeing another side to them.

The cocoon is a natural phenomenon, just like the cocoon in which a butterfly begins its life. The butterfly's cocoon is a living part of the caterpillar, kept alive by its constant patch-ing. But when the butterfly is about to emerge, the cocoon dries up and becomes a dead shell. Just like the butterfly, we grow a cocoon early in our life to protect ourselves. But if we can see and feel its layers in the light and warmth of basic goodness, it will fall away of itself and we can step out. This falling away is unforced and unmanipulated. It is a natural process, just as bark peels from a birch tree as it grows from within. The cocoon falls away when we see it in contrast to the freshness of a moment of basic goodness, much as we may realize that the air in a room is stale only when someone opens the window to let in a fresh breeze, or we may realize that it's getting dark only when someone comes in and turns on the light.

To step out of the cocoon and connect with the sacred world, we have to begin with ourselves. First, we have to *pay attention to the details of our most ordinary experience.* It is in the *details* of your ordinary experience that you will find basic goodness. You will never find it just by believing in it because someone else says it is so, nor by striving for some alternate reality, some other world, nor by vaguely perceiving generalities. You can only experience basic goodness here, for yourself, by paying attention to the details of your sense perceptions in the present moment—moment by moment.

For example, whatever kind of experience you are having at the moment, the fact is that you *are experiencing.* You can feel the beating of your heart, the in and out of your breath, the weight of this book in your hands. Perhaps you hear the sound of the wind whistling past the chimney, the hum of the refrigerator, or the traffic down in the street. If you look around, you may see people's faces or automobiles or the pictures on the wall of your room or the little flowering plant that needs watering.

But you have mental and emotional reactions to all these things that take you away from the direct experiences of your world. You consider them good or you consider them bad, or maybe you're indifferent to them. You feel excited, or you feel blue. You may be so caught up in your judgment or your mood that the fact that you are experiencing at all seems very unimportant to you at the moment. But think back to a time when you had just recovered from a bad fever—how fresh and pleasing simply eating a meal or taking a walk was.

The Epidemic of Mindlessness

In order to pay more attention to the details of our lives, we need to slow down, to stop and be with ourselves for a while. But when we do that, we often just follow our thoughts and feelings along wherever they take us. We very quickly find that we are no longer present. We have lost our sense of being in this particular room, sitting in this particular chair. We have lost the sights and sounds and smells of our immediate surroundings.

Instead, we think about what happened a moment ago or a few hours ago or yesterday or years ago. We recall memories to make ourselves feel better. We replay over and over a deal we lost to make it a deal won; a challenge we avoided becomes a victory. Or we plan for what we expect or want to happen later. We are not present with our immediate experience, nor are we aware that we are thinking: our thoughts are just dragging us along. In this sense, we are *mindless.*

In the popular comic strip "Jump Start," a young nurse who is always busy at work or with some project or other finally has a moment to herself. She says, with a sigh and a bright smile, "No TV. No radio." Then: "At last I am alone with my thoughts." In the closing panel, grimacing and holding her head, she ends, "Boy! It's noisy in here." This is the problem. When our environment is not distracting us, our own thoughts drag our attention hither and thither so that we still cannot be wholly in the present moment. It is not that thoughts themselves are the enemy: we *can* think and be aware of our environment and our own living presence all together, but we don't.

Being mindless, absent from our bodies, our feelings, and even our thoughts in the present moment—being on automatic pilot—is the activity of the cocoon, and it is our condition in daily life almost 100 percent of the time. Some people think it is very clever to be mindless: to be planning a future deal in their thoughts while they are walking down the street, watching TV, or talking to a colleague. Some deliberately cultivate mindlessness to distract themselves from the tedium of their jobs. Musak is played everywhere to relax us and entertain us so that we won't be bored or we won't have to become aware of silence. We sometimes have to hear this mind-dulling drone even while we wait to speak on the phone. Entertainment has become largely the social cultivation of mindlessness—leading us into a fantasy world so that we need not be present to the concerns of our daily drudgery.

Ellen Langer, a psychology professor at Harvard, has spent many years researching the roots of mindlessness and its costs in daily life. In her book *Mindfulness,* she summarizes this research and says, "Mindfulness and mindlessness are so common that few of us appreciate their importance or make use of their power to change our lives." Her book is about "the psychological and physical costs we pay because of pervasive mindlessness and, more important, about the benefits of greater control, richer options, and transcended limits that mindfulness can make possible."

Many people come to near the end of their lives and ask, with a tinge of regret and nostalgia, "I have done many things, but did I really live?" Or they lament, "Life seems to have slipped by without my really noticing it. It went by so fast." Mindfulness is really living your life, not letting it slip by without noticing it. It is paying attention to your life in all its nitty-gritty, slimy, mucky, joyful, and occasionally brilliant detail.

Only at the moment when we are attentive to our lives, mindful of our lives, are we really living at all. Nadia Boulanger, a French music composition teacher whose many famous students included Aaron Copeland and Leonard Bernstein, once commented, "Life is denied by lack of attention, whether it be to cleaning windows or trying to write a masterpiece."

Paula, a Shambhala student, was first brought face-to-face with her life and mind in the Kimberley region of northwest Australia, the most remote and rugged area of the country, on an Aboriginal reserve. She had received a grant to tour the area's schools and to present workshops on a communication technique using drama. She had done this work for several years but had only once before been on an Aboriginal reserve. As she describes it:

> There was much in the Aboriginal way of life that completely turned my American cultural pride inside out. I thought I had thoroughly divested myself of that vulnerability by being a left-wing, New Agey, anti-American whatever. The society I was dealing with was so in contrast to my conceptual world that

"I" became totally undermined. It was by no means an ideal social order, and if I were to go back now years later, I am sure that I would see this even more. The important point is that gradually my mind became apparent to me. It was swirling, distraught, contradictory, a cacophony of ideas, statements, worries, ambitions, fears, hopes, delusions, and so on. And it was constant—no gaps at all. I started to feel desperate and inwardly crazy. I am grateful now.

The Aboriginals told me they thought whiteys were sick. They were always trying to smoke me in a purifying fire or dump me in some sacred pool. They were very kind. Then they started asking me why I wasn't in my own country with my own people. It made no sense to them, and pretty soon it made no sense to me.

One day, in a state of extremely heightened confusion, I walked a little from this bizarre desert settlement. I sat on the edge of an enormous cliff overlooking hundreds of miles of flat red desert dotted with mounds resembling large, nippled breasts. There was a tremendous amount of sky, horizon, and air. Great expanses. And I heard my mind—it felt small, cramped, and painfully claustrophobic. The space felt real. My mind felt sick. The thought arose that if I could let my mind go into all that space, mix it with that space, there would be relief. Let it go with the breath. Just that. Mix my mind with vast space. Maybe I even did it for a moment, but it was fleeting. I knew I could not do it on my own and that I needed someone to teach me how to do this.

Like Paula, when we first sit down quietly with ourselves, our thoughts and feelings seem to run wild. *They* seem to drag *us* along with them. Try this exercise: put this book down and, for five minutes, while sitting in a comfortable but firm chair, try to be aware of the sensation of your backside pressing on the chair. As well, try to be aware of your thoughts. Do your thoughts keep trying to pull you away from the simple task of being mindful of your backside? Do you keep forgetting the exercise and have to start over?

You most likely found that, within a few seconds, your mind was caught up in a thought or an emotion. You were no longer mindful of the sensation of your body, and you had even forgotten your intention. Each time you remembered and brought your attention back, it was probably only a few seconds before you were lost in thought again. This may not have been exactly your experience, but it is close to the experience most of us have the first time. Many people are quite shocked to discover how little influence they really have over what is going on in their own minds—the part of themselves that they believe most certainly to *be* themselves.

How much more difficult it is to remain mindful in the middle of an office meeting! Being mindful in daily life, with all the demands that our environment and our habits of thought place on our attention, is asking too much of ourselves at first. It is like giving a rank beginner a pair of skis and putting him at the top of an Olympic downhill race course: a curve or a bump would send him flying. This same kind of careening out of control would happen if we were to say to ourselves, "Gee, that's a good idea. I will be mindful from now on." Within a few moments, we would be lost in the next thought and bouncing back and forth helplessly, having altogether forgotten our intention to be mindful.

If you tried the exercise, you probably discovered the untamed quality of your mind. It was probably constantly running from one thing to the next or was stuck in a groove from which you could not budge. The mind does not seem to want to be with immediate experience at all. So we need to train our mindfulness, to *practice* mindfulness. This is a very important beginning step. If we don't initially tame the wildness of our mind, we will have no way to experience the richness and power of our world.

Training Mindfulness

Mindfulness, the antidote to the mindless activity of the cocoon, is part of the American tradition of psychology and therapy, going back at least as far as the great Harvard psychologist William James, who said at the turn of the century, "The faculty of voluntarily bringing back a wandering attention, over and over again, is the very root of judgment, character and will. An education which should improve this faculty would be education *par excellence*. But it is easier to define this ideal than to give practical direction for bringing it about."

More recently, therapists and physicians such as Jon Kabat-Zinn have shown how mindfulness is a key element in working with chronic physical pain and psychological suffering. Kabat-Zinn, who was featured on Bill Moyers's television special "Healing and the Mind," is director of the Stress Reduction Unit at the University of Massachusetts Medical Center. In his book describing this program, *Full Catastrophe Living,* he says, "Knowing what you are doing while you are doing it is the essence of mindfulness practice. . . . This leads directly to new ways of seeing and being in your life because the present moment, whenever it is recognized and honored, reveals a very special, indeed magical power: *it is the only time that any of us ever has.*"

Mindfulness and insight-awareness practices also lie at the heart of Buddhist and Taoist training, and Christian teachers and scholars have begun to reclaim mindfulness meditation as the root of Christian prayer. According to Father Laurence Freeman, spiritual director of the World Community for Christian Meditation, "What all religions share is a deep tradition of meditation that stems from the original teachings of their founders. In the experience of meditation, we all face the human struggle with ego and distraction."

Father George Timko, a Greek Orthodox parish priest, says, "Christianity became trapped at some point by thinking that prayer is verbalization and asking. That's a wrong understanding of prayer. The Greek word *prosevkomai* [translated as "prayer"] . . . simply means to be in a mindful state of awareness. *Theoria* [usually translated as "contemplation"] is watching, observing, simply looking. It is an interior looking of the mind, of paying attention without expectations."

The ability to guide our attention to be present to our experience is our human birthright. Doug Boyd, author of *Rolling Thunder,* spent many years living with native medicine peoples in a number of cultures. His story of the year he spent with Native American healer and shaman Rolling Thunder is both down-to-earth and evocative. Boyd emphasizes the key role of mindfulness in shamanistic rituals of all kinds. Spotted Fawn, Rolling Thunder's wife, spoke to Boyd about the drums that she heard incessantly throughout the night during peyote rituals: "The drums speak," she said. "They talk to you and they help you. They keep you there. I remember times I would start to drift away, 'space out' as they say, and the drums would say, 'Pay attention, pay attention, pay attention.'"

Boyd observes, "This reminded me of the night of the purification ritual at the hot springs in Carlin when Rolling Thunder had conveyed those words to me without speaking. Rolling Thunder, like . . . perhaps all "medicine people," gives first priority to the capacity to control attention, to maintain 'one-pointedness of mind.' There can be no healing, no meditation, no meaningful spiritual experience without that highest of disciplines."

All of us *can* learn to be aware of our lives as we live them. Rediscovering and coming to know our basic goodness through being mindful is a natural process that is available to anyone. The beliefs of a particular culture and the way children are brought up may facilitate this process or may serve to thwart it, but the experience is available to any human being.

But becoming mindful does take practice. To train our mindfulness, there is a very simple technique to help us be with ourselves thoroughly and deeply. This is the practice of sitting, or mindfulness practice. It allows us the time and space to discover who we are, to discover and face the details of our wild untamed mind and our fears, and to discover the basic goodness of ourselves and our world.

Practice always involves simplification. Practicing the guitar means doing lots of scales, and training to be a football player means doing a lot of practice sprints, blocks, and tackles. Just as you cannot pick up a guitar and instantly play beautifully, there is no instant mindfulness. Practice takes effort, but with the right vision and intention the effort can be joyful because it feels wholesome and good. Practice *is* only practice, however. The point of playing scales is to be able to play the guitar; the point of the sitting practice of mindfulness is to be mindful in daily life.

Mindfulness is not a tool for therapy, a spiritual exercise, or an educational technique. It is a natural function. *It is, more than anything else, what makes us human.* We all have the capability to be mindful of our body, feelings, perceptions, and thoughts as they happen, unless we are diseased or brain-damaged. But most of us use this ability only partially and intermittently, hardly realizing that we are doing it. There is no training for mindfulness in our upbringing, and we therefore do not realize the fullness of living and the creative potential that its practice can unfold. We practice mindfulness—"bringing back the wandering attention over and over again" —simply so that we can be present in our lives as they happen. Only when we are present can we begin to see our cocoon, to feel the fear that keeps it going, and perhaps to be refreshed by glimpses of the sacred world.

We will summarize the basic instructions for mindfulness sitting practice: Sit cross-legged on a firm cushion on the floor, or on a dining table–type chair with your back straight and upright, your shoulders relaxed, and your hands palm down on your thighs. Keep your lips slightly parted and your eyes open with your gaze down. Let your body relax while keeping good posture—not too tight and not too loose.

Now turn your attention to your breath. As it goes out, let your awareness go out with it—let go, actually try to go out with the breath. At the end of the out-breath, let your attention return to your body and posture. Notice the next out-breath, and so on.

Don't try to control or manipulate your thoughts and emotions. Whatever thought, emotion, image, or sensation arises in your mind as you sit, acknowledge it, touch it thoroughly, and then let it go. And try to keep your sense of humor!

From time to time, as you sit there, you can take a brief break from the technique: for a few seconds, just relax and think that you are not practicing mindfulness. Then begin again with a fresh start.

You might try this alone, but it is always better to get personal instruction from a qualified teacher. It is helpful to schedule a time to practice during the day when you will not be interrupted. Make a commitment to practice sitting mindfulness for a specific period of time, perhaps twenty or thirty minutes; if you practice less than this, you really will not have time to let your mind settle. And continue practicing until the end of the time period you have set aside, unless your house is on fire! You might practice three days a week or every day, whatever is manageable for you. Often people manage to find as much as an hour a day to sit during some periods of their lives.

A crucial aspect of sitting is to have an attitude toward the practice that is free from striving for results, or expecting any particular experience. The much-loved Zen teacher Suzuki Roshi used to call this state of mind "beginner's mind." He said,

> Our "original mind" includes everything within itself. It is always rich and sufficient within itself. You should not lose your self-sufficient state of mind. This does not mean a closed mind, but actually an empty mind and a ready mind. If your mind is empty, it is always ready for anything; it is open to everything. In the beginner's mind there are many possibilities; in the expert's mind there are few.

In the beginner's mind there is no thought, "I have attained something." All self-centered thoughts limit our vast mind. When we have no thought of achievement, no thought of self, we are true beginners. Then we can really learn something. The beginner's mind is the mind of compassion.

Sitting practice is a way to be kind to yourself and to have the courage to find out and to be who you are. It is a way to stop running from your anxiety, running to catch up or keep up with your neighbors, running to fulfill your own and others' expectations for you, running away from knowing your own mind and heart, running toward your death and rarely ever tasting the richness of your life. Anne wrote to us of her first experience of a two-day session of group sitting practice.

I guess what I remember about the first day is the total surprise of having all these thoughts go on and on in my mind while I was focusing on my breath; and realizing that I wasn't creating these thoughts— they were happening on their own. I didn't sit down to think, I sat down to focus on my breath and go out with my breath. So that was a revelation just to realize that thoughts arise and move with their own energy.

On the second day I had my first experience of the gap between thoughts—going out with my breath and staying out there for a moment. There was an absence of any barriers or sense of separateness between me and the point on the floor where my eyes rested. I felt a sharp shock that this was so. It was the first time that I experienced the fact that I am not just this cubic unit named Anne.

It felt as if all my life I had lived with a pair of binoculars attached to my eyes backward so that everything seemed out of reach and always slightly off balance. Every time I tried to capture the beauty in my life, it seemed always just beyond my grasp. As I was sitting that day I saw things clearly for the first time. What a shock! That momentary glimpse of how life could be and that it is possible to truly experience the world purely as it is, I shall never forget.

Quite often, as we continue to sit, the more superficial memories and fantasies become boring and wear out their welcome, and deeper feelings come to the surface. Emotional energy that has been blocked by constant inner chatter or constant busyness finally has a chance to call on your awareness and ask for attention. In the privacy and safety of sitting practice, nothing is pushed away as bad or invited as especially good. Whatever occurs, you can treat it exactly the same—touch it, thoroughly acknowledge its presence, feel how it feels and what mood it brings with it, and let it go gently and without force.

This evenness toward all our thoughts, hidden desires, or deep prejudices is a fundamental expression of gentleness and fearlessness. We are gentle and kind to ourselves: nothing is rejected, nothing pushed away as childish or silly or too wild. And we are fearless: we do not hide from anything but look directly at our experience just as our eyes are open and we are facing forward in the physical posture. This is the beginning of warriorship. For if we can be gentle and fearless toward ourselves, we can then be gentle and fearless toward others and toward the world. There is tremendous human dignity in just sitting upright, facing our inner lives directly, without manipulation or judgment.

Going away from home to practice alone for a few days or a week, or maybe even longer, can help to deepen your experience of sitting. Sometimes the very thought of being alone with the mind is so sad and lonely that we can't imagine doing such a thing. Being alone, really alone, maybe for the first time—without even a telephone to call a friend—can even be frightening. But something surprising and magical might happen.

Perhaps you will discover a little sore spot on your heart, a little feeling of tenderness for yourself and your plight—your sorry state. You may feel so sad that you fall in love with yourself. It's lonely. You can't share yourself with anyone yet. But that sadness slows you down and makes you sensitive to your world. You start to feel the space, and you start to come alive. You start to appreciate yourself—being alone with your self is so rich. You start to appreciate the whole world of colors and sounds—the trees, the greenery, the chipmunks and birds, even taxicab horns, for that matter. These sensations call you to pay attention to the details of your experience and wake you up out of your deep sleep. The world becomes alive and bright, and the more you can open to it, the more you can see. So when your sad and lonely and joyful and tender retreat is finished, you may venture back to your world a little tentatively, but you may see with new eyes—the eyes of basic goodness.

Of course, during a first experience of sitting practice (and usually for long after that) practitioners may struggle with all kinds of negativity arising within their own minds. Doubt frequently attacks. After the initial joy and relief of finding that you can be with yourself, you may begin to wonder why you are doing it. Your speedy or depressed mind may come back in full force and accuse you of wasting time, of being naïve, of losing contact with reality. Your body may discover all kinds of new pains, usually caused by tension. Doubt is a universal experience for everyone on a path of warriorship. Such twists and turns are to be expected, and because these negative feelings come from an aspiration to be genuine, they are themselves an expression of basic goodness.

But many people just feel deeply relieved to sit and practice mindfulness. They feel a sense of fresh air, of open spaciousness. Even if their life is very difficult and they feel great pain, just to *be with* the pain for the first time, no matter what turmoil they find in their thoughts and feelings, is profoundly healing. This realization is itself the discovery of basic goodness. For many students, a glimpse of basic goodness is a tremendous relief, like letting go of a huge burden that they have carried for many years. Some people weep at their momentary freedom from anxiety. Others associate the experience with childhood memories of joyful times when they were truly themselves. Some feel an intense, almost physical warmth in the heart, as if they were actually connecting with their hearts for the first time. For others, it is like coming home to a warm hearth after a long hard journey. Once you have glimpsed basic goodness or even just vaguely felt its reality, it gives you a sense of direction for your life.

CHAPTER 7

The Joy of Being Fully Present

Mindfulness in Daily Life

W E PRACTICE MINDFULNESS in sitting practice precisely so that we can carry it into daily life. The challenge is to extend your mindfulness practice from its foundation in sitting practice to action in the world. The whole point of mindfulness practice is to be present without losing mindfulness in the middle of daily-life activities. Sogyal Rinpoche says, "I cannot say it strongly enough: to integrate meditation in action is the whole ground and point and purpose of meditation. The violence and stress, the challenges and distractions of modern life make this integration even more urgently necessary."

Mindfulness in daily life is not the same as self-consciousness. When you are self-conscious, you are split into someone who is acting and someone else who is watching. You are in two minds—and are filled with doubt. Self-consciousness can become a problem for practitioners of mindfulness, especially if they take a heavy-handed, "religious" attitude toward it. In that case, "mindfulness" becomes another reason to beat themselves over the head, to doubt their basic goodness.

Mindfulness actually means being 100 percent *one* with what you are doing and what you are saying. Your mind and body are joined, synchronized, and in harmony: they are one.

Your mind is no longer constantly racing ahead of your body, planning and scheming, nor dragging behind as it tries to dwell in yesterday. Nor does your mind stand aloof and watch your actions as if from a distance. Instead, your body and mind experience the world *together*. Your attention is fully in the present, mindful of sense perceptions at the very moment you have those perceptions. As you reach for a coffee cup, your mind pays attention to the color of the cup, the smell of the coffee, the feel of the solid curving handle between your fingers, its weight as you pick it up.

When you practice in this way, mindfulness becomes a source of joy rather than worry. It brings joy because when you let go of the doubting watcher and can just be with your life as it is, much more energy and vitality are available to you. Practicing mindfulness in the midst of activity, however, takes some effort and discipline. When you're not used to it, mindfulness does not come as naturally as your heartbeat, although it is a natural function. First, you have to form a deliberate *intention* to be mindful, although the effort you make doesn't have to be heavy and dutiful. Mindfulness in action can have both humor and a light touch.

In a discussion group, John told of a moment of mindfulness that occurred to him while he was driving down the street:

> I was in a sort of sullen, gray, mildly depressed, mildly anxious mood. Just closed in my little world. No big deal, just stuck. Out of the blue, I remembered a photography class, where we practiced looking at colors. Out of a corner of my eye, I noticed something—I think it was the green leaves on the trees. Suddenly, wow! There was a world out there!

It was as if a curtain had been pulled back. Suddenly, a huge, colorful world was just *there*. My dull mood simply evaporated. It wasn't exactly dramatic; it felt very simple and ordinary. But it made a powerful difference to me. For several minutes afterward, I was able to practice mindfulness with real delight.

You can begin to bring mindfulness into your daily life by retaining your mindfulness as you rise from your practice cushion and leave the space. At this point, do not use your breath as the focus of mindfulness. Rather, pay attention to the soles of your feet as they press on the floor and the way your legs feel as they walk. Next, you can practice mindfulness of body in the midst of simple physical tasks such as pouring milk into a bowl of cereal, carrying wood in for the stove, or typing a letter. Pay attention to each detail of your movement while remaining present, so that your mind and body are doing the same things. As you pour the cereal into the bowl, notice how the bowl feels and looks—the colors, the light reflected on it—how the cereal sounds hitting the bowl, what happens when the milk touches the cereal, and so forth. There are innumerable details for you to notice.

Mindfulness of Speech

Mindfulness in daily life includes mindfulness of speech, which is a very important practice. Speech is the link between body and mind. If body and mind are not joined, they communicate different messages. Since we cannot manipulate our body as we can our words, our body will give us away. Bodies communicate in many ways. Posture, gestures, facial tension, the way you walk or enter a room—these visible communications may say something quite different from the words you speak. If this is the case, your speech will inevitably be deceptive to yourself and to others.

Being fully present in the moment, with mind and body joined, is the basis of genuine speech. Speech, at its most superficial level, involves only the literal meaning of words. But when someone is speaking, vastly more is happening than the literal meaning of the words. We choose particular words, but the sound and tone of our voice as we speak also have meaning. The rhythm, pace, and precision with which we speak and the quality of the silence between words also communicate meaning.

When you speak mindfully, you actually hear and feel the words as they come out of your mouth. You feel the place in your body where they originate. They may come from the heart center in your chest or off the top of your head or from a tight little knot in your throat. You may speak with feeling for what you are saying, or you may speak as if you were reading a press release. You may be speaking too fast, so that the words come tumbling out before you know what you are going to say. Do the words come out sharply like bullets, or do they have a gentler quality? Do they stroke the listener or strike him? You can be aware of all these aspects of your speech when you speak mindfully.

Ask yourself if you are saying what you mean to say. Are you being fundamentally honest and direct in your communication? Or is there some deception in your words or attitude, toward either yourself or others? If you're not communicating what you feel, you'll create a lot of confusion in your relationships. The purpose of speech is to communicate, but even in a request as simple as "Please pass the salt," there is almost always something besides words. There can be communication of hatred or love, of cold indifference or appreciation. When your body and mind are working together, you speak differently from the way you speak in your cocoon.

Words have power: they are not merely bearers of dictionary meanings. They carry the wisdom of generations. When you say "I love you so much" or "The sky is very black" or "Just thinking about it makes my mouth water," your words carry a whole world of subtle meanings. When you speak with synchronized mind and body and open heart, listening to and feeling your words, you tune in to that flow of power, and you become a conduit for it. With body and mind together, you say neither more nor less than you mean, and the words you speak have clarity and the power to affect your world. When you speak automatically, by contrast, you have only the power of a mechanical doll or a broken faucet.

Practicing mindfulness of speech, or elocution, in a group can reveal some of our most deep-seated resistances to knowing ourselves. People can be invited to read exercises or poems, clearly enunciating and differentiating each vowel and consonant. When people take part in elocution practice they hear how they are speaking, and feel how they are forming the words in their mouths, throats, and bodies. Perhaps this is the first time they have ever realized how they speak. So much of our habitual identity is embodied in our speech that when we are asked to change the way we speak, our personal arrogance can come out. Even though they have volunteered to do this exercise, at first people often show tremendous irritation and resistance. However, some remarkable changes take place in people even in the course of just one ten-minute exercise. Kathy took part in an evening of elocution during a week-long residential program of Shambhala warriorship training. Her experience of elocution practice may be extreme but it is not atypical:

> The night of elocution practice I was irritated beyond belief. I thought the elocution was long and painful and I stormed to my room thinking, "this practice is not for me, it's absurd." I hated everything that I was doing here. I was going to talk to someone tomorrow and leave. I don't remember ever having felt so irritated, or ever having so little faith about the Shambhala path. The next morning, though, I woke up and began to say aloud 'the rain in Spain stays mainly in the plain.' [This was not one of the exercises!] I burst out laughing. I couldn't believe how good and cheerful I felt. This was not like me to wake up like this. I didn't know how I got to this flip side of the coin of my state of mind. I left the room taking pictures of trees and plants and mushrooms as I walked the path on my way to breakfast. Everything at breakfast was delicious. What the hell happened? At the talk that night the director said that irritability opens things up. It was a magical connection. I had never before felt that flip in that kind of way. Never.

Mindfulness of Your State of Mind

Mindfulness in daily life can include mindfulness of your state of mind, being attentive to your state of mind or to your mood at the moment. Does your mind feel closed and claustrophobic, or open and expansive? Do you have a lot of speedy thoughts racing along like a highland stream, are your thoughts slow and thick like a stagnant pond, or are they

something in between, like a broad river? Are you in a religious frame of mind today or more murderous? Simply note
your state of mind at the moment, seeing how it changes in
response to changing circumstances, seeing how little you are
normally able to "control" it.

Our state of mind always affects what we do and say, but
we hardly ever acknowledge this. We usually believe our ob-
servations about the people around us without taking into
account our own mood. When we are tired and grumpy, we
believe that our irritable judgments are accurate. When we
are cheerful and optimistic, we might dive into a situation
without careful forethought. When we feel flat and bored,
the world seems to have little to offer. All this comes from
not paying attention to our state of mind.

When we do become mindful of our state of mind, we may
begin to notice a simple sense of presence that is mindful of
what we are thinking, saying, and doing, without judgment
or commentary. This mindfulness beyond thought is sometimes referred to as the "transcendental watcher" because it
is altogether beyond cocoon mind. It is *always* there, but as
soon as we become caught up in our thoughts and actions, we
lose touch with it.

When you try to practice mindfulness, distractions will
likely come along pretty quickly. Don't worry about it. These
distractions are reminders. Simply remember mindfulness
again—it might be two minutes, two hours, or two days
later—and then again pay attention, mindfully, to whatever
you are doing. When you are not deliberately practicing,
mindfulness will come to you from time to time, suddenly.
This is a result of your previous practice, and such moments
will come more often as you practice more. Acknowledge
your moments of mindfulness when they occur and remain

mindful for as long as you can without struggling. The more you do this, the more often mindfulness will return.

The key to bringing mindfulness into your daily life is relaxation in your efforts. Forcing mindfulness will not work. If you try too hard to hold on to mindfulness, you will turn it into a struggle. You'll be thinking about mindfulness rather than actually doing it. Your thought will again be divided from your action—this time, in the name of mindfulness. Where mindfulness arises in the middle of activity, acknowledge it and let it go, just as you would any other thought. If you try to grasp it, you will lose it; if you let it go, it will come back. Just as you once learned to walk as a child and then trusted that you could walk, you can trust that mindfulness will return. Just like walking, mindfulness is a natural function: once you have learned to be mindful, you don't have to keep checking that you are doing it.

When you are mindful, you are here, actually living your life, and your mind and body function harmoniously together. Practice itself develops trust in the effectiveness of practice. Gradually, a "residue of mindfulness" develops naturally in you, a general atmosphere of mindfulness in which you need not struggle. Your mind can appreciate resting in mindfulness, almost naïvely, and you become familiar with the sense of being present.

Awareness

As you continue to practice mindfulness, both in sitting practice and in daily life, your practice expands to include *awareness* of the outer environment as well as the inner environment of your thoughts and emotions. The distinction between *mindfulness* and *awareness* comes from the Buddhist tradition of practice. The Sanskrit word for mindfulness is *shamatha,* which literally means "development of peace" but is sometimes used to mean "taming the mind." The Sanskrit word for awareness is *vipashyana,* which can also be translated as "insight." Mindfulness is the attention to detail and settling of mind. Awareness is the more global sense of space, openness, and clarity that develops out of mindfulness as your practice strengthens. Awareness is the insight that sees the holes in the cocoon, sees that the cocoon is mostly make-believe, and sees through it. The precision of mindfulness to actually see the cocoon, and the openness of awareness to see beyond the cocoon, are both necessary aspects of practice in action, like the two wings of a bird.

The development of awareness fundamentally means a greater and greater recognition of space. Your sense perceptions open so that you can literally be aware of more of the space around you and the perceptions arising in that space. You can begin to include a larger space in your awareness. This is a relaxed, natural process, not strained or focused. Your awareness expands of its own accord, and you can just let it happen. You can feel the space around and within other people, feel the living space that surrounds trees and rocks and encircles the earth. You recognize psychological space in your own being, as if your mind and heart were full of holes constantly letting in the fresh air of unfamiliar and perhaps strange ideas and feelings.

In daily life, when we look with awareness, we literally include the space around us in our attention. We notice peripheral sights and sounds—and they no longer feel like distractions to our mindfulness. When we are talking to someone, we notice the spaces within, between, and around the two of us and the subtleties of our exchange. We slow down and hear the silence between our words. When we slow down, we don't need to react defensively or with speed.

In the summer of 1971, shortly after he first met Chögyam Trungpa, Jeremy was doing garbage-collection duty at the contemplative center that he was staffing.

> Trungpa Rinpoche was teaching there all summer and was staying in a cottage in a nearby village. I went over to his house to pick up his garbage. The door to the living room was open. Rinpoche invited me in and offered me tea. As I sat at the table with him, I became very self-conscious and nervous. The space around me seemed to get smaller and smaller, and my attention narrowed down to the table in front of me and to Rinpoche, sitting opposite and smiling. Embarrassed and struggling to find something to say, I began to complain about the sloppiness of other staff and the dirtiness of the center. After a few minutes, Rinpoche cocked his head to one side as if he were listening and then interrupted me, saying, "Is that a lawn mower?" I stopped and listened, and indeed, there was the sound of a lawn mower way off in the distance.
>
> At first, I felt a surge of irritation that he seemed not to have been listening to me, but then suddenly my awareness expanded. I felt the whole room around me, and I became aware of the evening sun shining outside and the fields around the house. My body relaxed, I sat back in my chair, and I was able to continue to talk with him about the general situation at the center and its possibilities, while dropping my nervous complaining. When Rinpoche drew my

attention to the sound of the lawn mower, he actually increased my awareness of the room around me and of my body sitting at the table, instead of diminishing my awareness, as one might suppose.

When awareness opens, you are able to relax and see the larger patterns of your own and others' behavior. You can see more of the whole context, the bigger picture. It is like being able to see all around you—360 degrees—rather than just straight ahead. You begin to see with your whole being rather than with your eyes alone. Through the practice of awareness, you connect mind with body. You can pay attention in this way and still talk to a friend. Even as you sit typing at a computer monitor, for example, you can be aware of the room around you, the sounds coming from the street, the larger space above you, and the solid chair, supported by the earth beneath you.

Awareness also brings attention to the inner environment that the emotions carry with them. If you pay attention with awareness, you will notice that each emotion brings along with it a trail of other thoughts, emotions, and moods— feelings of expansiveness or contraction, of sadness or joy. We do not have merely an angry thought about a friend: our anger has something behind it. It brings all kinds of assumptions about the friend's attitude and behavior, for example; it may bring jealousy and even passion along with it. Strong emotions always bring fear and grasping. When you look directly at your emotion, with clear insight, you will see that it is fleeting and insubstantial, having no permanence other than your attempt to hold on to it. Seeing this, you can begin to let go of the fear and feel the energy of the emotion as it is.

When we lack awareness, we too often jump to conclusions about people without slowing down enough to look at them, feel how they are feeling, see what they are going through. When we are more aware of the inner environment of our emotions, we no longer get them so mixed up with the outer world. We don't take our own emotional reactions about people to be the objective truth about them, and we don't confuse our past associations with people with their present situations. We remain open to what other people have to say and show right now, regardless of our past interactions with them. Awareness enables us to discriminate between authentic and inauthentic words because, with awareness, we not only hear the words that are being spoken but sense the meaning and feeling behind those words.

A colleague, for example, might make a comment to you that on the face of it seems insulting, and you might impulsively react with a corresponding insult. When you are aware of the demeanor of the colleague, however—the tone of voice, and so on—you can see that the felt insult is actually an expression of his own insecurity and that you have the possibility of reacting with compassion. With the freshness and openness that awareness brings, you can let go of your own self-righteousness. You can feel the energy of your own and your colleague's emotions, and genuine communication can take place.

Sense of Humor

A natural sense of humor develops when we acknowledge the sudden, unpredictable flashes of awareness and insight. A sense of humor comes from opening to broader perspective on a situation. It can often arise from seeing the situation through someone else's eyes, whether it be a black cat or one's own daughter.

A friend recounts the following story:

> Early in our marriage, my wife and I sometimes got into some pretty ferocious fights. Somehow, we seemed to be talking on completely different levels. We just locked into something that neither of us could seem to stop, once it got going. One day, we were in a frenzy of shouting and insulting each other. I picked up one of my wife's favorite vases and threatened to hurl it at the wall. I looked across the room, and there was our black cat sitting on the back of the sofa, staring at us. At that very moment, he yawned.
>
> Seeing that cat's open, blank stare was like hearing a crack in my mind. It opened up the space. Suddenly, I realized how emotionally indifferent that cat was to all that was going on between us, even though he seemed to be watching us with intense curiosity. I felt an urge to laugh that was so strong not even my anger could suppress it. I suppose I realized how comical the whole fight was. My wife stared at me for a moment, and our anger just dissipated. The whole room as well as our mood lightened up.

Sense of humor is a necessary ingredient if we want to follow any spiritual path. Down-to-earth straightforwardness is the ground of all practice. We have to keep our feet firmly on the earth if we are to open our minds and hearts into the subtle meanings and energies of our world without getting carried away into pretentious fantasies about ourselves. When we begin to realize the basic goodness in ourselves, we might take our discovery much too seriously. We become solemn, religious, and lose our sense of humor. Humor does not mean telling jokes or being comical or laughing at others. A genuine sense of humor is appreciating reality with a light touch and a sense of perspective. Once, Jeremy sprained his toe and could hardly walk. He parked his car outside the post office in a fifteen-minute spot in the pouring rain.

> When I came back from the post office, the car wouldn't start. I hobbled to a phone booth about fifty yards away, getting soaked in the process, and called for help. I returned to the car, cursing, to wait for a tow truck. After a few minutes, I felt a shadow over my left shoulder. A policeman was banging on the window, glowering at me. I explained that the car would not start and I was waiting for a tow truck. He pointed to another parking spot a hundred feet away and helped me push the car to it in the rain. I climbed back into the car drenched and fuming. Our twelve-year-old daughter, Vanessa, who had been sitting inside all this time, looked at me with amused concern. "Why are you so irritated?" she asked. Suddenly, I saw the whole episode from Vanessa's perspective, and we both exploded with laughter.

Perceiving Vastness in the Details

Awareness is experiencing the space in our environment, which opens us up to the bigger world. When the precision and one-pointedness of mindfulness is joined with the openness and insight of awareness, perception of the heart opens. We can see, hear, smell, taste, and touch the details of the world around us without being caught up in them, fascinated by them, or repelled by them.

We can recognize the living, dynamic, responsive quality of the physical space of the world. When something has physical space in and around it, it becomes illuminated. If you go to an old junk shop and find a valuable antique vase on a shelf surrounded closely by hundreds of other objects—in front, in back, and all around—you probably don't see it very clearly. But if you take that same vase upstairs and put it in a spacious room, on a pedestal, with special lighting, the sacredness of the vase becomes apparent. The space around it illuminates it, and you can experience its beauty.

We can feel ourselves to be immersed in a living, spacious world where each detail has its own place and meaning. When you look at a peony, you first see the whole flower, its color and shape. As you keep looking, you see the petals and veins and stamens and pistils. When you look more closely still, you see the segments and shading in the petals, until you begin to feel you could go deeper and deeper into those details. Then you can begin to feel a sense of vastness, a connection to vast space and to all other things. Gradually, you recognize that the space "inside" is no different from the space "outside." As Suzuki Roshi says, "The inner world is limitless, and the outer world is also limitless. We say 'inner world' or 'outer world,' but actually there is just one whole world."

CONTEMPLATIONS

Mindfulness of Body   This exercise can help you to become mindful of the inner sensation of your body and to join mind and body together. A good time to do this is after sitting practice. Sit on a firm chair without leaning back or on a stool. Plant your feet on the floor firmly and place your hands on your thighs. Feel the sensation of the bottom of your feet as the floor presses up against them. Feel the sensation of your feet, from the inside. Don't judge whether the sensation is "good" or "bad," whether you are sensing what you are "supposed" to be sensing. Whatever you do or don't sense in your feet, pay attention to that for a moment. Now, move your attention up your shins and calves, again resting there for a while.

Now, continue to move your attention through your knees and into your thighs, hands, and forearms, resting for a moment at each stage. Move your mindfulness up your torso and upper arms to your shoulders—up through the back of your neck, over the top of your head, down your face and chest, and into your heart, coming to rest there.

Now, let the inner sensation of your entire body, as you just went through it, come into your awareness. Try to have a sensation of your whole body as one unit. Hold that sensation for as long as you can—perhaps a few minutes.

After you have done this exercise, you may decide to remember to do it from time to time during the day. When you do remember, choose a part of your body—any part (your right forearm, for example)—and notice the inner sensation of that part. Keep the mindfulness of this inner sensation for a few moments while you continue your other activities. Notice any change in your perceptions.

Mindfulness of Action   Choose an ordinary action that you often do. It can be anything, but keep it simple. While you are doing it, be mindful of every detail. Maybe you choose cutting an apple. The first thing you do is prepare your space. Set down the cutting board; look at the details of the wood, how the grain goes, and how the previous cuts have marked it. Feel the texture of the apple, how it smells, how the colors of the skin subtly shade into one another. Feel the sensation of your arm moving to pick up the knife, your muscles tensing as you grasp it; feel its weight; look at its shape and sharpness. Hear the crunch of the knife as it slowly goes through the apple. See and smell the juice; feel your mouth starting to water. Keep going: the details you can notice are endless. When you notice that thoughts or the sound of someone talking has taken away your mindfulness, simply return to your activity of cutting, just as in sitting practice you return to the breath.

Mindfulness of Speech   Choose a favorite poem. Read it out loud to yourself.

Now, read it aloud again, paying attention to each vowel and consonant, to each syllable and word and phrase. Speak each distinctly and precisely. Read slowly, word by word. You can definitely exaggerate. Sit up straight while you are doing this.

Feel the difference between the two styles of reading.

Read it out loud one more time. This time, don't exaggerate the precision so much, but keep it in mind. Speak with a dignified, uplifted body.

Now, have a friend listen. Repeat the poetry readings both in your usual manner of speaking and in the slow, precise way. Feel that both your readings are communicating to your friend.

You can try this exercise in daily life. When you remember to, pay attention to how you are speaking without trying to alter anything about it. Pay attention to the quality of what you are saying, the loudness or softness, the speed, the tone, the feeling in what you are saying, and the meaning you are trying to convey. Now, try to be mindful of your speech, and speak more precisely, as you did in the reading exercise. Do you feel any difference in what you are saying or in how it is being received by the person you are talking to?

Joining Mind and Body   Next time you are in a café or diner (or bus or train), try to join mind and body and notice how your perception changes. As you sit there, instead of losing yourself in your thoughts, feel the presence of your own body. Now, take a moment to look at and listen to the details: to what people are wearing, the way they are moving, the tones of their voices, the sounds of traffic outside, and the smell of slightly stale coffee and the sweetness of the doughnuts. The place itself suddenly comes alive, as if you had awakened from a dream for a moment. You are actually *here;* the world is actually *here.*

Awareness of Space around an Object   Choose an object you find particularly beautiful and care about. Put it somewhere free of clutter, against a plain background. Spend some time looking at the details of it. Let yourself appreciate its lines, its color, its texture, its quality. Now, soften your gaze, relax your focus, and see the space around the object. You might notice an energetic quality to that space. Notice how you feel about the object and any change of perception when you relax your focus.

When you think of it, you can do this exercise on the spot, with anything your gaze falls on. First, just look at the object in your usual focused way. Then, as before, soften your gaze, relax your focus, notice the details of the object and the space around it, and notice any change in your perception of and feeling about the object.

CHAPTER 8

Opening to the Energy of Emotions

MINDFULNESS AND AWARENESS are the basic tools with which we continue on our warrior's journey into authentic living; synchronized mind-and-body is the vehicle; and fear is the stepping-stone and the gateway. As you practice awareness in your daily life, over and over you will find yourself on the edge between opening out to your world and fearfully closing back into yourself. This is the edge of the cocoon. The cocoon is not some solid "thing" so that either you are out of it or you are not. The cocoon is a dynamic quality of the mind and heart—the constant tendency to freeze and turn inward instead of opening out. For example, suppose you are in a difficult relationship and trying to decide whether to leave it or stay with it. It is not that one or the other decision is the "right" one, the one that is out of the cocoon, while the other decision would be staying in your cocoon. It is your state of mind at the very moment when you are considering your decision that matters: is it tight, frozen, fearful, or simply open to the uncertainty of not knowing what the outcome will be?

Stepping out of this frozen state happens at each moment. It is not necessarily a big deal. It need not be a struggle. It may be just a fleeting, almost imperceptible, insight about your stubbornness, perhaps, or your grasping. If you can catch such insights, you can choose to acknowledge them. This is where the practice of mindfulness and awareness is essential: you slow down and become precise enough to be able to catch brief cracks in your defenses, then relax and open enough to acknowledge them.

D. H. Lawrence beautifully describes the gentle step out of the cocoon into a fresh world in his poem "Escape":

> When we get out of the glass bottle of our ego,
> and when we escape
> like squirrels in the cage of our personality
> and get into the forest again, we shall shiver
> with cold and fright.
> But things will happen to us
> so that we don't know ourselves.
> Cool, unlying life will rush in,
> and passion will make our
> bodies taut with power.
> We shall laugh, and
> institutions will curl up
> like burnt paper.

The world that we encounter each time we open our awareness beyond the barrier of fear is full of challenges. Being a warrior does not mean that everything will go evenly and smoothly. We are not trying to anesthetize ourselves— quite the contrary. We wish to become aware of the world as it is, without a plastic skin to protect us. Once we open our- selves to it, something new can always appear to press our emotional buttons, rouse our habitual reactions, and chal- lenge us to be mindful warriors and not mindless cowards.

The habitual reactions always cover fear. The difference between the warrior and the coward lies in their attitudes toward these sharp points of fear: the warrior pays attention to them and eventually can be delighted by them; the coward covers them over or runs from them. It takes daring and courage to be genuine, to stay on the path of warriorship, to stay with the sharpness and awkwardness of who we are and how we are.

These painful points can come about not just because we are more sensitive to the world but also because we are more sensitive to our own reactions. When you practice awareness in the world, you may find yourself reacting with volatile emotion to small events that previously you would have brushed off insensitively. You may feel embarrassed by this or thrown off balance. Who is this person? you may wonder. When an associate is late meeting you for an appointment, anger and resentment might flare up as if from nowhere. You might feel surprising new flames of passion when meeting an old friend. You might feel deeply depressed over a seemingly small setback at school or work.

This experience is different for everyone. You may listen to other people and hear them for the first time. You may find that people you know are quite different from the way you always thought of them. You may realize how strange your husband or wife really is to you, or you may realize that there is some truth in the criticisms that your boss or teenage child makes of you. The affection your friends show may feel a little too intense; friendships may seem not to flow so smoothly as you look at your friends with fresh eyes. You may see more clearly the aggression and manipulation of your colleagues at the office.

Tom, a newspaper editor, seemed in a state of shock in a

group discussion after he had been practicing for a few months. "Nothing is working anymore. I feel awkward and loud. I see how I boss people around. But I don't know how else to do my job. I see people being brutal to each other, and I don't know how to stop them. How can I go to work without my masks? What's wrong with masks anyway? I feel as if I'm being turned into a wet rag." Others in the group nodded in sympathy. They, too, were having a rough time.

We want so much to be free from pain rather than face the simple truth of our lives. But spiritual training isn't intended to make you feel good continuously. You're not doing something wrong if you sometimes feel pain. Your life is bound to feel more painful at times—perhaps a great deal more painful—as you begin to wake up to who you really are. It is like when you sit too long with your legs tucked under you and one leg goes to sleep; as it wakes up, you get a prickly, painful sensation of "pins and needles" as feeling returns to it. Or when you go to the dentist and get a shot of anesthetic, your jaw goes to sleep; as it wakes up and feeling returns, it can be very painful. Like feeling physical sensation return to a sleeping limb or jaw, waking up to who you are, feeling who you are, can be prickly and painful.

Sara, in another group discussion, told us:

> I had tried to be a good, loving friend to Joseph for two years. One day, I looked at him and realized that I didn't really like him and didn't want to be with him. I just felt numb around him and always had. This was really a shock to me. I didn't want to hurt him, and I felt sad both for him and for myself, but our relationship was a sham. I knew I had to end it, but I would try to do it kindly. I realized that I had

known this for some time but simply couldn't face it before. Now, my feeling of wanting to be genuine is stronger than my fear of being honest with Joseph or my fear of being alone.

Feeling the Raw Energy of Emotions

When we are afraid to face our fear and embarrassment, we relate to others with habitual and stereotyped "emotions." We usually experience the emotion, and believe it, without feeling the underlying fear that it covers. We become angry when we feel insulted, without acknowledging the "me" that we are trying to protect. We feel passion toward someone when he or she nourishes our pride and rubs "me" the right way. If the emotion is too intense, too real, we're likely afraid of *it* as well as the deeper fear that it hides. The energy may feel threatening simply because it hurts, or it may feel overwhelming because it's so delightful and passionate. It may feel painful because it is unfamiliar and scary, and we get confused trying to figure it out. We are afraid of losing control, of having our mask stripped. We narrow the emotional energy of our relationships and communications; we fix it and diminish its power. Then we give it a familiar name—like anger, passion, or depression—and conceptualize it into story lines: "It won't work out, it's not practical, it's not what I had in mind," or, "You are the only one in the world for me, my true soul mate, what miracle could have brought you to me?" We may eventually become afraid to feel deeply at all. We may resist the energy, try to escape it, or react defensively to it, which creates further pain. We fear that we may become lost in our emotions and lose our dignity. We try to repress them, losing sight of the fact that, without emotion, nothing moves us.

The key to warriorship is to become aware of the energy of emotion as it arises and of the fear as well as the softness and tenderness that accompany the emotion. Let go of the fear, refuse to hold on to the energy as "my anger" or "my passion," and you can feel the raw, unfiltered *energy*. This energy always has a quality—texture, vibration, temperature, and so on. You can look at the details of how it feels in your body without giving it an accompanying story. Where there is intense and painful emotion, there is also tremendous living energy. The raw energy at the heart of emotions is what propels us through life and along the path of warriorship. The Vietnamese Buddhist teacher Thich Nhat Hanh writes:

> When we are angry, we are the anger. When anger is born in us, we can be aware that anger is an energy in us, and we can accept that energy in order to transform it into another kind of energy. When we have a compost bin filled with organic material which is decomposing and smelly, we know that we can transform the waste into beautiful flowers. . . . We need the insight and non-dual wisdom of the organic gardener with regard to our anger. We need not reject it or be afraid of it. We know that anger can be a kind of compost, and that it is within its power to give birth to something beautiful.

If we act out our emotions mindlessly, however, they dominate us as if something foreign were possessing us. When, for example, you feel anger rising and just let it blaze up, you may think "I am *really* angry." By losing your mind to anger, you have lost contact with your energy. You have shifted your attention from the pure energy to the "I" who thinks it is angry. Your idea that "I am really angry" takes over, and you may make a habitual response of shouting, hitting, throwing things, or storming away and stewing in a dark rage.

Thich Nhat Hanh says:

> In expressing anger, we might be practicing it or re-hearsing it, and making it stronger in the depth of our consciousness. Expressing the anger to the person we are angry with can cause a lot of damage. . . . Awareness can be called upon to be a companion for our anger. Our awareness of our anger does not suppress it or drive it out, it just looks after it. This is a very important principle. Mindfulness is not a judge. It is more like an older sister looking after and comforting her younger sister in an affectionate and caring way.

Opening to Our Emotions with Gentleness and Fearlessness

Being with the energy of our emotions without habitual reactions begins with an attitude of loving-kindness. We need to accept, as they are, the difficult situations and challenges that stir our emotions. Emotions are not *things* that we can possess or that can possess us. *They are patterns of energy linking our body-mind with the larger world.* When you open to your emotional responses with gentleness, you can let them be there without trying to cover them over or manipulate them with a story line about why you're feeling this way, what caused it, how you messed up, and so on. If you feel angry, forlorn, impatient, or any other intense emotion, then really *feel* the energy of anger, forlornness, or impatience. Make friends with it, listen to it, and let it tell you what it has to say. Karen remembers:

> When Vanessa was three, she would have the most uncontrollable, hair-raising tantrums imaginable. She would fall on the floor, usually under the dining room table, and kick and scream as loud as she could, and would get more agitated if anyone tried to touch her. It was really frightening for her and for me as well (especially if she did this in the grocery store, where we had to deal with suspicious, hostile eyes). I couldn't talk to her or hold her, so all I could do was stay by her and wait quietly. Finally, she would scream, "Mama, get me out of here." She was really feeling the energy of the emotion but was stuck. Then I could comfort and rock her until she calmed down. She needed warmth and kindness to be able to relax again and not be overwhelmed by the intense energy.

We need to treat *ourselves* that way. It is said in the Shambhala teachings of warriorship, "That mind of fearfulness should be put in the cradle of loving-kindness." Gentleness is not weakness or timidity but the flexibility to let go of fixed opinions and rigid feelings. When you let yourself be in the emotion, begin to go toward the emotion rather than just experiencing the emotion coming toward you, a relationship, a dance, begins to develop. Then the most powerful energies become workable rather than taking you over because there is nothing to take over if you are not putting up resistance.

Gentleness alone is not enough, however. To really stay present in a tight spot, feeling an emotion beginning to flare up, we need to be fearless as well as gentle. Fearlessness is the quality that dares to engage the enemies. What enemies? you may ask. It isn't supposed to be nice to talk about enemies on a spiritual path. But whatever threatens to steal our awareness and cast us back into the cocoon—our own harshness, cowardice, grasping, or laziness—*are* enemies of awareness. Gathering your strength and fearlessness in the face of a difficult situation will enable you to remain steady and gentle as emotions begin to flare. This steadiness is the firm ground for maintaining awareness as you experience intense emotions, keeping you from being swayed by your own reactions or the reactions of others. Bravery is the steadfastness to stay with it.

Fearlessness doesn't come from obliterating fear: it comes from opening to the tenderness and vulnerability that underlie all fear. Fear is always shaking, cranking up to try to protect something. When we slow down, when we relax with our fear, we find sadness, which is calm and gentle. Our fear covers the sadness and tenderness of our heart, which feels affection for those whom we love and connection with the reality beyond our cocoon. When we open our eyes, we can feel that the world itself is full of sadness and suffering. We can see the way we pass on our own habits of fear and denial to our children and the way habits of hatred and brutality are passed on from generation to generation. We see how we try to hold on to people and things as if they would last forever, though we know they will not. When we feel the sadness in our heart and in our body, that is the first hint of bravery.

It takes courage to be fully present with our own emotional energy and the energy around us, whether the feeling is anger, sorrow, or passion, or a nameless mixture of these. It takes courage not to turn away from an emotion or try to diminish its intensity. But if you really stay with your anger, your passion, or your jealousy and ask of it, "What do you really *want?*" you may find that it is pointing in an altogether unexpected direction.

CONTEMPLATIONS

Thoroughly Tasting Your Emotion   When an emotion arises, notice what happens in your state of mind. You can experience its energy directly if you pay particular attention to the intense and sharp feelings, catch moments where there is a shift or crack in the energy, see the spaciousness of the situation, remain steady and feel the energy rather than manipulate it to fit your particular idea of it. At what stage do you give the emotional energy a name? Once you name it, see how you create an elaborate story line about how you feel, why you feel that way, who "made" you feel that way, and so on.

Perhaps you feel sad because you're missing an ex-lover. The energy of sadness arises, and you quickly name it "loneliness." Then you start to analyze why you're lonely and why the person is gone. You think you still want to be with the person, which makes you feel even more forlorn. Then you feel the person rejected you, and you start to get resentful. Your mind takes off in all kinds of ways and escalates the situation until you're feeling thoroughly miserable and hopeless. Whether it is loneliness or another emotion, just notice the whole process as it arises, as you name it, and as you create your story.

You might choose to practice awareness of an emotion such as the "elation" you feel when you meet an old friend rather than the loneliness of missing someone. We do not suggest that you try to dig up old, hurtful feelings or linger longer than usual on emotions that arise. The point is not to try to intensify the emotion or otherwise manipulate it but simply to be aware of it as it arises and as far as you can as it develops all the way through. Making an effort to apply awareness in this way is itself an expression of your basic goodness. That effort may itself change your experience of the emotion so that you do not experience it with quite the habitual heaviness of grasping. Whatever does happen, touch it, feel it, and let it go.

Accepting Negative Emotions   At a time when you are feeling anger or depression or some other "down" emotion, try to notice any additional feelings of judgment that you put on top of the emotion. When you feel depressed, for example, do you feel bad about feeling this way, on top of the depression? Try instead to look at the emotion as an expression of your basic goodness and health. How might you react to the emotion differently if you did not judge it as "negative"? This additional layer of negativity is what Chögyam Trungpa used to call "negative negativity," saying that "this secondary, commenting kind of intelligence of double negativity is very cautious and cowardly as well as frivolous and emotional. It inhibits identification with the energy and intelligence of basic negativity." Can you see the depression as pure energy and let yourself feel it wholeheartedly, without judgment— without condemning yourself for feeling "depressed" and thereby making yourself feel even worse? Can you see the insight that the depression stems from? Can you find the genuine sadness in your depression? Can you look at your sadness fearlessly, without extra comment, be gentle toward it, and appreciate its wisdom?

CHAPTER 9

The Genuine Heart
of Sadness and Joy

WHEN YOU STAY IN TUNE with your own heart and feel its quality without judging it or impulsively reacting to it, you will discover beneath all the emotional highlights a deeper, tender, more constant feeling. At the core of the heart is a sense of profound, unwavering sadness and joy that comes from being truly open to the world and responding deeply to it.

Understanding the role of sadness on any spiritual path is a profound insight of the teachings of Shambhala warriorship. A sense of genuine sadness seems to be missing from our society altogether—*genuine* sadness, not anger or righteousness or self-indulgent depression, but *sadness* for our real plight and the horrifying danger human society is in. So much spiritual teaching and so many systems of therapy nowadays seem to be oriented toward finding contentment, joy, love, wisdom, and all the other wonderful things. Sometimes, they seem like just another version of the "unalienable right to the pursuit of happiness." People who feel genuine sadness are told that they are sick. Psychologists list sadness as one of the symptoms of clinical depression, and the latest wave of self-help books label depression—and by implication, sadness—as one of the most common diseases of our time.

Perhaps, though, people are genuinely sad that their lives feel so empty, that the society they were born into is such a mess, and that they and others are suffering so much. People feel this kind of sadness for others, even without being aware of it. It is the sadness of knowing the degraded world of the *setting sun* and its contrast with the possibilities of the *great eastern sun*. Perhaps we could listen to the message that the epidemic of sadness is trying to tell us about our society. Perhaps sadness is not *merely* a disease, due to "chemical imbalance." Rather than being ashamed that we feel sad, we could rejoice that we *can* feel sad and thereby share the joys and sorrows of others.

Some years ago, Jeremy directed a Shambhala program in France. It was a ten-day residential program, and the fifty participants were from all over Europe. The habitual ways in which people keep separate from each other, without really feeling the struggle of each other's existence, did not quite work there. The participants felt very stretched, tired, and emotionally raw, as well as inspired and opened. Halfway through the program, a young woman came to see him. She launched into a series of complaints about how irritating it all was. She didn't know why she had come—or why she had borrowed money to come; she thought the people were being mean to each other.

Then she started to cry, saying how hypocritical she felt at the difference between all the wonderful things they were studying and how people actually behave most of the time. She said she realized how she had put her irritation onto others—blaming them—but that the problem really started in her. Jeremy felt much loving-kindness coming through her

pain and felt her longing for the group to live kindly together. Perhaps this was the first step in building a good
human society, they speculated. Then people could be honest
with each other, see their hearts more nakedly, and be gentle
with themselves and others. Finally, she admitted that she
was afraid of what would happen when she went back home
after the program, afraid that she would just close up again.

So often in contemplative retreats, the participants express
a longing to love, to be kind and gentle to others and give to
them—as well as a fear of this very kindness and giving.
Many people weep, feeling that they are not ready, feeling the
huge gap between what they want to be and what they are,
feeling *bad*. Yet caring and longing to give are present in that
very heartbreak. The perception of each other's basic goodness is already there.

Beth, a single mother and businesswoman, writes:

> When my daughter was about eleven years old, I was
> sitting at dinner with her one evening. She was chat-
> tering on about school, and I was ignoring her, feeling
> irritated and preoccupied, as I often do at dinnertime.
> Funnily enough, on this occasion I was thinking
> about the cocoon, which I had just heard about the
> previous weekend. I glanced at my daughter, and
> suddenly I *saw* her cheerful, eager face. It was as if
> the whole room was suddenly lit up and stood out
> like a cutout from a pop-up book. I heard her voice,
> listened to what she was saying, and felt her excite-
> ment about what had happened at school that day. It
> woke me right up, and cheered me up, but I was also
> struck with sadness to realize how I loved her and
> how I so often forgot that she is a real person, with
> her own longings and excitements.

We all have compassionate, caring energy in our hearts. We are all capable of sympathizing with some other being, whether it be human or animal. We can feel the joy and pain of another being, in the clarity of our heart. This is our pain: that we know we can love, but we think we do not know how to love or whom to love. We are afraid to love even ourselves. When we see that others feel the same way, it can break our heart. And from that broken heart of sadness and longing and joy, we can look at others and feel their heart of sadness and longing and goodness. There really is no difference between their longing and our longing. Seeing and feeling such longing and kindness—and fear—sometimes we might weep. Yet, at the same time, there is a quiet joy, because that broken heart is at last opening.

The sadness of an open heart has nothing to do with depression or self-pity or self-indulgence. Sadness is the heart's response to change. A golden leaf floats gently to the ground, twisting and turning as it falls, catching the autumn sunlight. Slowly turning, it finally comes to rest on a patch of moist green moss crossed by sunlight and evening shadows. If we watch that leaf with a sad, gentle heart, we may feel profoundly connected to it. It is in itself neither beautiful nor ugly, and it does not belong to us. It is just a leaf falling with the changing season. We can see it falling, and we can appreciate it; but we can't possess it, nor can we hold on to the poignancy of that moment. This is true of everything in life. Our daughter has at last grown up from a bouncing, playful toddler to an intense young woman, and we can never possess her no matter how much we love. When we do not try to possess our children but touch the sadness of watching them change, we can also take delight in them as they grow

into being who they are—even if it is not quite what we expected.

Everything is changing around us all the time. In that
sense, everything is dying. We ourselves are changing and
dying, as is everyone we love and everything in the world of
beauty and grace. We cannot hold on to our lives and ourselves as we are now and try to stay that way. We are changing, and our lives are changing. This is the beauty of life, the
joy and sadness of it. Jennifer understood this profoundly
when she attended a meditation-training weekend:

> Friday night, I went to a party with my husband,
> Richard. Late that evening, he told me that he had
> had an affair with another woman. Neither of us had
> had an affair before this time, though I had been in
> and out of love with various men over the previous
> couple of years. I was devastated when he told me.
>
> We went to the program on the Saturday morning.
> The day was intense for me; everything was very one-
> pointed. I experienced a great deal of rage. Alone, on
> Saturday night, I made the conscious choice not to
> shut Richard out, to see him as he was rather than as
> I wanted him to be.
>
> Sunday was much the same as Saturday, but with
> more of a brokenhearted quality. Then, while I was
> sitting on Sunday afternoon, I began to have a sensa-
> tion of falling. I knew that I was right there, but the
> sensation of dropping through a tunnel was very
> vivid. It felt bottomless, with nothing for me to grab
> on to. I was terrified, crying. I had an impulse to run
> from the room, but I held on, knowing that I would
> be having an interview with the director soon. Fi-

nally, I was escorted into the interview room. The director looked at me and asked what was going on. I described what was happening. She leaned forward in her chair and said, "That's warriorship." I returned to my sitting cushion, the meditation weekend continued, and then it ended. And life goes on, with all of its ups and downs. But something happened in that moment when I had sought reassurance and had found, instead, my own sad and tender heart, my own dignity. There's no turning back.

Sadness is often accompanied by tenderness—and this is profoundly joyful. Joy and sadness are inseparable. People cry at weddings or out of sheer joy when they are happy. We feel quiet, soft, tenderhearted joy when we are sad and thoroughly in touch with ourselves. Holding a newborn baby— whether it be human, animal, or even a tree sapling—brings joy at the new life blossoming but, at the same time, a certain inexplicable tender and sad heart. Sadness is joy, and joy is sadness, and if you try to avoid one, you will never experience the other. "Experiencing the upliftedness of the world is a joyous situation," Chögyam Trungpa wrote. "But it also brings sadness. It is like falling in love. When you are in love, being with your lover is both delightful and very painful. You feel both joy and sorrow. That is not a problem; in fact it is wonderful. It is the ideal human emotion."

Sadness is a feeling of aloneness. Feeling joyful, you want to share your joy with others, but you cannot really fully share it because joy reveals itself only through experience. The only way others can share joy is to discover it themselves in their own intimate and personal experience, in their hearts. The only way you can share your joy is through your presence and through communication of your genuine connection with others. However much we may want to help others and give them something of the joy and refreshment that we have found on our path, we know that they have to find their own way. We can guide them, but we can never do it for them.

The tenderness of a sad-joyful heart softens the brittleness of intellect, like rain falling gently on the hard earth that has been dried by the hot sun. A friend of ours, a hardheaded logician, had left his family at the end of August to spend the autumn in a writing retreat. He wrote to us:

> At the end of September, the aspen leaves had turned to brilliant gold; the days were warm, but the evenings were chill enough to light a wood stove. I invited my wife and four-year-old daughter to drive up and spend a Saturday with me. The intensity of the retreat, the beauty of the surroundings, and the spontaneity of the visit, as well as the fact that we had not seen each other for a whole month, all contributed to a delightful, joy-filled day. As my wife and daughter drove away down the dirt road at the end of the day, I waved until I could see the car no more. Tears came to my eyes, and the feeling of sadness and joy in my heart can barely be expressed, except perhaps in a poem such as this, by the Japanese poet Jakuren:

> > Loneliness
> > The essential colour of a beauty
> > Not to be defined
> > Over the dark evergreens, the dusk
> > That gathers on far autumn hills.

An open heart realizes that the human heart *is* sad when it is genuine. Early American blues and Spanish flamenco—songs of love and separation of any time and place—reveal a sadness that is less an expression of depression or misery than of the depth of the human heart. In the best of these songs, there is always something timeless and beyond the personal drama. It rings true to us, and we feel glad. The root of the word *sad* is the Latin *satis,* which is also the root of the word *satisfied.* So sadness is related to being completely full, completely satisfied. When we eat dinner with close friends—not at a "dinner party" but at a genuine feast of friendship—a sense of sadness sometimes dawns as the evening wears on. It comes from the feeling of fullness and quiet joy that is present in the atmosphere and because, in being together in this way, a hint of the inevitable parting is always present.

We need to learn to have soft, tender, sad, and broken hearts. We can cry together, and then we can love each other. When you love, start small, then expand. Love a dog and then you can expand to your children, your spouse, your friends, your colleagues, your government officials, the gods, and all the rest, including the birds and the bees. Nothing need keep us from falling in love. Fall in love with whatever you can—with a frog or tree bark or an ant or your best friend. It doesn't really matter. By loving, we include the world in a bigger sphere, where all can be included. Buddhist teacher Joseph Goldstein describes genuine love as "a universal, nondiscriminating sense of care and connectedness. . . . Love is inclusive and powerful—not the near-enemy of attachment, but something much deeper—infusing our awareness, enabling us to open to and accept the truth of each moment; and [it is] service that feels our intimate connectedness with all things and responds to the wholeness of life."

Genuine love for your world is not sentimental, but it is precise. The details of your world become as sharp and penetrating as if you had a hair on your eyeball—the jet plane glittering far overhead in the blue sky; the brilliant red leaf lying on the sidewalk, moistened by an autumn drizzle; the sound of your daughter calling "Hello-oo!" as she returns from school; a paper cup lying trampled on the canteen floor; the strong, sweet smell of cheap perfume lingering in the dentist's waiting room; the magnificent stand of two-hundred-year-old trees being cut down for newsprint or to make way for a plastic condominium.

It is as if we discover a new organ of perception, perception of the heart, though it has been there all the time, covered by the unceasing turmoil of emotional upheavals or the rigidity of a heart hardened by decades of being ignored. When the raw heart of sadness and joy is open, there is genuine insight, which sees things just as they are, positive or negative, painful or pleasurable. But as well there is tranquillity because, as long as it remains open, your heart has the space and peace to accommodate many possibilities. This tranquillity and insight leads you into that profound trust in your world, which we first discussed in chapter 2, and your heart and mind can open to its sacredness and power.

CONTEMPLATIONS

Radiating Loving-Kindness   The purpose of this practice, derived from the Buddhist tradition, is to develop the energy of *maitri,* or loving-kindness, and radiate it to others. It is best to do the practice after a period of sitting while you are still on your cushion. Try it only after you have some familiarity with the basic mindfulness practice.

It has several steps:

1. First, reflect on your understanding of the basic goodness of yourself and others—the universal, unconditioned basic goodness. Let your mind just rest in that openness for a moment.

2. Recall a situation in which you felt content, free from hostility, ill will, and stress—in which you felt well-being and happiness. Imagine this situation as vividly and clearly as you can. Recall where you were, the people involved, what you were doing, and so on. Take a few moments to establish the scene firmly in your mind. Now, turn your attention to the physical sensation in your body as you recall that situation. Feel that sensation—its warmth, vibration, color, however you feel it. Now, give it a name—"happiness," "well-being," "contentment"—whatever feels right to you.

   Still paying attention to that feeling of bodily well-being, let the details of the remembered situation fade. Just stay with the overall mood and the feeling of well-being. As you stay with it, allow yourself to feel it intensely. Allow the feeling of well-being to increase, thinking "May I be happy" or "May I experience well-being" or whatever name you have given the positive feeling that you generated.

3. Think of someone who is alive today, with whom you have had a good relationship, toward whom you feel kindly and who has been kind to you. (It is better at first not to choose a lover or a parent. Begin with someone with whom you have a basically positive connection, whom you can quite easily wish well without getting caught up in strong emotions.) Hold the image of that person vividly in

mind. Recall the feeling of happiness that you generated in step 2. You may particularly experience this feeling as focused in the center of the chest—the "heart center." Feel that you are radiating that good feeling from your heart center to the person you are thinking about, thinking, "Just as I wish happiness for myself, may _____ be happy."

4. When you feel some familiarity with radiating *maitri* to people toward whom you feel positive, you can try radiating it to people toward whom you feel neutral or with whom you have had negative encounters. Again, recall the image of that person, radiate well-being toward him or her, and think, "May _____ be happy," or, "May _____ experience well-being" (or whatever). Don't force it. Be gentle, and stop if you begin to feel that you are not being genuine.

5. The final step is to radiate *maitri* without a specific direction. Again, generate the feeling of happiness and well-being in yourself. Now, let that feeling radiate out in front of you, behind you, to both sides of you, above and below you. Without losing the feeling of well-being in your own body, focused slightly in your heart center, just feel it extending out into the space all around you. As it radiates out, let it touch whatever beings it encounters, whether they be humans, animals, plants, or the earth itself. As you radiate well-being, think, "May all beings enjoy happiness."

Just as the sitting practice of mindfulness is practice toward developing mindfulness in daily life, so the sitting practice of developing *maitri* is practice toward developing *maitri* in daily life. When you have practiced *maitri* in sitting and feel some familiarity with it, you can begin to practice it in daily life as well. When you are with someone toward whom you feel kindly, and who has positive feelings toward you, quietly recall the feeling of well-being that you generated in your practice and radiate that feeling to your friend. Move on to radiating *maitri* in more difficult situations when you feel ready.

Sending and Taking   This exercise is an extension of the exercise on developing *maitri,* loving-kindness. It is based on the Buddhist practice called "sending and taking." In it, we send well-being to others and we accept their pain into ourselves, using the breath as a vehicle. While doing the *maitri* exercise, you may have found that, as you radiated kindness to others, you began to think of all the pain in the world—the suffering of others in less fortunate circumstances or the suffering of a friend who is sick. This exercise will help you to work with the sadness of realizing others' pain. Usually, we try to keep pain away from us, so that we might remain happy ourselves. This practice is based on the fundamental fact that we are interconnected with each other and cannot separate ourselves from the pain and troubles and stresses of others.

The exercise is very simple: Having practiced the development of *maitri* for a while, you can radiate *maitri* on the out-breath.

On the in-breath, open yourself to admit the pain and sadness of the world. Allow into your being the suffering, anxiety, stress, and darkness of all those trapped in the setting-sun world. Let yourself feel the sadness of all this. After your breath comes in, simply let go of that suffering. Transfer your attention to your feeling of well-being. On the out-breath, breathe out basic goodness, well-being, health, and benevolence from your heart to others and the environment.

This practice is a recognition that you really are not separate from others, that the pain of others is your pain, that you cannot generate well-being in yourself unless you are willing also to work with the pain of others. You cannot truly isolate yourself and pretend that the sadness of the world does not affect you. So you allow the sadness of others to come into your being without putting up barriers, just as your breath naturally comes in if you do not try to stop it. In exchange, you give away well-being.

This practice can be difficult: you might experience a great deal of resistance to letting in pain. It might make you feel quite claustrophobic. However, you do not get stuck on your sadness because it is just for one breath. Then, on the out-breath, you relax and breathe out goodness again. Likewise, you cannot get stuck on your joy, because on the in-breath, you allow sadness into your heart again. This is a good practice to help you realize the inseparability of sadness and joy, since your in-breath and out-breath are really all part of one breath, which is part of the atmosphere that we all share. If you have any difficulty with this practice, wait until you feel some relaxation and familiarity with basic mindfulness practice and the practice of radiating *maitri*.

This practice is effective and quite magical in helping you to let go of your self-centeredness and open your heart to sadness and joy and to actually care for others. "Give your sanity to the world; keep your neurosis to yourselves" is one of the slogans of Shambhala warriorship.

CHAPTER 10

Letting Go

I have had my dream—like others—
and it has come to nothing, so that
I remain now, carelessly
with feet planted on the ground
and look up at the sky—
feeling my clothes about me,
the weight of my body in my shoes,
the rim of my hat, air passing in and out
at my nose—and decide to dream no more.

—"Thursday," *by William Carlos Williams*

*I*N THE PREVIOUS CHAPTER, we spoke of a way of perceiving that we called "perception of the heart." Perception of the heart feels the depth of the world as well as being touched by the subtle details and qualities of everything. Though the details are deeply felt, they are also clear and sharp, for the open heart is tender and sensitive. But it takes courage, strength of heart, to remain open in this way. So often, when our heart begins to open, we freeze. Something tightens up in our muscles, in our blood, in our nervous system. It can be quite subtle. We hold on to some idea or old feeling of what *should* be, how we *want* things to be, how things *were,* or who *we* are. So opening the perception of the

129

heart is not once and for all; we have to do it again and again and again. The heart opens, we see a fresh world, then we freeze. And then we have to let go. It is as if opening the heart brings us to the edge of a cliff. There beyond the cliff we see a beautiful green valley, with flowering trees and a broad, clear river running through it. And we actually have the wings to fly out like an eagle over the valley. But at the last moment, we freeze. Now, we have to jump. We have to let go.

When the heart opens, we see others, we feel the hearts of others. It is the only moment when we truly know that others exist, and not just as props in our own story line. But as soon as we see this, we pull back and hold on to "me." We have to let go of our subtle feeling of "me-ness." Letting go includes letting go of memories of past successes and failures, old wounds, and beliefs about the world. If we are remembering the past, we are reacting to it, living in it; we are not living in the present, *now*. Letting go is not easy to do. Our habit is to hold on to what we think we know. We try all kinds of ways to hold on forever to the significant moments of our lives. We take snapshots. We write journals, we go over the moment again and again to fix it in our memory. Sometimes, it seems as if the memory is more important than the moment itself, just because it does seem more fixed. We can remember and relive the memory in our minds over again, whenever we wish, although usually the freshness has gone. What made that moment so special has gone, and we can't get it back.

We live in concept, caught in the webs of logic and reasonableness that we have spun. We created the idea of a good life; now, we have to live it, but maybe it is not so good. We thought we had managed to avoid discomfort, but maybe we have not. Some of us may live a fairly easy life until we die;

others may be confronted constantly with terrible challenges and horrors. Yet we all are confronted with challenges if we open our eyes and see them. The more willing we are to let go, the more challenges come to us that put us on the spot. Each moment of our lives is a moment of letting go, letting some part of us die, so that the next moment can be born afresh. We all are confronted with a challenge at the moment of physical death, and at that time, comforting philosophies are of no use to us at all; they count for nothing at that unique moment of nowness.

Anthony tells a funny but poignant story about refusing to let go:

> Last night was a Saturday night, and it being a non-work night, I stayed up rather late. I forgot to reset my alarm clock, and the damn thing went off as if it were a working morning. I woke up out of a deep sleep and blindly thrust out to turn the alarm off. It was one of those "twilight zone" experiences. I'm sure you've had the experience of suddenly waking up and not knowing where you are, what day of the week it is, what you have to do this day, and so on.
>
> What was really interesting for me is that a few days earlier, I had had a good fight with my wife. One of the ways I react to being hurt is to go into my "silent treatment" behavior, which I suppose is a type of passive-aggressive approach. Well, when I got up so suddenly, I actually found myself trying to remember, along with the above-mentioned things, if this was a day I still had to maintain my silent treatment. What a riot! This struck me right between the eyes in terms of "letting go."

We have to let go of trying to possess the world altogether, of trying, in a sense, to possess our own lives. No matter what the state of the economy, we can never truly possess our own security. We may become unemployed, all our savings running out; we don't know how long our health will last, however healthy we feel at the present. We like to think that we have control over our lives and that we have important choices to make, and in some ways we do. But in the context of a larger vision, we do not have such definite control, and the choices we make may not be the ones that really determine how our life goes. When we let go of all these hopes and anxieties, we are left naked. We respond to whatever situation we are in from our tender and vulnerable heart, not from the hard knot of certainty.

When Vanessa was fifteen, like many teenagers, she went through a period of anger and pulling away from her family. Things got more and more tense for several months. Whenever Jeremy would ask her what was going on with her, she would say, "Daddy, trust me, *please.* I *need* to do this." Jeremy says:

> Over and over again, I had to let go of thinking of her as "my little girl" and thinking that I had to keep track of her every move. I did, in fact, feel glad that she had the daring to branch out and experience a larger world and trusted that she would come through it strengthened. Nevertheless, the anger and fear would rise up again and again, along with vague images of her getting into some unknown, terrible trouble. Again and again, I would have to practice letting go of these images, as well as the anger and fear, and respond to what was actually happening.

We have to let go. There really is nothing else we can do, not because of any moral law, not because any teaching says so, but simply because the past has already gone, and if we cling to what has gone, we cannot be fully with what is here now. If we cling to the beauty or joy or horror of the past, then we cannot feel the beauty and joy and horror of the present moment.

Letting go is not easy because it goes against the grain of who we usually feel we are. It can be extremely painful. It isn't "giving up" on something—on the difficult issues in our lives. Nor is it just being loose. We need a sense of discipline to let go into the moment, balancing tight and loose. This can be worked with in sitting practice. During practice, we can begin to let go of our thoughts and our heavy emotional patterns. We let go of a little bit of this and a little bit of that, and each time, we feel relieved and unburdened for a moment.

Letting Go Is Relaxing

Letting go is relaxing and appreciating the ordinary world we live in. But it can be sloppy and aggressive if it is not based on the discipline of mindfulness and awareness, and cultivating gentleness and fearlessness. Letting go is not trying to get away from the limitations of our ordinary life. Rather, it is being in tune with the environment, however challenging it may be, and relaxing into that. It is letting go of our uptightness in the face of challenges, letting go of the barrier of anxious watchfulness that usually separates us from our environment. But this does take the discipline of being fully present: a musician can only truly let go and improvise beautifully when she has fully mastered her instrument; a Formula One racecar driver can only be top-class if he can let go of all hesitation in his driving, but to do this, he must know his car through and through.

Letting go is by no means the same as repressing or trying to get rid of painful emotions, like the false idea of "detachment," in which you become distant and unfeeling. On the contrary, we need to let go of the *barriers* to feeling. We need to go toward our feelings with gentleness and fearlessness, rather than becoming more detached from them. We can let go of the crusts of habitual responses that cover the heart's deeper feeling of tender sadness and genuine caring.

Letting go takes energy: you can't be mushy and sweet about it. It is fearless warriorship as well as gentle warriorship. To let go of our uptightness and self-centeredness, our righteous anger, our feeling of being victims, our phony optimism, or whatever our habitual thoughts may be, far from trying to be detached from them, we have to feel these things, touch them, hold them. Then we can let them go.

To practice letting go, you have to *capture the moment of holding on*—holding on to your past, your depression, your passion, whatever—holding on to your cocoon. The moment that you realize you are holding, first stay with it, continue to hold, and acknowledge that you are holding. Hold, and then you can let go. Surrender: give it up, give it all up. Hold, intensify that state of mind and heart, let go, and relax. That is the precise action of the warrior.

Let go of the *idea* of letting go and just *do* it—that's the point. If you *try* too hard to let go, making a project out of it or trying to foresee the result of letting go, then you'll get stuck—because you'll have to let go of *that* project, too. It's like the Chinese finger puzzle—you slip your fingers into a tube and try to get them out—the more you pull on them, the more stuck they get. This is the catch-22 of letting go:

you can't let go if you try *too hard,* and you can't let go if you don't try *at all.* The only solution is to take a chance and relax. You have to be fearless about it and then gentle. Be a warrior. Trusting the basic goodness of your world is the key. You don't just let go into voidness, but into a rich and trustworthy world. It is important to trust that you are not letting go into a dead nothing, or into a hostile world, but into something much fuller and richer than the world you are letting go *of.* If you don't trust that you are letting go into a sane and sacred world, even if it is unfamiliar and feels strange, then you'll be too frightened to let go in the first place.

Fresh Perception

When we let go, with open heart and clear mind we can perceive whatever occurs freshly, *at that very moment that it occurs.* We use the phrase "first thought, best thought" to highlight that *first moment of fresh perception,* before the clouds of judgment and personal interpretation take over. "First thought" is "best" because it is not yet covered over by all our opinions and interpretations, our hopes and fears, our likes and dislikes. *It is direct perception of the world as it is.*

Although we call it first *thought,* it is not necessarily a thought that comes in words. It is the very first inspiration, however it expresses itself to us. It may be just that first view as you come around the bend on a mountaintop and see the valley laid out below. Then, of course, we may start thinking second and third thoughts, such as, "Oh, wow, isn't that beautiful," or, "How stupid that I didn't bring my camera."

Before we have any thought at all, we have the ground or space of openness we have been calling basic goodness or the open dimension. We may experience this as a blank state of mind, before we know what to do or say. We might even feel dumb or naive or childlike at that moment. Out of that openness, energies, colors, sounds appear. A spark happens, and then there is a moment when we feel some connection happening. We might feel that our heart has been touched. This is the moment of first thought.

Through the practice of mindfulness-awareness, we can begin to see how a flash of direct, concept-free perception of color, sound, and so on, is very rapidly followed by the conceptual recognition of that direct perception. This usually happens much too fast for us to catch it, and we become conscious only of the conceptual label, with the original perception vaguely filtering through. To use the previous example, when we come around a curve on a mountain road, often we first become conscious of our commentary, "Oh, what a beautiful valley," and only then do we actually look carefully at the scene. *First thought* refers to that very first moment when the mind recognizes the direct perception *before* it is labeled with a concept. That "thought" is a direct response to the perception; it is pure and accurate and unadorned by interpretation. Therefore, it is the "best thought."

First thought is always elaborated—again, very quickly—in a mushroom cloud of conceptualizations and interpretations that carry our consciousness further and further away from that initial direct perception. Normally, in the cocoon, we live in our interpretations, completely out of touch with direct perceptions. We do not have to be advanced practitioners of mindfulness to see the interpretive process at work. It is happening constantly. All we have to do is pay attention mindfully to how our inner chatter responds to everything we see, hear, smell, taste, and touch and how it interprets the world to fit its version of reality. When we let go of those interpretations, we experience first thought and perceive the world directly, without the filter of language.

You can discover first thought by relaxing into the present moment in a very simple way. Perhaps you are sitting in an airport looking down from a balcony onto the crowds milling around below. Suddenly, your inner chatter stops. You are right there for a moment, and you actually see and hear. You see the pattern of motion; you hear the hubbub of voices and machines; you have a sense of timelessness and completeness, gentle sadness and joy: first thought.

You may also discover this moment when you are suddenly shocked. Perhaps you have had the experience of slipping on ice. Without any thought, your whole body and mind become unified to prevent a fall. At that moment, you feel completely alive and present. Afterward, you may get a sudden rush of adrenaline and say, "Whew, that was close," but the energy and wakefulness linger for a while. Or maybe you're casually walking down the street thinking your thoughts when you turn the corner and run into a tree. At that moment, your mind stops for an instant, your thoughts are gone, and your mind opens to space. A friend, Julie, discovered the clarity in a shock that wasn't so beautiful:

> I was speeding down the highway, and my mind was several miles ahead, thinking of my little boy, who would be wondering why Mom was late picking him up at school. Suddenly, on the side of the road, I saw a car that had been sliced in two by a lamppost. A woman was lying on the ground beside the car. I couldn't tell whether she was alive or dead. She was surrounded by firemen and curious onlookers. All my thoughts of being late and what my child would think

of my being late and how fast I must drive and how much traffic there was melted into a pure blankness in the horror of seeing such an accident. Although I did not dwell on the vision, for some time afterward my perception was extremely clear and sharp.

The first moment of waking in the morning can be an opportunity to notice first thought because the mind is not yet caught up in the daily routine. We rarely catch the actual moment when we awaken from sleep, but sometimes you may experience a kind of blank in which you don't even remember where you are or who you are. This moment might be frightening or joyful, but you will have a vivid perception of the room around you, a moment of first thought. Second thoughts quickly follow: You feel "I"; you think, "Who am I? What am I?"; and suddenly—there you are. Your name comes to mind, your profession, family, debts, and so on.

Taking photographs, you can capture the vivid first moment of experiencing something, just as it is. But first, you, the photographer, must open your mind and see: the afternoon sun glancing off a bright yellow-green moss-covered rock in the middle of a clearing in the pine forest; a long, horizontal bulbous cloud dark with rain, yet brilliantly lit underneath by the evening sun; white mist over the bay, through which the faint outline of an island, a boat, and a lone seagull suggest something out of nothing; a pile of steaming brown cow dung surrounded by yellow dandelions. In order to capture these moments, you look through the viewfinder not only at the objects themselves but at the space and light shining around and within them. Afterward, when you put the camera down and look at the ordinary world, it suddenly seems bright and vibrant, too.

When you take a photograph, just before you click the shutter, your mind is empty and open, seeing without words. When you stand in front of a blank sheet of paper, about to make a painting or do calligraphy, you have no idea what you will produce. Maybe you have some plan for the painting or you know what symbol you want to calligraph, but you don't know what will appear when you actually put brush to paper. What you do out of trust in open mind will be fresh and spontaneous.

Opening to that uncertain open space that we experience as a blankness in our minds and letting first thought naturally arise is the way to begin any action properly. At the moment when you are about to make any gesture, before you actually do it, you can let go of your expectations and open to first thought. When you are about to drink a glass of water, do you just reach for it and grab it and swallow it down? Can you practice a moment of first thought, clear perception, as you reach for the glass; and again as you touch it; and again as you lift it; again as you move it toward your lips; and again as you taste the water on your tongue? When someone speaks sharply to you, do you immediately fire back, or can you touch a moment of first thought before you respond? Likewise, when you go about your daily business, make coffee, go to work, use the copier, attend a meeting, walk down the street, eat dinner, have an argument with your partner or make love, if you would open to first thought, each of these occurrences in your life *could* be fresh and direct. The same process happens, very fast, at every moment of our lives. We can experience any moment as first thought. We have to catch first thought again and again. *There is no ultimate point where you don't have to pay attention anymore.*

The moment of first thought is a moment of *nowness* because it occurs only right *now*. You cannot hold on to first thought: you can only touch it and let it go, again and again. The only time you can do it is *now* and *now* and again *now*. You have to do it and do it and do it. There is no shortcut or quick fix. If you keep practicing in this way, gradually you will become more accustomed to first thought. You will recognize it more easily. Like the face of someone you love who has departed, the flavor of first-thought freshness will be present as soon as you remember it, and the flavor of it will, once again, open your genuine heart of sadness and joy.

CONTEMPLATIONS

Discovering Perceptions and Interpretations Sit in a public place, like a café or a waiting room. Remember your mindfulness and awareness practice. Let yourself slow down and look around with open eyes and ears. Pay attention to details in the environment—colors, shapes, objects, people. What is the first detail that catches your eye in each person you see? The tattered red jacket on that young man, with an eagle imprinted on the left shoulder? The whimsical expression in the right eye of the elderly woman drinking coffee? Notice how quickly you have a feeling about the first detail: "That jacket is dirty and ugly." "What's wrong with her eye?" Notice the vivid detail and your interpretations, but do not judge either of them.

Next, notice everything around you of a particular color—blue or red or the color of your choice. Do you just see the color as color, or do you label it immediately with your second thought: blue—it's a hat; blue—of the sky; blue—bird. Try to see just color without naming anything.

Now, walk down a street, observing everything on the

street as much as you can. See if you can just see without naming each thing you see. Notice how your thoughts take off from a simple observation and immediately start a whole interpretation and story line about it. See if you notice the momentary gap between what you see and what you think—your interpretation of the simple perception.

Playing with "First Thought" Place a blank white sheet of paper on a table in front of you. Let your mind settle by practicing mindfulness of breathing for a while. Hold a Magic Marker a foot or so above the paper. (A jumbo marker would be good.) Relax your mind so that you're looking at the blank sheet of paper and your thoughts are quiet. You are going to make one dot on that sheet of paper with your marker, but you don't know exactly when and you won't try to control it. Sit there with your arm poised, marker pointing down, ready. Wait. Suddenly—your arm goes down, and the dot is made. Notice the moment the mark appears: first thought.

Letting Go of Dark Feelings Recall a situation that you recently experienced that made you feel fearful, tight, and claustrophobic—that evoked dark feelings. Imagine the situation as if it were in front of you now, on a movie screen or in a bubble of light. (You can imagine that the bubble is a soap bubble and that the situation you are contemplating is projected into it like a hologram, if this helps.) Examine the scene clearly, in full color. See all the people taking part in it, hear what they are saying, feel what you felt in that situation. Let yourself relax with gentleness toward the situation.

When you have established the scene and recalled your feeling for it clearly, pop the bubble of light so that it shatters

into many tiny pieces of colored light. You are not harming
any of the people in that situation, just popping the situation
itself. Let all the pieces of the scene go free, along with your
heavy, dark feeling about it. Enjoy the dance of energy and
color that it creates. Notice the contrast between the darkness
and heaviness of the original scene and the joyfulness of the
dancing shards of light. It might even make you laugh.

Practicing Letting Go   Hold both of your arms out in front
of you, relaxed, bent at the elbow, your hands open and palms
up. Clench your fists tight. Gently open your fingers until
your hands are completely open again, as if you were offering
a small gift to someone or letting a butterfly fly away.

Now, clench your fists again. This time, clench them as
tight as you can. Feel the muscles in your arms and shoulders
getting tight. *Quickly* relax your grip, and open your hands
completely.

Do this again and clench even tighter. Think, "Tighter,
tighter, tighter" for thirty seconds. Now, suddenly open your
hands; think, "Let go." As you let go, you might let out a
little sigh or a soft "ahh."

Do this again. This time, notice your state of mind as you
clench tighter and let go.

If an emotion arises that comes from your cocoon, such
as jealousy or resentment, imagine that you are holding the
emotion in your clenched fist. Hold, tighten, let go.

Finally, imagine that you are holding in your hand your
most valued and precious possession. Hold, tighten, let go.
Now hold on to your most dearly held belief: hold, hold
tighter, let go.

CHAPTER 11

Raising the Energy of Windhorse

FEELING YOUR GENUINE sad-joyful heart and letting go of fixation, as we have described in previous chapters, is the way actually to tune in to the living reservoir of energy that exists all around you and within you, all the time. In the Shambhala teachings, this living energy as it is expressed in each person is called that person's "windhorse." It is powerful and dignified like a horse; forceful, swift, and unpredictable like the wind. When you step out of the cocoon, you can ride this energy. If you feel hopelessly stuck in your cocoon, connecting with windhorse can help lift you out.

Wind represents the brilliant living energy all around us and within us. It has a meaning very close to the Chinese term *chi* or the Japanese *ki*. According to *The Encyclopedia of Eastern Philosophy and Religion,* "*chi* literally means air, vapor, breath, ether, energy. It is also a central concept in Taoism and Chinese medicine. In the Taoist view, *chi* is the vital energy, the life force, the cosmic spirit that pervades and enlivens all things and is therefore synonymous with primordial energy."

The Navajo believe that every visible object in the world has an invisible aspect that is called "Holy People." There are Mountain People, Star People, River People, Rain People,

Corn People, and so on. These Holy People are symbols for the consciousness within all things, which the Navajo call the "Holy Wind" (*nilch'i*) . In humans, this invisible aspect is called "the Wind within one" (*nilch'i hwii 'siziini*). These "Holy Winds," the Navajo tell us, are not at all distinct: all are really part of one Wind, and the living energy of Wind flows in and out of even the most apparently solid objects. According to Peter Gold, author of *The Circle of the Spirit: Navajo and Tibetan Sacred Wisdom,* "Holy Wind is a glittering, pulsating, breathing fusion of all the animating and enlivening energies of a living cosmos. It is the power behind the Universal Mind [awareness] permeating all the elements and phenomena of the cosmos."

The use of the term *wind* to symbolize universal living energy is common to many peoples throughout the world. Wind suggests forces that normally can be observed only by their effects, just as the physical wind can be detected only by movement of trees or clouds; one cannot directly *see* the physical wind. Likewise, one cannot perceive *chi,* or *wind,* directly, but one can certainly experience its effects.

The horse represents the fact that humans can ride on the energy of wind. This living energy is not merely an abstract philosophical idea or a sentimental religious belief but can be an actual experience available to all of us. The grace and power of the horse gave early peoples the ability to travel great distances; it was as close as humans came to flying, before the airplane. The horse is often a sacred symbol, representing, according to Chögyam Trungpa, "any wild dreams that human beings might have of capturing a wild animal. If any human beings would like to capture the wind, a cloud, the sky, if anybody would like to ride on mountains or dance with waterfalls—all of those are incorporated in the symbol of the horse."

An Exercise in Raising Windhorse

To enable you to feel something of the quality and energy that come from raising windhorse, we suggest a simple exercise that uses your intuitive feeling and creative imagination. One cannot really convey the magic of a genuine practice in writing because it is living energy, not merely an idea, that must be pointed out. The practice of raising windhorse can be passed on fully only by personal instruction. It is the same with any practice, from sitting meditation to healing to playing the guitar to learning to light a campfire: the living human wisdom is learned directly only from a living human. However, doing this exercise with open mind and heart can help you to raise windhorse in a direct and natural way.

Raise up your physical posture. Sitting on a meditation cushion or a straight-backed chair is fine for this simple feeling-visualization exercise. Feel your head and shoulders strong and uplifted, as if they were reaching up to the sky. Make your spine straight and taut, but not too tight. Keep your chest soft and your heart open.

Imagine and feel that you are surrounded by a bank of living power and energy all around and above you. It has depth and richness, and vibrates. To help you visualize it, you might feel that the energy has a slightly golden hue, like the sky at dawn. It is living energy—warm and quivering. It is loving, sharp, and awake, with great affection for the earth and all that exists. But it is also razor-sharp and cuts all aggression and hatred. This energy is very real, and you can call it down because *you are a part of it.* You are not conjuring up something. Rather, you are opening to what is already there and allowing it to open you further. You have perhaps felt it in those sudden, unexpected moments of openness that happen in sitting practice or in daily life.

The energy is particularly strong in front and slightly above you, as if you were looking up at a master teacher or someone you profoundly respect and admire. He or she might be sitting on a platform and gazing down at you with an expression of warmth and affection, yet seeing you just as you are, with sharp and uncompromising wakefulness. Or you could be raising your face to the sun on a bright summer morning.

Visualize that the energy is descending and enveloping you, like gentle rain. As you feel the energy descending, raise yourself up toward it—raise your posture and your energy, as if you longed to go toward that energy. Raising windhorse has been said to be a person's wakefulness meeting the wakefulness of the universe. The energy enters you and descends through your head and fills your heart: head and heart are joined.

Now feel-imagine that the energy and power around and within you are becoming overwhelming. Let your mind and heart go into that energy. Let go as you have learned to let go of your thoughts in sitting practice. Let go of your feeling of separateness, of dwelling in your body, of any inadequacy or psychological impoverishment. There is no preparation for letting go. Just let go. *Abruptly.*

As you let go, feel that you are riding out on waves of energy. You are not separate from the power bank of energy that is descending and enveloping you. You are connected to the world. Forget yourself and ride the waves of energy, and expand out and out, radiating kindness as far as you can. This is the key point of the whole practice: cutting your own aggression and fear, to receive the benevolent energy of the cosmos into your own heart and radiate that positive feeling to others.

Wherever you are, that is your sacred place, your palace. Whether you are in the middle of the street, in a one-room apartment, in an expensive home, on a factory production line, or at home with your parents, that place is sacred and the center of your world. In it, you are the monarch. As you sit in your sacred palace, touch back on your own genuine heart. Imagine and feel that you are a monarch with a broken heart—confident and joyful, as well as genuinely sad. You can radiate goodness and benevolence from your broken heart and bring healing and caring to others.

We will summarize this exercise of creative feeling and imagination in a short verse that you can read aloud; or you can record and play it back so that you can follow it as you listen:

> Feel a power-energy bank all around, descending, enveloping, opening.
> Feel love so full and affectionate and energetic.
> Feel the *quality* of your world.
> Feel the vast space, power, and energy.
> Feel uplifted and raise yourself up—your posture as well as your humor.
> Raise yourself up and cut all thoughts of impoverishment.
> Feel your tender heart and affection.
> Let go into it. *Abruptly.*

Feel you are riding on waves of energy.
Actually connect your body cells with the air cells
    and energy cells,
so you feel not separate from the world.
Feel like a king or queen of your world.
Feel like you live in your sacred palace.
Feel like you can love and cherish and take care of
    your fellow kings and queens.
Now expand your experience of energy further and
    further.
You can do this on the spot, in an instant, if you are
    not afraid.

The Experience of Raising Windhorse

There is magic to windhorse. This "four-legged miracle"
gives you the strength to leap from cowardice to bravery. Just
as, when you slip on a patch of ice, your awareness is suddenly completely there, windhorse abruptly cuts through daydreams and scheming. Raising windhorse opens a gap in your
steady stream of setting-sun thoughts and brings you to the
present moment. It might feel as if you were intoxicated or
suddenly shocked, as if you had come face-to-face with simple wisdom beyond words.

Any kind of challenging situation, whether large or small,
is an opportunity to leap through hesitation and raise windhorse. Ted, a project engineer in the Bay Area of California,
says, "I try to remember to raise windhorse just before I enter
the door where I work. My work is often hectic and demand-
ing. During my drive to work, I cannot help thinking about
what I have to do that day and often get quite worked up

about it. Taking that moment to raise windhorse just before I go through the door cuts all that thinking and anxiety, and I go in with a fresh mind."

You have to be brave to raise windhorse. You cannot do it if you prefer to stay in your cocoon; in that case, the energy can feel sharp and threatening. Certainly, windhorse has no concern for the ego's comfort.

Karen, who was an actress for many years, says that the first time she raised windhorse, she felt a tremendous shock, as if she were being physically wrenched open, her heart exposed:

> As I sat there, I felt like a mountain, full of energy and power. I had the outrageous confidence to feel like a majestic queen of the universe, sitting on her throne. Then the doubts started their attack. Was I feeling arrogant, proud? How could I let anyone see this strength? Would it overwhelm them and me? I felt much more comfortable feeling small and humble. I became terrified of that confidence. I felt cracked open and very vulnerable. My heart felt exposed, and I wanted to close it up again. I didn't want to go into that energy, let alone ride it. When I was on the stage, I could take on the role of a queen or some extraordinary character and feel comfortable settling into the power and elegance of that role. I was "allowed" to do this because it wasn't really me. In the context of the play, I could experience and communicate the reality of that power. But raising windhorse at first was terrifying because there was no mask. It was not a temporary role. It was direct and shocking, but very real.

When you are not afraid of the energy, you can raise wind-horse in a flash. It does not take time; you don't need to prepare for it. To raise windhorse, you don't need to be in a special place or a particularly positive mood already. Wherever you are and whatever your state of mind, at that very moment, you can raise your windhorse. If you are feeling depressed or nervous, raising windhorse can lift you out of that cocoon.

Jeremy first experienced the practical effect of windhorse in 1978, a few months after we learned the practice. As vice president of the Naropa Institute, he led the staff working on accreditation candidacy with the federal accrediting agency. One of dozens of groups being examined, they arrived at the O'Hare Hilton Hotel in Chicago, where the meetings were being held. They had rented a hotel room in which to rest and prepare, and had a few hours to wait. For many nights before the trip, they had stayed up into the early hours of the morning preparing their documentation and were exhausted. All of them had minor psychosomatic stomach or head problems. The long, hard work of so many people now seemed to depend on their performance, and this weighed heavily on their shoulders. Jeremy relates:

> When the time came for the meeting, we raised windhorse together. I felt the swirl of energy, and delight was so powerful that it was almost intoxicating—so much so that I took the wrong exit and landed in a janitor's closet, with the rest of the team piling in behind me. We almost collapsed with laughter right there among the brooms. We were having a great time for a bunch of folks in their thirties about to go into a very serious examination.

As we entered the examination room, we were shown to our seats by the chairman of the examination team that had visited the institute in the spring. He was there to support our application, but he looked as anxious as I had felt during the days of preparation. Around the huge oval table sat about a dozen men and women who looked very imposing—heavy-duty academics and bureaucrats. They were friendly, however, and seemed genuinely curious about us and our institute. In spite of our tiredness and nerves, we were all quite relaxed, joking with the examiners and rising to all their challenges. After the interview was over, we were amazed at the confidence and sharpness that we had expressed in the meeting. The meeting was a success, and the institute received the credential it had worked so hard for. We were quite sure that our success was due in no small part to the fact that we came into that meeting with windhorse—soft yet confident and with a sense of humor—and were able to ride the energy of our nervousness.

Windhorse Is Universal

The energy of windhorse is recognized universally, even when it is not called by that name. A connection with windhorse is the basis of charisma. Many cultures speak of this energy. In Arabic, for example, it is known as *baraka,* "a kind of charisma or spiritual electricity, because it is a kind of power that seems to energize those who receive it, even when they return to secular lives and mundane tasks."

Mihaly Csikszentmihalyi, former chairman of the depart-

ment of psychology at the University of Chicago, has spent
a lifetime studying experiences of windhorse, although he
calls such moments "optimal experiences" or experiences of
"flow." In these experiences, people report, their lives seem
at least momentarily fulfilled. Csikszentmihalyi interviewed
thousands of ordinary people in a wide variety of different
occupations for his studies.

One of his interviewees, a dancer, described her experience
of dancing thus: "A strong relaxation and calmness comes
over me. I have no worries of failure. What a powerful and
warm feeling it is! I want to expand, to hug the world. I feel
enormous power to effect something of grace and beauty."
Another dancer said, "Your concentration is very complete.
Your mind isn't wandering, you are not thinking of something else; you are totally involved in what you are doing.
. . . Your energy is flowing very smoothly. You feel relaxed,
comfortable and energetic."

A rock climber commented, "You are so involved in what
you are doing that you aren't thinking of yourself as separate
from the immediate activity." Another climber said, "One
thing you're after is the one-pointedness of mind. You can get
your ego mixed up with climbing in all sorts of ways and it
isn't necessarily enlightening. But when things become automatic, it's like an egoless thing, in a way. Somehow the right
thing is done without you ever thinking about it or doing
anything at all. . . . It just happens. And yet you are more
concentrated."

These remarks capture the characteristics of windhorse:
the synchronization of mind and body so that thoughts are
not separate from action, the feeling of relaxation and calm
combined with a sense of power, the joy and warmth toward
others, and the loss of the sense of a separate watching self.

Just before he died, pianist Arthur Rubinstein was interviewed by Mike Wallace. Wallace asked whether, given the modern belief that mind is just the brain, he was sad that his wonderful talent would be entirely lost when he died (a strange question indeed!). Rubinstein replied that he knew nothing about death or the brain. He knew, however, that whenever he played, something tangible reached out from him and touched the audience, lifting their spirits. Through that "something," he felt that he communicated directly with the audience. Rubinstein was clearly not talking merely about the physical propagation of sound through air. He was describing the power of windhorse.

Windhorse need not be restricted to special moments of optimal experience of enjoyment and fulfillment. It is an energy that you have probably already experienced many times, before hearing about windhorse. Windhorse does not discriminate between presidents and bank clerks, between men and women, between paupers and millionaires. Your own power and warmth, your windhorse, is available to you whenever you remember to connect with it, even in the darkest moments of fear and depression. It can be roused by anyone who is willing to let go of ego-centered concerns and open to it with bravery and humor. Csikszentmihalyi's work demonstrates that such moments are not rare or limited only to the most accomplished but occur in the lives of many. Whether they occur by chance or through our own effort depends, however, on whether we train. It is rare to know how to rouse this energy spontaneously and increase it. "Raising windhorse" is the practice of deliberately opening to this energy and rousing it in your own being.

CHAPTER 12

Raising Windhorse in One Stroke

Do you know a word that doesn't refer to something?
Have you ever picked and held a rose from
    R. O. S. and E.?
You say the NAME. Now try to find the reality it
    names.
Look at the moon in the sky, not the one in the lake.
If you want to be free of your obsession with words
and beautiful lettering, make one stroke down.
There's no self, no characteristics,
but a bright center where you have the knowledge
the prophets have, without books or interpreters

           —"The Name," by Jalalaudin Rumi

Traditional Art Forms Can Raise Windhorse

WINDHORSE IS RAISED whenever we carry out any action mindfully and wholeheartedly. When body, mind, and heart become *one,* and our clarity and loving energy are expressed in our action, *there* is windhorse. Many traditional practices of arts can help us raise windhorse and, in some cases, have been practiced with this purpose for many centuries. Because of the effort and wisdom that have been put into these practices over the generations, they can be particularly potent. Many of the art forms associated with cathedrals—for example, stone masonry, painting, and wood carving—originally had the capacity to rouse the windhorse of the practitioners.

An example of a traditional art form that has been passed down unchanged for centuries is kyudo, the Japanese art of archery. This very simple practice is well known to many through Eugen Herrigel's classic *Zen in the Art of Archery*. It originated as one of the main fighting methods of the samurai, but for six hundred years, it has been taught, unchanged, as a practice for synchronizing mind and body and raising windhorse. The power of the weapon has been harnessed into the power to overcome aggression.

A master of this art, Shibata Kanjuro Sensei, is the twentieth in a family line of bow-makers and master archers for the emperor of Japan. He came to North America first in 1980 to teach kyudo to Shambhala students, at the request of Chögyam Trungpa. Had he stayed in Japan a few years longer, he would have been appointed a "Living Treasure of Japan"—the highest cultural honor of that country. In North America, he was so impressed by the practice attitude of Shambhala students that he returned again and again. He took up permanent residence in the United States in 1985 and has taught kyudo in North America and Europe ever since. Sensei exhibits a combination of humbleness and power. In ordinary activities, he conveys a light humor and joy of life that are not inhibited even by his conventional Japanese manners. When Sensei is in the *dojo* ("practice hall"), however, it is another story; there, he can display a fierceness that is awesome.

Shibata Sensei emphasizes over and over again that

"kyudo is mind," slapping his lower abdomen (his *tanden,* where *kokoro*—which means something like "mind-heart-spirit"—is said to reside). By this, he means that kyudo is practiced not for the competitive or sport aspect but as a way of polishing *kokoro;* letting go of negative emotions, confusions, and fixation on self; and rousing windhorse. As Sensei says:

> The ultimate goal of kyudo is to polish your mind. It is the same with zazen [Zen mindfulness practice]. You are not polishing your style of shooting, but the mind. The dignity of shooting is the important point. Without the right mind, no matter how long you shoot, this dignity won't be gained.
>
> Rather than being a question of hitting the target due to good form or good style, if your mind is correct, you will naturally hit it. This is the case for anything that you do, not just kyudo. If you are always wondering about the target or the result, then nothing good can come of it. If you always look at . . . your own feet, your basis, then things will naturally go right.

In kyudo practice, the archer stands only six feet in front of a large target, usually made of a hay bale. Hitting the target is not the point, although later you do shoot at distant targets. Steve, a Shambhala student and kyudo instructor, describes making a shot:

> First, the practitioner assumes a solid stance like a tree whose branches extend naturally to heaven but whose roots are planted firmly in the earth. The

upper torso has a sense of upliftedness, as if a string were lightly pulling the head to the sky. When the yumi [bow] is fully drawn, the moment of release ripens naturally, of its own accord, as energy flows up and out from the *tanden,* the center of the body near the navel. The mind follows the path of the arrow, allowing itself to rest in the space. There is a sense of "lingering," like the deep resonance of a temple bell after it is struck.

Over and over, he or she practices the apparently simple form: taking a stance like a huge oak tree, joining heaven and earth; raising the bow; pushing the bow forward and extending the string; holding that, hold, hold, and—release! It is said that it can take ten years just to learn to release the arrow properly. The buildup of intensity and the energy arising at the release feel very much like raising windhorse.

A practice taught in Shambhala to invoke windhorse is the practice of executing the "primordial stroke of confidence." This practice is something like calligraphy or *sumi-e* drawing in spirit. The practice was recognized by both Chögyam Trungpa and Shibata Sensei to be identical in essence to kyudo. It is outwardly very simple: standing or kneeling in front of white calligraphy paper, with a bowl of black ink and a calligraphy brush, you make one stroke down on the paper.

There is first the empty sheet of paper. The blank sheet of paper symbolizes the open dimension, before anything has happened. It is the empty canvas of an artist, before he or she knows what to paint. It is the target in kyudo. It is the open sky, clear and very big, able to accommodate the entire earth, sun, moon, and stars, a peaceful sunrise or a violent storm. It mirrors the mind and heart that are open to all possibilities. It may be the openness in your mind just before you say something to a friend but are not sure what. It may be the moment of silence just as a meeting begins or just before you leap down a ski slope. Yet your mind is not completely blank because you have the intention, perhaps even the longing, to say or do something.

Suddenly, you make a first connection with reality—first thought—the first dot of black ink as the brush strikes the paper. The downstroke symbolizes a warrior's weapon—a two-edged sword that cuts all aggression and hatred and, at the same time, cuts itself so that no sense of self-importance or self-righteousness remains, no idea that you are a victor over something or someone. When you do the stroke whole-heartedly, you have no separate sense of self. The stroke cuts through your conceptual thoughts and cloudy emotions, joining your mind and body, and opening a crack in the cocoon. Finally, as you abruptly lift the brush from the paper, you open your mind further to the energy and magic of wind-horse, which can enter through the gap in the cocoon.

The primordial stroke is not merely a stroke of calligraphy. Rather, it is a particularly powerful and magical practice for our time that was discovered by Chögyam Trungpa—a message from awake mind. It is a specific way to rend the setting-sun veil that normally prevents direct experience of sacredness and windhorse. When asked on one occasion what the stroke symbolized, Chögyam Trungpa replied, "One." His questioner continued, "One what?" "One with everything" was the succinct answer.

A similar understanding of making a primordial stroke is expressed by the Sufi poet Jalalaudin Rumi in "The Name," quoted at the opening of the chapter.

Although there are further depths of meaning to the practice of the primordial stroke of confidence, there are parallels to it in the brush stroke of Chinese and Japanese painting and calligraphy. According to François Cheng:

> In the eyes of the Chinese painter, the execution of the brush stroke is the link between man and the supernatural. For the brush stroke, through its internal unity and its capacity for variation, is one and many. It embodies the process through which man returns in painting to the original gestures of creation. (The act of executing the stroke corresponds to the very act which draws the One forth from chaos, which separates Heaven and Earth.) The stroke is simultaneously breath, yin-yang, Heaven-Earth, the ten thousand existents, while at the same time taking on the rhythm and secret instincts of man. . . .

A renowned calligrapher once told a Chinese emperor, when asked how to hold the brush, "If your mind [*kokoro*] is correct, the brush will be correct. This holds true for any of the Ways. If one's mind is crooked or warped, so will be one's technique. When a calligrapher writes 'no-mindedly' in the here and now, the brush strokes are vibrant; if one is distracted or full of delusion, the lines will be dead no matter how well they are constructed."

Raising Windhorse Gathers Authentic Presence

By practicing raising windhorse, you gradually accumulate a quality of *authentic presence*. Authentic presence is a translation of the Tibetan term *wangtang,* which literally means a "field of power." Authentic presence grows in your system as your genuine confidence matures and you are able to open yourself again and again to the energy of windhorse. Authentic presence develops in a simple cause-and-effect process from letting go of ego fixation, of obsession with yourself and who you are, and of grasping for power and possessions. All *you* have to do is let go, relax, and open your genuine heart of sadness-joy. Then the dawning of authentic presence is as automatic as action and reaction. Authentic presence dawns gradually, and in the Shambhala teachings, the gradual dawning is divided into four stages, called qualities, or dignities.

The first quality, meekness, is the ground of authentic being. Whatever their accomplishments, people with authentic presence remain genuine, modest, and without pretense. They are self-contained and alert. Because they do not have an inflated image of themselves, they are inquisitive and interested in the world around them.

Meekness is neither cowardly nor shrinking. Like a tiger in the forest, a traditional image for mindfulness and meekness, the young warrior stays close to the ground—connecting her feet with the soil, watching, feeling, moving, with heightened awareness. It is feeling the hairs on your back stand on end, having your ears alert and open in all directions, smelling the electricity in the air, watching, waiting. It is using all your senses, listening, and looking and touching your world with interest and inquisitiveness, and staying mindful in the moment, alert like a frightened doe, nerves as sensitive as bruises. Then, suddenly, without your doing anything, a crack will appear in the cocoon, and you can slip through.

The second quality is perkiness. *Webster's Collegiate Dictionary* defines "to perk" as "to grow in vigor or cheerfulness, especially after a period of weakness or depression." This definition brings us very close to the sense of the word *perkiness* as a quality of authentic presence: it is the cheerfulness one feels at the moment of leaving behind the depression caused by doubt and hesitation. Perkiness has a sense of playfulness that treats everything with a light touch of humor. A person who has developed this quality is not casual, however, but is thoroughly trained in mindfulness and continually exerts himself joyfully. Perkiness is a fresh and uplifted state of being in which body and mind are completely in harmony. Its youthful zest overcomes all doubt and laziness, as well as the feeling that it is not worthwhile to keep going forward into new challenges.

Someone who lets go of the cocoon mind enjoys leaping from first thought to first thought. People who have the bravery and willingness to be genuine can enjoy their lives and their world, enjoy their challenges, and welcome the challenges of difficult situations. With the quality of perkiness, they can take delight in facing difficulties head-on and seeing what happens.

The third quality, outrageousness, enables warriors to enter completely into any situation without trying to measure their own ability to respond to it adequately or to guess the outcome. To accomplish what is needed, people at this stage of authentic presence are not afraid to go beyond conventional responses or the limits set by habitual norms of thinking or behaving. They are able to appreciate the whole picture and not be trapped into taking sides.

Extending yourself outrageously, allowing a gap in your time and space, you have no need to hope or expect anything; you are completely beyond "poverty mentality" or fear of making a mistake. Someone who can fly so far above the cocoon of the setting sun could be called "outrageous," in the sense of going beyond boundaries, not being limited by conceptual barriers or petty expectations. Nevertheless, the outrageous warrior never departs from the tiger's meekness and genuine decency and the uplifted discipline of the dignity of perkiness.

The fourth quality, inscrutability, is remaining-in-nowness. People who have accomplished inscrutability are able to let go altogether of their own logic, beliefs, and ways of doing things. At this stage, they overcome the boundary between themselves and the world and identify fully with other people and with earth, the weather, the forests, the sky, and the elements. The inscrutable warrior joins the vast unbounded space discovered in outrageousness with the practicality of earth by becoming completely one with the elements, earth, water, fire, and wind. Inscrutable warriors are able to perform all actions effortlessly and elegantly. Their actions support like earth, bind like water, nourish and promote growth like fire, and refresh and cause circulation like the wind.

When we are still going steadily step-by-step through the gateway of fear to emerge from our cocoons, we are fundamentally at the level of meekness. However, at any stage on the path, we can see the seeds of all these qualities in our everyday life. The qualities build on each other, so that someone who has developed the quality of perkiness has not renounced or gone beyond the quality of meekness. It is not like learning math in school, where once you have "covered" algebra, you hope you never hear the word again. Meekness, the quality of being thoroughly grounded and open, is learned—or relearned—and used again and again. Furthermore, perkiness is a natural outcome of the accomplishment of meekness, and outrageousness is a natural result of accomplishing perkiness. In this sense, all the qualities are already contained in meekness, just as the teenager is already contained in the youngster, and the mature person in the teenager. The qualities do not have to be striven for; they are not some kind of credential. They simply characterize the natural development of authentic presence in anyone practicing mindfulness and awareness and continually raising their windhorse. We will revisit the dignities of authentic presence in later chapters, as we discuss the way a spiritual warrior acts in the world.

CHAPTER 13

People of Authentic Presence

*A*UTHENTIC PRESENCE IS easier to point to by example than to describe. However, it is not a mysterious or an especially rare quality. We have probably all met people with some degree of authentic presence. Men and women of great authentic presence are characterized by simplicity and humor, not burdened by holding a lot on their minds. They have a simple smile and genuine cheerfulness, combined with a seriousness that approaches sadness. Yet they also have a sharp edge: they have cut through pretension and learned to live humbly and directly, and their presence challenges others to be without pretense as well. Such people, whether formally well educated or not, often have tremendous discipline in their chosen way of working in the world. They sparkle with rare liveliness and spirit. They may be people in positions of high visibility and great power, or they may be completely anonymous, ordinary people.

Nancy Wake Forward, an Australian, was a young journalist in Europe before the Second World War, fun-loving and enjoying the high life of Paris. She became one of the most decorated women of the war. On a trip to Vienna, she saw the degrading treatment of the Jews and determined to become involved in the French Resistance movement. She says of those early days, "Back in Paris, I would think of all the chaos in Germany. But what could an inexperienced girl like myself do or hope to achieve when so many brilliant, well-informed men had failed to make an impact on the outside world?" Her involvement in the Resistance began slowly, smuggling documents and helping downed Allied pilots. Then she trained in London and became a secret agent and saboteur. The Nazis dubbed her the White Mouse (the title of her autobiography) because she was so hard to find.

On one of her many escapades, Nancy traveled through German lines on a stolen bicycle with no license and no identity cards to fetch a radio transmitter. She cycled three hundred miles in seventy-two hours and had to be lifted off her bike when she returned. She recalls, "I got through German lines because I looked innocent and polite, you see. They were holding up everybody. I went through with a little string bag on the end of my bicycle with a couple of leeks or carrots, and I was just a little housewife." When asked if she was ever afraid, she replied, "Never. Why should I be afraid of a situation? Afterward you might say, 'Ah, that was a close call.' But your reaction has got to be good. If you're going to be frightened and shivering, you'll never get away with anything."

She kept her sense of humor through all this. At one point, she had the French underground commandeer a bus for her to sleep in. She said, "I said to this lovely young man, I'm *sick* of this ground! I want a bus! So the men started stopping buses and making the people get off. It had to be one where the two back seats faced each other." They took the fourth bus they stopped; Nancy Wake put a mattress over the back seats and used parachutes for sheets. In addition, each night she'd shed her grimy, mannish uniform for a blue or pink nightgown.

In person, even in her seventies, Nancy was outspoken, even fierce, and possessed a great gusto for life. One official document said, "[H]er irrepressible high spirits were a joy to everyone who worked with her." Recently, she told a reporter, "I'll tell you something absolutely wonderful. Some fans in New South Wales want to name a race horse the 'White Mouse.' I was thrilled pink. The woman says the horse is very naughty and I said she takes after me. Don't you think that's gorgeous? Lots of funny things happen to me, so I don't lead an uninteresting life."

The authentic presence of an accomplished warrior has the power to benefit many people. It comes from a profound letting go of inner grasping after personal gain. It is a field of power that we recognize in the subtle radiance of genuinely wise leaders, such as the Dalai Lama, leader of the Tibetan government in exile and Nobel Peace Prize winner. Their presence can at times be powerful to the point of seeming majestic. At other times, they can be unpredictable or wrathful or even appear like a child.

The stories of many of the early Christian saints often illustrate tremendous authentic presence, but even these stories include behavior that cut through the conventional minds of the day. Saint Symeon of Emesa, a sixth-century canonized saint, was just such a "Fool for Christ." On one occasion, he was employed to sell beans for an innkeeper, and instead, he distributed them free to the people. He would throw nuts at people praying in church, walk about naked, throw stones at passersby, and associate with prostitutes. He had a mischievous sense of humor, but he also worked miracles. He was buried as a madman, but shortly afterward, when his coffin was reopened to grant him a decent burial, his corpse was not to be found.

People of great authentic presence often do not fulfill the usual image of a holy man or woman. They are not bound inwardly by conventional understanding, to the extent that their contemporaries might consider them unorthodox or too outspoken. They have no need to hide their real humanity behind a veneer of specialness or holiness. Yet however outwardly unconventional *or* gracious their appearance, they have given up grasping for personal comfort, and so without pretense or needing to crank anything up, they are able to radiate loving-kindness.

Maya Angelou, author of *I Know Why the Caged Bird Sings,* strikes all those who meet her as a person of great authentic presence. When she speaks, from the minute she takes the stage, the audience—which often numbers in the thousands—is electrified by her power. Yet somehow she is able to establish what feels like personal rapport with each of them. Angelou tells how she was raped when she was seven and, for five and a half years afterward, did not speak at all. "I was a giant ear," she says. She went on to become a singer and dancer, playwright, poet, and author.

During her talks, she can be completely uninhibited, frequently breaking into spontaneous song, dance, and poetry. The large hall throbs with her energy. She says, "People always recognize the truth no matter how it is spoken," a statement of which she herself is a vivid illustration. People are moved to tears by her full, radiant, "tell-it-like-it-is" presence. Yet it is beyond ordinary charisma or mere celebrity. It is clear that she has done plenty of work on herself, which she characterizes as "trying to be a Christian." She says that her response to people who say they are Christians is, "Already?"

When someone once asked her how she got from her impoverished background in rural Arkansas to where she is today, she said simply, "By being grateful." Her confidence is as strong as her humility, and she talks about confidence as one of the most important virtues: "With confidence, you can do anything; without it, you can do nothing."

In *The Sword of No-Sword,* John Stevens describes the life of one of the greatest Japanese Zen sword teachers of modern times, Yamaoka Tesshu, who lived from 1836 to 1888. Tesshu was a remarkable poet and painter as well as a master swordsman and renowned teacher of swordsmanship. In the last eight years of his life, he produced more than a million works of painting and calligraphy. Stevens says of these works, "Many were obviously dashed off in a frenzy of Zen enthusiasm; still, there is no trace of stagnation or a taint of constructed characters. Wonderfully constructed, his paintings too are a joy to contemplate, and has anyone brushed better Zen cartoons?"

Tesshu established the Muto Ryu (no-sword system) school of swordsmanship. According to Stevens:

> Tesshu insisted that no-sword swordsmanship was ultimately pure spirit. Near the end of his life Tesshu's movements were extraordinarily supple and he could defeat an opponent without even touching him. Students had sore spots on the places where Tesshu had merely pointed his sword at their bodies.
>
> A week before his death, Tesshu called all his trainees together for a final practice session. Tesshu told them, "I'm dying. My physical strength is gone.

I am barely able to stand. Not a trace of competitiveness remains. I'll now prove to you all that Muto Ryu swordsmanship is a thing of the spirit. If any of you displays the slightest reserve today, the Muto Ryu will perish with my death."

Without regard for Tesshu's terminal illness, one by one, eight or nine disciples came forward and attacked him ferociously. The first student attacked, and just as he was about to bring down his sword with all his might, he was spun around and crashed to the floor by a tremendous force. Yet Tesshu had not physically touched him. The other students went flying in the same way. Tesshu proclaimed, "This is the sword of no-sword."

Tesshu shocked the conventional society of his time by his love of sake, or rice wine. Stories of his sake-drinking exploits and his sense of humor were legion. On one occasion, when Tesshu was drinking with his companions, they dared him to try to ride a horse so violent that no one could get near it, let alone ride it. According to Stevens, "Tesshu walked straight into the horse's stall, grabbed it by the tail, and started yanking. 'Look out, you madman' the others yelled as they headed for cover. To everyone's surprise, the animal no man could tame meekly followed Tesshu out of the stall and stood at bay in the middle of the stable."

Tesshu was renowned and popular. There was a constant stream of visitors to his home. "Callers included those who merely wanted to borrow money or to have some petition presented to the emperor," Stevens says, "but most came for instruction and counsel, and not a few hung around just to absorb a bit of the tremendous energy radiated by Tesshu's presence. . . . Despite the constant crush of visitors Tesshu's door was always open and all were received with courtesy." Yet his popularity was of no concern to him. "Whenever Zen attempts to win converts or compete with other sects," he said, "its true spirit is lost. Nothing I have done was for the sake of popularizing Zen. . . . If just one person carries on the right transmission, I will be satisfied." Tesshu served in the imperial household for ten years, and because of his freedom from corruptibility, he was deeply trusted by the emperor. A fellow minister once said of him, "He doesn't need fame, fortune, status, or even life itself—how do you deal with such a man?"

A Meeting of Two Remarkable Men

Chögyam Trungpa and Gerald Red Elk were two men of great authentic presence. Outwardly, Chögyam Trungpa lived an ordinary life: he married and had children; he drank and fell in love; he entered into human life with an extraordinary intensity of joy and sadness. His life was a feast of celebrations and an open secret: he had no privacy and no hidden corners. He used to recount with great delight that an auto accident that had changed the direction and style of his teaching in the West was a crash into a joke shop. Yet he was able to bring Buddhism as well as the Shambhala teachings—the path of awakening in daily life—to the West with power and integrity. Because he lived an ordinary human life alongside them, he was able to *show* his students how to wake up rather than merely preach at them.

He was short and overweight and walked with a limp, as his left side had been partially paralyzed by the auto accident. Yet when he entered a room, one felt a tremendous sense of power joined with humor. His love for his students could be almost too much to bear. A friend told us that once, after he had been away for a while, he went into a room where Chögyam Trungpa was sitting with a few friends. Our friend went up to give him a hug. "I felt so much warmth and love from Chögyam Trungpa," he told me, "that I felt a physical shock and found myself closing off and pulling back. I just couldn't stand to be loved so much." Because of his radiance of love and his fierce authenticity, he was loved intensely by thousands of students and often feared by them as well.

His own generosity in leading his students beyond their hesitations seemed to have no bounds. One very brilliant student, Joshua, a Harvard-trained writer who had a great sense of humor but was also very sharp and cynical, became very ill and wrote a long letter a few days before he died. The letter was addressed to Chögyam Trungpa Rinpoche, but it was also intended for his fellow students. A few paragraphs of this letter here convey so well Chögyam Trungpa's humor and directness:

> Dear Rinpoche,
> You continue to astonish me right to the end. What amazingly good karma for me to have met you. Over the years, I have not been what you would call a great student. . . . And yet you have never abandoned me— never, not for an instant. And I have somehow managed to hold you in my heart. . . .
> Do you recall when you told me to "pull up your socks" I replied "I don't wear socks," and you shot back, "Then pull up your pants." That was the moment I knew I had met my teacher.
> Do you recall that Sasaki Roshi gave me a "very

difficult koan" to "protect my mind" at the first semi-
nary [a three-month residential retreat introducing
students to Vajrayana Buddhism], and when I arrived, without my having mentioned it, the first thing
you said was, "Forget the koan."

Do you recall the time—even now thinking about
it makes my heart beat—when you stood at the top
of the murderous flight of stairs at 1111 Pearl and you
asked me, "Are you ready?" ("ripe," you meant), and
when I hesitated for a moment, you plunged down
the stairs! I leaped to catch you at the landing and
tore my sports coat on the banister. I felt totally bewildered and dejected and said that I hoped I would
someday have another chance.

"Sure," you said, and plunged down the remaining
steps to my complete surprise. O Teacher—at any
price, even your own body, your life.

We've really had fun together.

As well as being warm and benevolent, Chögyam Trungpa
could be wrathful, challenging people suddenly and unexpectedly but with piercing accuracy. He often created friction
and feistiness among his students—friction that ignited a
flame of power and energy so that they could leap to another
level of genuine understanding. When he detected hypocrisy
or self-deception, he could radiate black air that made one
freeze or want to turn and run for cover. He overflowed with
stark compassion that was uncompromising with conventional niceness or what he called spiritual materialism—
wanting to make a new cocoon out of spiritual teachings or
practice.

In 1984, Chögyam Trungpa had an extraordinary meeting

with Gerald Red Elk, an Oglala Sioux shaman-chief, another man of great compassion and authentic presence. Gerald Red Elk's adopted American nephew Roger La Borde wrote:

> At one time he was a very angry man. He hated the white man and all that the white man had done to his people. He was lost in alcoholism. But nearly twenty years ago, as he was near death, he prayed to the Great Spirit to be spared. He promised that if he was allowed to live he would change his life and help his people. . . . Gerald did keep his promise. He helped his people, and his people included everyone. He told me one day that he realized that after the Great Spirit had let him live there was only one race of people on this earth—the human race.

Gerald was deeply concerned that the bad state of mind of the present civilization was causing tremendous turmoil on the earth and that much worse was to come. Every four years, he would meet with other native elders at a special place in the Rocky Mountains near Denver, Colorado, to read messages from the gods—the Star People, as he called them—etched on the rocks. The recent messages had depicted the gods weeping—warning of the terrible suffering of the earth itself. "They're telling us, for the future," he said. "Some things are going to happen, and people will have to be in a very good state of mind, so they could be strong, so they could reason without panicking, and at the same time they could learn what all those grasses and trees and (they call them weeds) what those plants are all about, because all of them are medicine and are edible."

Gerald Red Elk visited the Denver area in 1980 to read the

medicine rocks, and when he was there, he asked to meet Chögyam Trungpa. "I wanted to meet a Tibetan lama," he said later, "because we understand the heart of what they are. We call anybody in that state of mind a 'common man of the earth' because they live the laws of the earth, they understand, and we could communicate without talking."

Since Chögyam Trungpa was not available to meet Red Elk, Jeremy was asked to do so. He came into Jeremy's office one late afternoon. Tall and stooped, he wore baggy polyester pants and a short-sleeved shirt with a row of ball-point pens in the breast pocket, clipped onto a plastic pocket guard. He looked a little like an aging truck driver. Jeremy relates:

> We sat down against opposite walls in my small office. Red Elk began by saying that he believed that the Tibetans had knowledge about the Star People that complemented the knowledge his people had of them. Together, he felt, the two peoples could help the world in the coming bad times.
>
> Red Elk's voice was very soft and low; I could hardly understand what he was saying. I had not then heard of the Star People, though they sounded somewhat like the dralas, to whom Chögyam Trungpa had very recently introduced us. Yet I was completely transfixed by his presence. The room seemed filled with kindness and generosity and an almost magical enchantment. I felt, as we sat there, that he was pouring love out toward me, even as he spoke about almost incomprehensible things. As the sun set, the room grew dark, but I did not want to get out of my chair and turn on the light for fear of breaking the spell.

Chögyam Trungpa was still unavailable that night, and Red Elk left town early the next morning. It was four years before their paths finally crossed, when Gerald Red Elk was again in Colorado to read the medicine rocks. The meeting with Chögyam Trungpa took place only a few months before Red Elk died.

It was on a bright summer afternoon in the Rocky Mountains at an encampment for training in Shambhala warriorship practice. At the beginning of their meeting, Chögyam Trungpa and Gerald Red Elk talked briefly about the weather. Trungpa looked at the sky and said, "I think it is going to rain tomorrow." Red Elk replied, "I think it will probably rain in a few hours." Trungpa responded, "I think it will rain tomorrow morning." Red Elk said, "I think it will rain soon." Throughout the meeting, thunder rumbled.

Red Elk presented Chögyam Trungpa with a turquoise stone, which represented the nature of the universe; a red stone, the nature of the gods; a green stone, the earth; and a purple stone, medicine. They spoke together for about forty minutes, Red Elk showing Chögyam Trungpa drawings of the rock messages. Both commented on the similarity of the drawings to the animals portrayed on Chögyam Trungpa's Shambhala standard: the tiger, snow lion, garuda, and dragon. "I think we can work together," Trungpa said. "It is very magical." He gave Red Elk a copy of *Shambhala: The Sacred Path of the Warrior,* which had just been published. Red Elk exclaimed, "The sacred path of the warrior, this is what we believe in. The honor is there. The honor is there." Later, Chögyam Trungpa said, "He understood the whole book just from the cover," while Gerald Red Elk commented, "We understood each other completely without needing to say anything."

The two sat quietly together for almost an hour. At the end of the meeting, they embraced, and Chögyam Trungpa said, "I think something extraordinary will come out of this." As Gerald Red Elk walked slowly back down the valley, a slight rain began to fall. As they walked away, Roger La Borde says:

> Huge raindrops began to fall, the biggest I think I have ever seen, and I grew up where thunderstorms were common. A large electric-blue bolt of lightning struck the ground several hundred yards away. I actually saw the spot where it hit the ground. As we drove away a monsoon (or so it seemed) commenced. I said to Gerald as we were driving out to the main highway that I knew that sparks would fly during the meeting, but I didn't expect it to be lightning! Gerald's response was that the night before he had had a dream of rain and lightning during the meeting, which he took to be the gods' approval of the meeting.

As they walked away, meanwhile, Chögyam Trungpa remained seated outside his tent, saying, "It's so sad, so sad." The rain fell more heavily as Red Elk continued down the road. The attendants tried to encourage Chögyam Trungpa to go inside his tent, but he continued to sit outside, under the tent flap. The rain seemed to let up, and Trungpa picked up his stick and said, "Well, I guess that's enough." The rain stopped for a minute.

Then Trungpa began to shake, and he started crying, sobbing. He picked up his stick again and slammed it on his knee. At that point, a torrential downpour—the heaviest rain anyone had ever experienced—flooded the valley. Our nephew Carl told us, "We were standing in the center of the campground getting ready to take down the flag for the evening. It had been a beautiful, warm, sunny afternoon. Suddenly, a big, black cloud moved across the valley and seemed to stop over us. We were told to go to our tents—just forty or fifty feet away—to get our raincoats, but it started to pour, and before we could even get to the tents, we were soaked. The cloud just emptied on the camp and then moved away."

During this time, Gerald Red Elk was being driven away from the property by Roger La Borde. A few miles down the road, Gerald Red Elk had Roger stop the car. He walked out into the middle of a field and gazed toward the encampment grounds, over which the storm cloud could be seen. After many minutes, he turned and silently returned to the car.

Chögyam Trungpa still wouldn't go into his tent. Attendants inside and outside the tent pushed up the roof with poles to try to keep the rain from collapsing it. As the downpour increased to a formidable deluge, the grounds were no longer visible, and a curtain of water completely surrounded him. His attendants were yelling pleas that he come inside the tent. But he shook his head. As he continued to sit, finally a rainbow formed in the valley. It was as if, in the play of the rain and hail, the lightning and sunshine, the elements had sealed a magical connection between two true master warriors.

Gerald Red Elk became ill with cancer shortly after this meeting and died a few months later. When Roger went to visit Red Elk in his hospital room just before he died, the first thing Red Elk said was, "How's Rinpoche?" He and Chögyam Trungpa never met again.

In this chapter, we have given examples of people who have attained some degree of mastery on the path of warriorship and who exhibit an authentic presence that has a powerful effect on their world. However, authentic presence is not only for a few, rare individuals or some far-off state of being that is difficult to accomplish. Authentic presence accumulates naturally when you are kind and brave; when you see and let go of fixations about yourself and your world, and of the aggression that comes from defending these fixations; when you genuinely care for others; and when you keep your sense of humor.

CHAPTER 14

Experience of Many Dimensions

T o GO FURTHER and deeper toward understanding and feeling the sacred world, the *real* "real world," we need to look at what we believe about *how* our world—the ordinary world of rocks, trees, bugs, and people—is and how it comes to be. Many of us may think that these questions don't really matter nowadays, perhaps vaguely feeling that science has solved all that. Yet we all do have some belief that guides how we feel about our world and how we perceive it. Especially those of us brought up in Western culture grow up with two rather limited but extreme choices. We can believe in scientific materialism—that nothing-but-matter is all that is really *real,* and all that happens is nothing but blind chance. Or we can believe in an omnipotent God, who, though creating it all, is also beyond it all.

Scientific materialism is profoundly nihilistic in saying that *fundamentally* nothing exists in the universe other than lifeless, mindless matter; cold, lifeless, empty space; and meaningless, objective, linear time. In the words of Nobel Prize winner Francis Crick, "You, your joys and sorrows, your memories and ambitions, your sense of personal identity and free will are, in fact, no more than the behavior of a vast assembly of nerve cells." In this view, "sacred" is a subjective fantasy, a weak-willed attempt to escape the harsh truth that, in reality, the cosmos itself is lifeless and meaningless.

At the other extreme, the transcendent God, who is the one and only god and creator of the physical universe, dwells in a realm altogether separate from the earthly realm. This is the "Heaven" realm, in which our mind or soul may dwell eternally after the death of our physical body. So this belief creates a profound duality between mind and body, between the earth realm and the "Heaven" realm, and between "secular" and "sacred."

Perhaps most of us are guided by a vague hodgepodge of these two extremes, or vehemently deny one or the other of them, but we all *do* have *some* relation to them. Monotheism, the belief in one almighty God, and the unbridgeable split between mind and body that comes with it, is still a powerful force in our society. But the nihilistic view of materialism is becoming more and more dominant. Nihilistic materialism is the basic philosophy of the modern world. Because of this nihilism, most people in modern society are simply unable to accept the evidence of their own senses that their cosmos itself is alive with wisdom and sacredness. Or if they do feel the sacredness, they have to believe this is "just in the head" since science now knows that the physical world, of tables and chairs, stereos and computers, rocks and trees, bodies and brains, is meaningless. We are taught by our science teachers, by popular magazines, and by eminent scientists on TV that "scientists know that such things are just not possible." Even those involved in spiritual pursuits often do not realize the extent to which they were deeply conditioned by the nihilism of materialism as they grew up.

Both materialism and popular monotheism are terribly impoverished views of the universe. However, many scientists today would agree with Candace Pert, herself a highly re-spected biochemist, when, in a conversation with Bill Moyers in *Healing and the Mind,* she said, "There's another realm that we experience that's not under the purview of science." This "other realm of experience" is the realm of subtle en-ergy, feeling, and awareness, perceived with the open heart of sadness and joy. In this and the following chapters, we want to take a close look at this realm and how we can open to it fully. First, let's see how it fits together with the conventional dogmas of materialism and monotheism.

The great American scholar Huston Smith, who is best known for his classic book *The World's Religions,* also wrote a less well-known book, *Forgotten Truth: The Common Vision of the World's Religions.* In this book, he suggests that there is an inner heart of all religions and spiritual traditions that recognizes several levels of reality and experience. He calls them "levels," but they could just as well be called "realms," "spaces," or "dimensions." As well, many other scholars of spirituality—for example, Aldous Huxley, author of *The Pe-rennial Philosophy,* and more recently, Ken Wilber—have pointed to the multidimensionality of experience. The num-ber of levels varies from writer to writer, from at least three to more than twenty-seven. Huston Smith describes four levels.

These writers agree that what we are actually dealing with is a *continuum, or spectrum,* of human experience that we can divide conceptually into as many parts as we please, depend-ing on our particular philosophy. At one end of this contin-uum, there is the *outer,* or terrestrial, dimension. This is the mundane world that all humans perceive with their un-trained five senses, perhaps aided by scientific instruments. Perhaps we could say it is the lowest common denominator of human experience. It is the dimension of experience in which all that exists are bare facts, value-free and meaningless, and subjective opinion. It is the world of the scientific materialist, in which all is nothing but space, time, and matter. It is the world in which, as novelist and philosopher Iris Murdoch said, "People play cricket, cook cakes, make simple decisions, remember their childhood, and go to the circus." But it is a world that denies the subleties and insights of feeling, which cause people to, in Murdoch's words, "commit sins, fall in love, say prayers, or join the Communist Party." At the other end of the continuum of experience is the *totality* of each moment, not conditioned by our thoughts and concepts, undivided, unbounded, infinite: we could call it the *open* dimension, experiencing the universality of unconditional basic goodness, first introduced in chapter 1.

In between the outer, terrestrial, level and the infinite, open, level of experience stretches more than usually subtle energy/awareness—the *intermediate* level, as Huston Smith calls it, following the lead of Plato. This is the level of experience in which the world is itself meaningful, with inherent value, quality, and power. It is the realm of qualities, felt with perception of the open heart of sadness/joy. It is a world that responds to our call, to our love, to our hate, or to our indifference. It is the level of the gods, spirits, and other beings invisible to the mundane eye but known to almost all ages and cultures. But it is also the level of ghosts and demons.

It is important to emphasize that all three levels of the continuum are *present within ordinary human experience.* The energy that we have called *windhorse runs through all three levels:* windhorse is experienced as physical energy that energizes our bodies, as the more subtle energy of feeling that opens our hearts, and as unconditioned energy that intoxicates our minds beyond any conceptual thinking. So the practice of raising windhorse joins all three levels in our experience.

How the Dimensions Interweave

It is very important to understand that these dimensions— outer, intermediate, and open—are not stacked one on top of another, as if we were going from the Earth, through the intermediate atmosphere, and into infinite cosmic space. This very common image is quite misleading. Rather, the three dimensions are completely entangled with each other. To help you visualize how these dimensions are interconnected, think of the analogy of dimensions (or scales of measurement) in the skin of your hand. If you just look at a patch of skin on the palm of your hand with your naked eyes, it looks like typical skin with many fine and a few deep lines. If you look at a small piece of that skin under a regular microscope—at another scale, or dimension—you will see a different world. You will see the single cells of your skin and lots of microbes and bacteria crawling around on the surface of your skin. If you go to yet a deeper dimension, by looking at that piece of skin through an electron microscope, you will see the atomic level—again, an altogether different world of atoms and space. Notice that these worlds, or dimensions, are embedded one within the other. And notice that while the initial patch of skin looked like skin belonging to a hand, seen under the regular microscope, it could have been skin from anywhere on your body, and again, seen under the electron microscope, it joined the atomic realm common to all things.

Or in another analogy, consider the relation between matter, light, and space. Space contains both light and matter.

Light is completely intermingled with space: you cannot have light without space, though you can have space without light. So in that sense, space is a more encompassing realm than light. And light is more encompassing than matter: light penetrates matter (for example, in the ocean), whereas there can be light where there is no matter (for example, in outer space). So space, light, and matter are completely intermingled in our one world, with space being the more all-encompassing, then light, then matter.

In a similar way to our analogy of the skin, the dimensions of being—from the outer; through the intermediate; to the unconditioned, or open—are completely intermingled. And like the atomic dimension of the skin, the infinite, unbounded, open dimension encompasses all the others. Because these dimensions intermingle, they are all within our ordinary human experience. To experience them, we have to train our perception to be open to more subtle aspects of our experience than usual, just as to see the hidden dimensions of the skin, we had to tune in to finer and finer detail.

The Open Dimension

In the following chapters, we will be looking closely at the intermediate dimension, since this is the realm least familiar and perhaps most threatening to us in the modern scientific-materialist world. But let us first explain what we mean by the "open dimension." Unconditioned basic goodness is, in itself, empty of all forms but full of all possibilities and potentials. The much-loved Zen master Suzuki Roshi describes very clearly this sense that the open dimension of experience is not anything we can point to "out there," separate from our own being, but is nevertheless full:

I discovered that it is necessary, absolutely necessary, to believe in nothing. That is, we have to believe in something which has no form and no color— something which exists before all forms and colors appear. This is a very important point. . . . It is absolutely necessary to believe in nothing. But I do not mean voidness. There is something, but that something is something which is always prepared for taking some particular form, and it has some rules, or theory or truth in its activity. . . . This is not just theory. This is not just the teaching of Buddhism. This is the absolutely necessary understanding of our life.

It is difficult to pin down openness in words because, in our experience, it is more basic than the discriminating intellectual aspect of mind—the aspect that distinguishes between opposites: one and many, good and evil, black and white, friend and enemy, our side and their side, existence and nonexistence. This is the yin and yang of Eastern thought: both together make the whole. They are only opposites in relation to each other.

The cognizing and conceptualizing, "thinking," aspect of mind always divides experience into opposites, and most modern people do not know that a state of mind more profound and basic than this kind of divisive thinking exists or could exist. It is presumed in our educational and political systems that the intellectual mind that creates opposite views, which then have to battle for the truth, is the highest function of the human mind. Is it any wonder we have wars! However, the fact is that all of us *are* capable of recognizing opposites and not being caught up in taking one side or the other.

That awareness which recognizes opposites is itself *beyond* opposites. When our thoughts and feelings are not caught up in opposites, but are able to encompass both sides and feel the whole, we harmonize them and bring peace. The intellectual mind *recognizes* opposites, and the open heart *accommodates* them as one. So the state of being we are talking about here is one in which heart and mind are awake and functioning together. There is a quality of human awareness that is not caught in opposites; this is clear. By developing the awareness beyond opposites, we can glimpse the open dimension within our ordinary world.

When we open our sense perceptions to the open dimension, the realm of basic goodness, we begin to see and feel more and more space. We sense that the appearances of forms, colors, sounds, tastes, and so on, of our ordinary world are not quite the solid "things" that we usually take them to be. Our experience of "things" softens, and we begin to see how "things" are related through the space they share.

We can sense the open dimension in our state of mind, also, when our thoughts are momentarily stilled. When, for example, you are just about to speak but are not sure what to say, your mind goes blank for a moment. However, your basic awareness is still there underlying the blankness. If you do not panic, at that moment, you can touch the unconditioned, open dimension in your experience. And you might find you have something quite remarkable to say. We touch the open dimension at the moment of first thought, nowness.

The Celestial Realm

In *Forgotten Truth,* Huston Smith includes the open dimension in the deepest understanding of the monotheistic traditions, thereby combining the theistic and nontheistic traditions into one scheme. The mystical, or contemplative, schools of all three monotheistic religions—Judaism, Christianity, and Islam—have certainly all recognized the open, unbounded dimension, which cannot be conditioned by names. And in all these traditions, including Eastern Orthodoxy but with the exception of Western Christianity, mysticism has not been a heresy, but a vibrant part of the life of the society of believers. These teachings understood that even the word *God* was limited and partial, since it described a *Being*, whereas there is a realm "above God" and "beyond Being," as Denys, a sixth-century Greek Christian writer, put it. This teaching, again, points to the unconditioned, open dimension, beyond one God or many, beyond being *and* nonbeing. As Karen Armstrong says, in *A History of God:*

> Though the idea of God as the Supreme Being had gained ascendancy in the West, other monotheistic traditions had gone out of their way to separate themselves from this type of theology. Jews, Muslims, and Orthodox Christians had all insisted in their different ways that our human idea of God did not correspond to the ineffable reality of which it is a mere symbol. All had suggested, at one time or another, that it was more accurate to describe God as "Nothing" rather than the Supreme Being, since "he" did not exist in any way that we could conceive. Over the centuries the West gradually lost sight of this more imaginative conception of God.

To accommodate the one God of the monotheistic traditions, Huston Smith places a "Celestial" level between the intermediate and open dimensions, corresponding to the "Heaven" of the theistic religions, the dwelling place of God. However, there really is no good reason to think of the one God of the Jews, Christians, and Muslims as a unique God or his abode as a separate, unique realm. All through the earliest period of Jewish and Christian history, there were many competing cults, all with their own gods and their incantations and rituals to invoke these gods. Yahweh, or Jehovah, the God of Abraham and Moses and later of Christ and Mohammed, was originally one of the many local pagan gods whose cult grew to remarkable prominence. It was not until the growth of rationalism during the Age of Enlightenment that the pagan (that is, non-Christian) gods of Europe and the Middle East were finally driven so far underground that they all but disappeared. Some were adopted into Christianity as "angels," "fairies," "saints," or "demons."

The God of the monotheists did come to transcend the local deity, Yahweh, and to symbolize a profound experience of oneness. The experience of many people, as they begin to feel the open dimension in their own lives, is an intuition of oneness, beyond the dualities of mind and body, inner world and outer world, and the separateness of individual beings. The intuition of oneness, a sense of the *whole* of experience included in one moment, is a profound and important aspect of the developing spiritual life of humankind. But it has too often been forgotten that this oneness is no *thing* in itself: oneness, or openness, is a fundamental part of *our* being, and we are a part of *that*. Too often, the mistake has been made of projecting this experience outward and objectifying it into an external God, and then tragically fighting over whose God is the real God. As well as the one God of the monotheists, there are, of course, many other gods—the devas of the

Hindu tradition, the yidams of the Tibetan Buddhist tradition, and so on.

The "Celestial" realm, then, is more reasonably thought of as the higher, or more transcendent, level of the intermediate realm of subtle energies. From this point of view, we could perhaps divide the intermediate realm into *three* abodes. There is the abode of ghosts and demons, and other forces and energies that have the intention to harm others. There is the abode of beings related directly with earth and those that dwell on it: protectors of localities, lakes, forests, mountains, and so on; ancestral beings; and protectors of the wisdom embodied in human activities. These energies protect and nourish the goodness and harmony of the life of earth as well as empowering human activity. Then there is the transcendent abode, of the gods, yidams, devas, and deities of all the world's religions. According to Huston Smith, this is also the realm of Jung's "archetypes." And some followers of Jung— for example, James Hillman and Thomas Moore—assert that the archetypes should not be considered as merely "subjective," psychological qualities but are in fact the *same* as the gods and should be thought of as having an "objective" aspect as well.

The Denial of the Intermediate Dimension in the Modern World

Finally, to return to the two narrow versions of belief about reality that most Westerners meet as they grow up, monotheism and materialism, these agree in their complete denial of an intermediate dimension to reality, the level of subtle, responsive, energy and power. To try to go into how this came about would take us too far afield, though it would be a fascinating detour into history nonetheless. It is enough for now to say that the denial of the subtle energy realm began as a combined effort of the medieval Western (not Eastern Orthodox) Christian Church and the newly awakening sciences of that time to destroy all vestiges of non-Christian (as defined by Church authority) beliefs and rites. The pagan teachings of correspondences between human, nature, and cosmos—"as above, so below"—of natural healing, alchemy, and so on, were ways of entering into communication and direct participation with the subtle energies of the intermediate realms. They were therefore a threat, or at least a nuisance, to both the Church and the new "natural philosophy," or science.

The result of this destruction of paganism was to create an unbridgeable gap between "Heaven" and "earth." Humans were no longer permitted to speak of their experience of the intermediate realm—their direct experience with pagan gods, or "angels." Joan of Arc was burned at the stake for "hearing voices" and refusing to deny them. And hundreds of thousands of others, mostly women, were likewise burned for their ability to heal or otherwise to communicate with non-Christian divine, or subtle, energies. People's only contact with the divine was to be mediated by the authorized representatives of the Church. What was sacred was only what was *sanctified* by authority. This then set the stage for the Church and the rationalists, representing Heaven and earth, respectively, to engage in battle. In this battle, the rationalists in the end asserted that Heaven was merely hogwash, while the Church insisted that the realm of God and the realm of earth were two utterly separate worlds, and therefore the discoveries of science had nothing to say about the realm of Heaven.

So far as we know, no other major culture in human history has blinded itself so completely to the presence of the intermediate dimension of being. The intermediate dimension is not "paranormal" or "supernatural." On the contrary, communication with this dimension is normal and natural in a healthy society, one that has not pathologically narrowed the scope of human experience, destroyed meaning, and lost heart. So let us now turn to look in depth at the intermediate dimension of subtle energies and forces. As we do so, we should always bear in mind that, because all is included in the open dimension of experience, the wisdom embodied in these subtle energies is not ultimately separate from our own wisdom.

CHAPTER 15

Patterns of Living Energy

The breeze at dawn has secrets to tell you
    Don't go back to sleep.
You must ask for what you really want
    Don't go back to sleep.
People are going back and forth across the doorsill
    where the two worlds touch.
The door is round and open.
    Don't go back to sleep.

—Rumi

Tuning in to Subtle Energies

IT *IS* POSSIBLE TO OPEN our minds and hearts and let go into the unfamiliar but very ordinary reality of the intermediate dimension. By expanding out of the cocoon of narrow-mindedness and fear, and learning how to raise windhorse and radiate authentic presence, we are able to tune in to the more subtle details of our world. Examples of seeing and feeling subtle energies are so common they actually become quite ordinary.

Probably you are familiar with a sense of intuition. Maybe you feel it in very small ways: As you walk to your car from the grocery, you may realize the school is trying to call you because your child is sick, or you may know who is calling before you pick up the phone, or you know when someone is thinking of you or that a friend is having a hard time. Usually, we experience such intuitions as a slight fleeting impression, at moments when we are not involved with something else. Mostly, even when we do manage to glimpse such intuitions, we dismiss them. Only later, when life has become more complicated because we ignored the intuition, do we think back and wish we'd paid attention. A colleague of ours totaled his car when the brakes failed as he went down a mountain road. That morning, he had ignored a nagging feeling that he ought to have the brakes checked.

Sometimes, these intuitive feelings become much more vivid, especially when intense emotions are involved. Experiences such as this happen often around death. A friend experienced, on several occasions, seeing the face of someone she knew in a clear and stark way, just before that person died. Karen intensely felt the presence of her mother in our home immediately after her mother died. But even at these times, although it is harder to dismiss the intuition, we still tend to distrust our own perception. Simple experiences of intuitive perception are numerous and familiar to all of us. The point is that we should not ignore them, for they open us to a new way of feeling the depth and power of our world. If we acknowledge that such things happen and let their happening challenge our comforting but narrow beliefs about reality, then the world will begin to reveal its vastness to us. We can begin to understand that we participate in a world far richer and more multifaceted and connected than we thought.

Jeremy's father is a civil engineer, a specialist in concrete, a religious agnostic, and very practical. One day, he told him this story, about something "that shook my whole world to its foundations." Jeremy relates:

> My father's mother was over ninety and was suffering from senile dementia. She could rarely recognize anyone except my father. But she was very fond of her daughter, Bettina, who was then dying of cancer. This was the same disease that my father's father, a doctor, had died from years before.
>
> The day after Bettina died, my father called the nursing home to tell the nurse but asked her not to tell his mother, since he would tell her himself the next day. The nurse said, "Oh, but she already knows. On her bedside table this morning there was a card which she had edged in black. And she had written the name *Bettina* in the middle. When I asked what it was for, she answered, 'Bettina died last night.' " When my father went to visit his mother the next day, he asked her how she knew Bettina had died. She answered, "Your father came to the window and held up a card that said 'Bettina died, same sickness.' "

We tell this story, not as a "ghost story," but as a demonstration of the power of the world to communicate with us, in whatever way it can get through. Stories about people's ability to feel the moods, images, or thoughts of others are so abundant and commonplace that they seem as natural as the splitting of the atom (which has not been as widely observed!). Such phenomena are less "mind reading" than being in tune with the sensitive receiving and transmitting organ that is our bodymind.

A story of the sword-master Tesshu, in *The Sword of No-Sword,* conveys the subtle perceptions that develop through profound letting go. "Tesshu developed a kind of sixth sense, frequently surprising his disciples by telling them exactly what they were thinking. When asked about this 'magic power,' Tesshu told them, "It is nothing out of the ordinary. If your mind is empty, it reflects the 'distortions' and shadows present in others' minds. In swordsmanship no-mind allows us to see the perfect place to strike; in daily life it enables us to see into another's heart."

There are many way to communicate other than speech. In *The Lost World of the Kalahari,* Laurens van der Post tells how he had been hunting with some Bushmen, and they had killed an eland, which was a cause for great celebration. He said to his companion, Dabe, "I wonder what they'll say at the sip-wells when they learn that we've killed an eland?"

"Excuse me, Master," Dabe said, bolder than I had ever known him, "they already know."

"What on earth do you mean?" I asked.

"They know by wire," he declared, the English word "wire" on his Bushman tongue making me start with its unexpectedness.

"Wire?" I exclaimed.

"Yes. A wire, Master. I have seen my own master go many times to the D.C. [district commissioner] at Gemsbok Pan and get him to send a wire to them when he is going to trek out to them with his cattle. We Bushmen have a wire here" he said, tapping his chest, "that brings us news."

More than that I couldn't get out of him, but even before we were home it was clear that our skeptical minds were about to be humbled. From afar in the dark, long before our fires were visible from a place where we stopped to adjust our heavy load, the black silence was broken by a glitter of new song from the women.

"Do you hear that, Master?" Dabe said, whistling between his teeth. "Do you hear? They're singing 'The Eland Song.' "

Whether by "wire" or by what mysterious means, they did know at the sip-wells, and were preparing to give their hunters the greatest of welcomes.

The musician Jim Nollman, who is also trained in ethology—the science that studies animal behavior—learned to use music to communicate with members of other species. In *Dolphin Dreamtime,* Nollman makes it clear that, in order to communicate with other species, we have to change our whole way of being; our way of seeing, thinking, and feeling; and especially our relationship to time. He tells of an experience of entering "buffalo time" when he was working with a film crew in Yellowstone Park. It beautifully illustrates the reality of communication through energy patterns.

The film crew was trying to get a film of Nollman communicating with elk through music. They could find no elk, but they unexpectedly came upon a herd of more than a hundred buffalo. Afraid that the buffalo might charge him, the crew tried to persuade Nollman not to go near the herd. He went ahead but heeded the warnings and moved cautiously, taking over an hour to advance three hundred yards. As he went, he strummed a repetitive drone of four notes on his guitar:

Slowly, ever so slowly, I shortened the distance between us. Then something strange happened. Suddenly, almost too suddenly, I stood no more than a hundred feet from the nearest animal. It was as if, all at once, I had been lifted right into place, without any recollection whatsoever of the long arduous hour of moving forward at a snail's pace. Perhaps it was nothing more than my own sensory reaction to the very hypnotic drone. Perhaps it was the shock of staring directly into the big brown eyes of a mountain of a buffalo. All my senses were being filtered through the lightheaded breeze blowing across the river valley at 8500 feet of elevation. All the shapes and colors appeared so sharp and vibrant. The prairie and the mountains seemed alive. I was nearly hallucinating—almost, but not exactly. It was not so much that any particular part of the landscape had dramatically altered—rather, that every part seemed more vivid. I had entered buffalo time.

He now stood directly in front of the herd. Three bull buffalo stepped to the edge of the herd.

The most uncanny thing happened. I beheld a dirty yellow glow pulse out from the herd, parallel to the three large bulls. It was like a ring, a smoke screen, or a fence expanding outward around the entire herd. It was luminous but it wasn't light; rather like individual bubbles or bundles of glowing energy. It was dots on fire. It stopped just in front of me, like a barrier or signal that defined the group territory: a boundary, a social aura, an energy extension of the herd's group body language. Yet it had no real substance. I felt it would disappear if I only blinked.

That I actually saw what I believed I saw was in no doubt, because when I put my left foot directly on the ring, the largest bull, who stood less than a hundred feet away, began to paw the ground with his hoof. I pulled my foot away. The bull immediately stopped pawing. To be sure that the connection was what I thought, once again I dropped my foot onto the glowing ring. Once again the big bull pawed the ground.

After Nollman and the buffalo did this dance several more times, the buffalo seemed to recognize that he had come in harmony, not in threat. Suddenly, Nollman found that he was surrounded by buffalo, and the ring had disappeared. He waited a while, and slowly the herd shuffled off down to the river.

The communication between Nollman the buffalo was two-way. He had offered his dance of friendship to them, and they had responded. As he says, the almost-hypnotic quality of the four notes affected him as well as the buffalo, but it affected him by opening his perception to the world beyond language. Communicating with the entire herd of buffalo through a dance of energy and music, Nollman had entered buffalo time.

Communicating with the Dralas

Many indigenous peoples have not lost their heart connection to the cosmos to the extent modern people have. They can still communicate with natural elements and forces and with each other in a way that we lost long ago because we ceased to be open to them. These peoples speak of all manner of modes of existence of subtle energy presences that have been given many names: gods, angels, devas, Japanese *kami,* and so on. It is very important to emphasize before we go any further that not all energy presences of the intermediate realm are benevolent. Most are neutral. Humans could make use of their connection with these neutral energies for positive or destructive purposes, depending on their training and intention. As well, there are intermediate-realm energies that have their own negative intentions. There are, in other words, energies that come from ego-centered aggression, as well as energies that come from awakened mind-heart. It is our connection with the open dimension of unconditioned basic goodness and with fundamental gentleness, that ensures that when we call on the subtle energies and forces in the intermediate realm, they will be beneficial to human society.

In the Shambhala tradition, these subtle energy presences are known as *dralas* (Tibetan: "above enemies"). Dralas could be neutral or benevolent, but our practice and connection with the Shambhala teachings, provided it is genuine, enables us to invoke them for positive purposes only.

Dralas are a form of energy as yet unknown to scientists—a union of spiritual, psychological, and physical energy. In chapter 3, we described these as patterns of living energy and wisdom in the world that you can connect with and draw strength, power, and energy from. They are the presence of the rich and powerful intermediate dimension within our ordinary world. They connect us with the depth of our world— that vast, fathomless dimension of formless energy and limitless wisdom and potential that supports our world and nourishes it.

Dralas are neither "otherworldly" nor "supernatural." Nor

are they merely "subjective" projections of the small mind-in-the-head. "It's all in your head" is an attitude that is thoroughly human-ego-centered, interpreting everything according to human perceptions and beliefs. A snake perceives no "tree" in its world, a fish perceives no "air," nor an ant "clouds." For us, knowing the dralas may be a little like a prairie dog perceiving a herd of buffalo. A cloud of dust, a thundering noise, vibrations felt through the ground—these might be about the extent of the prairie dog's experience.

Ed McGaa, Eagle Man, an Oglala Sioux, puts the dilemma this way: "What are the spirits? Who are they? In a way that question could be analogous to wondering what a grasshopper knows about a locomotive that goes whizzing by. No doubt the grasshopper might ask if it had the means or intellect to speak. No doubt the locomotive would be discovered to go quite beyond the grasp and comprehension of the crawling one who has but one summer's life span."

From the perspective of the open, unbounded dimension, it is a mistake to think of the gods or dralas as separate entities existing outside of us. Chögyam Trungpa writes, "One of the key points in discovering drala principle is realizing that your own wisdom as a human being is not separate from the power of things as they are. . . . There is no fundamental separation, or duality, between you and your world. When you experience these two things together, as one, so to speak, then you have access to tremendous vision and power in the world—you find they are inherently connected to your own vision, your own being."

However, on the relative level of perception of separate things, we *can* relate to the gods as if they were other than ourselves, just as we relate to each other as other than ourselves. Many people experience them to be as real as we are, if not more real—as real as the trees, weather patterns, galaxies, supernovas, and nuclear forces.

Don José Matsuwa was a Huichol shaman who lived in the Mexican Sierra Madre. Like all great shamans and teachers, don José had a sense of lightness and humor as well as fervor and power. In the video *Virarica: The Healing People,* don José, by then old and wizened, is seen lying on his back in the shade exchanging jokes with his young American apprentice, Brant Secunda. Brant comments, "The Huichols laugh more than any other people I know. Happiness and sadness are the same thing, they say, only happiness makes you feel better. I remember don José saying, 'Nothing I have taught you is worth anything if you leave here and can't tell a good joke.' "

Don José visited New York and California twice. On the first visit, he conducted a ceremony to bring rain to drought-ridden California—and rain indeed came. On his second visit, he said:

> The sacred feathers talk to me about why there has been no rain in this place [California]. In some places *Tayaupa* [the sun] burns your land, in other places *Tayaupa's* face is hidden. This place that you live in and many other places in your country suffer from drought, too much rain, shortages, many problems. There is a reason for this misfortune, for you have not been doing ceremonies, gathering together, thanking the earth, the gods, the sun, the sea for your lives.
>
> I see that many people here are so caught up in their own little lives that they are not getting their love up to the sun, out to the ocean and into the earth. When you do ceremonies, sending out your love in

the five directions—the north, the south, the east, the west, and the center—brings life force into you. That love brings in the rain. As it has been since human history began, people are wrapped up in their little worlds, and they forget the elements, forget the source of their life.

You must study these things I am saying, and with understanding, your life will become stronger. . . . Then, one day, the Sea will give you heart; the Fire will give you heart; the Sun will give you heart. And when you come to my village, I will know.

To open our hearts with love to the earth and the sun and the oceans, to the rocks and trees and animals, and then to receive back the heart and life force that we so sorely need is to connect with gods or dralas. We can meet dralas and dance with them only if we are not trapped in small-minded logic, in fixed ideas that we all got from books, teachers, and schools that themselves inherited them from the past. In this logic, we perpetuate a certain view of the world, a modern myth, without realizing that it is one particular creation myth among many. Our scientific or religious beliefs tell small patches of the story of the cosmos, but it is arrogant and foolish to believe that any one of them is the only myth, the final solution to the limitless wonder of the cosmos. A Zen koan puts it: "A monk asked Hui Chung of Nan Yang, 'Why do I not hear the teaching of inanimate objects?' Hui Chung replied, 'Although you do not hear it, do not hinder that which hears it.'"

Sometimes, when people first hear about dralas, they become quite frightened or highly irritated. They feel that they are being introduced to more than they bargained for, as if some primordial memory were being awakened in them. The mere idea of living in such a cosmos may be frightening at first, because we are so used to trying to contain our lives within a narrow, one-dimensional existence. It is not just the thought but the almost tangible energy of that memory that comes alive and seems threatening. When people initially take part in group ceremonies to invoke the dralas, they often have a powerful feeling of unreality in the space—that is, a feeling of unreality in relation to the narrowness of conventional reality. It takes daring to let go into that.

When you feel the boundlessness and depth of your own experience, however, you realize that the energy and wisdom of the dralas is not fundamentally separate from your own energy and wisdom. When you are in tune with the universe and the dralas, you are in tune with your own wisdom and power. If we can feel the presence of drala and communicate with that presence, we can bring this energy into our world and maintain its flow. Drala energy is able to heal, enliven, and resanctify our lives.

CONTEMPLATIONS

Trusting the Sky and the Earth   Go out to your garden or to a park or a field. Lie down on the earth, on your back, legs slightly apart, arms straight out from the shoulders, palms up. Relax your body step-by-step, from the top of your head down to your feet. Feel yourself dissolving into the earth. Feel the earth supporting you and sustaining you. Now, stand up. Stand firmly on the bare earth, with your feet spread apart—about the width of your shoulders—arms relaxed by your side as if you were a solid oak tree. Imagine you are putting roots deep down into the earth. Let your body relax.

Feel the solidness and reliability of the earth. Let it support your weight and carry you. Now, feel the sky above you. Feel the openness and spaciousness of the sky. Feel the energetic, living quality of the space above and around you. As you stand there, feel the strength of your head and shoulders, as if you were reaching up from the earth to the sky. Feel your body joining the sky and the earth, like that solid oak tree.

Awareness of Space in the Environment   The point of this exercise is to begin to realize the richness of the space around you and how it communicates with you. Go outside into a field or garden, or if you live in an apartment in the city, go to a park. Stand in one spot, pay attention to your breath for a few moments, and then pay attention to the sensation of your body. Now, notice the space around your body, and extend that awareness to include the space in your environment. Stay there for a few moments, letting your awareness go out into the space, and notice how you feel. Do you feel threatened, refreshed, agitated, nourished, healed? You don't have to put a name on how you feel—just notice how you feel, but if you do find it easier to give it a name, that's OK. Move to a second spot and repeat the exercise. Do the same at a third location. Notice the difference in how you feel in each space as you move from place to place.

Trusting the Elements   Hold a rock and feel its weight pushing down on your hand. Try to squeeze it in your fist and feel its solidness and unyielding quality. Lie on the bare earth, let your body relax, and feel that you are dissolving into the earth. Let the earth support you and feel its solidness, feel that it carries you and cares for you; feel that you are a part of that earth and that the earth's solidness and realness are a part of you. Stand in the rain, feel the wetness and the way the water refreshes and cleanses. Hold mud in your hand, squeeze it through your fingers, and feel the way the water binds the earth together. Feel the blood flowing through your body and feel your own wateriness. Look up at the sky. Feel the vast open space around you: let your awareness go out into the space, and feel that that space, as well as earth and water, is a part of you, and you are a part of it. Look at a clear sky at night and let yourself relax into its vastness.

Listening Our eyes can see the patterns of energy in our world, but we are used to focusing too sharply. Vision is habitual for most of us, but sound is unexpected: the chirp of the chickadee, the haunting lighthouse foghorn, even traffic that we have to put up with, the sounds of sirens and the horns of taxicabs. We can hear the most outrageous sounds if we listen. You can practice listening and hearing. Listen to tapes of whales and loons and hear their songs. Listen and hear tap drip, cereal pop, sound of children's chatter. Go outside and listen. Listen and hear the patterns; hear frogs, electricity, energy snaps; hear the silence of rocks and trees and bountiful rhododendrons.

Joining Inner and Outer Space Go outside to a place where you can see birds. Sit down, relax, and do sitting practice of mindfulness of breath for a few minutes. Now, look at a bird. Look softly, with a gentle, unfocused gaze. Pay attention to the way the bird moves—particularly the changes of its motion, from perching to flying, or sudden changes of direction. Try to feel that motion and that sudden change in your own body.

Paying Attention to Coincidence   For the next week, decide to pay attention to the coincidences in your life. Acknowledge any coincidences that occur, however small or seemingly meaningless. Don't try to interpret them, but make a quick note of them in a notebook and, having noted them, let them go. Read over the notebook at the end of the week. You might be surprised at how many meaningful coincidences occur when you are noticing them.

CHAPTER 16

The Gods of All Ages and Cultures

ALMOST ALL CULTURES throughout the ages and across the globe have had their own ways of understanding the dralas and how to communicate with them. In chapter 3 and the previous chapter, we saw how the drala principle is found in the ancestors, helpers, and spirits of the Native American tradition. And Chögyam Trungpa writes:

There are many . . . examples of invoking external drala [dralas in the environment]. . . . Some American Indians in the Southwest grow vegetables in the desert sands. The soil, from an objective standpoint, is completely infertile. If you just threw a handful of seeds into that earth nothing would grow. But the Indians have been cultivating that soil for generations; they have a deep connection to that earth and they care for it. To them it is sacred ground, and because of that their plants grow. That is real magic. That attitude of sacredness towards your environment will bring drala. You may live in a dirt hut with no floor and only one window, but if you regard that space as sacred, if you care for it with your heart and mind, then it will be a palace.

The extraordinary experiences at the Findhorn garden in northern Scotland may be one example in our time and culture of communication with similar intelligent energies of the intermediate dimension. Like the Native Americans mentioned by Chögyam Trungpa, the family at Findhorn was able to grow the most astonishing vegetables in the most inhospitable soil. Dorothy Maclean tells of communicating with what she calls "angels" at Findhorn:

> Yes, I talk with angels, great Beings whose lives infuse and create all of Nature. In another time and culture I might have been cloistered in a convent or a temple, or, less pleasantly burnt at the stake as a witch. . . . Being a practical, down-to-earth person, I never set out to learn to talk with angels, nor had I ever imagined that such contact would be possible or useful. Yet, when this communication began to occur, it did so in a way that I could not dispute.
>
> Concrete proof developed in the Findhorn garden. . . . This garden was planted on sand in conditions that offered scant hospitality and encouragement for the growth of anything other than hardy Scottish bushes and grasses requiring little moisture or nourishment. However, through my . . . contact with angelic Beings, . . . specific instructions and spiritual assistance were given. The resulting garden, which came to include even tropical varieties of plants, was so astonishing in its growth and vitality that visiting soil experts and horticulturists were unable to find any explanation for it within known methods of organic husbandry.

The drala principle is found, as well, in the pagan gods of the Greek, Roman, Germanic, and Nordic peoples; among African tribes and Australian Aboriginals; and in the Japanese kami, which are the basis of the naturalistic, shamanistic Shinto tradition.

When we hear about the gods or spirits, we often imagine that to know these gods is to experience some kind of visual or audial apparition in which beings appear, dressed in medieval garb, or speak to us in strange voices. Some people certainly do have such experiences. And it is often through such direct meetings that genuine shamans and realized people, as well as sometimes seemingly quite ordinary people, are able to bring fresh teachings and healing power to the ordinary earth realm. However, such actual visionary or auditory experiences are not the only way, or the most common way, to feel the presence of dralas. We do not need to look for or expect such experiences to find the presence of drala energy in our lives.

In a public TV interview, Kees Zoeteman, the Netherlands' deputy director general for the environment, revealed his ability to perceive "elves" and "gnomes." Later, Zoeteman reported that the reaction to this interview had been overwhelmingly positive.

> People were surprised and a little amazed. But I've been trying to tell people it's not just about gnomes, it's about nature spirits, it's about the world of the unseen. . . . There are countless beings around us that we cannot see, but we can feel them. . . . I can feel their warmth in my heart. You can connect with them and feel their energy. Basically, you can communicate

. . . It is good to call attention to this side of reality. If you open yourself up to this world, it's not crazy, it's enriching. We live in this technical world, in concrete buildings where you have to focus your energy inward in order to endure. The [intermediate] dimension has been lost.

For example, let's look at how the gods entered into the ordinary lives of the Greeks. In modern culture, when we speak of gods, spirits, or angels, we usually think of *our* relationship with them as some kind of personal, subjective experience. For the Greeks, however, the gods were beyond subjectivity and objectivity. The gods were *how they experienced the world.* Every thought, every feeling, every passion, every word, every action, had an immediate connection with the divine. A poet or a painter could not express any thought or action without referring directly to the gods as experience. There were not two worlds for the Greeks—our world and the world of the gods. The gods weren't like a distant star that might clarify our world or might withdraw from our world. There was no separation: they *were* the world. The gods are not personifications of natural forces or human qualities for the Greeks. The Greek gods do not *personify* anything but are *themselves* the splendor of the world of appearance.

For the Greeks, humans exist only in relationship to the gods. Humans were born in relationship to the gods, lived in relationship to the gods, and died in relationship to the gods. Motivations and actions came directly from the gods. Even our most secret motivations, they said, are decided by the gods. So the point is not to try to see or hear or touch the gods. The whole point is to surrender yourself to them unconditionally. That is the Greek version of relating to dralas.

Let's take Hermes as an example. Hermes is the divine presence—we could say the drala presence—of sudden happiness, luck, or a good find. He is an auspicious occasion, but he is also mischief. From Hermes comes benefit or gain for which we have worked for a long, long time; but also from Hermes comes a windfall, just like that, without any reason. Every time *we* would say, "Ah, I found it," the Greeks would say, "It's a gift of Hermes." That is the difference between our way of thinking and that of the Greeks: we always say, "me," "I have found this," while for the Greeks, it is the world that comes to us, it is a gift of Hermes. That doesn't mean that there can't be great work, a lot of effort put into it. But we can put great effort into a project with no result or with great result; there are no guarantees. The result, even after great effort, is still a *finding*. So in this way, Hermes is luck. It is the happiness of a moment. It is the joy of the present. It is a happy occasion. It is like the trick of the naughty boy. It is said that it is Hermes who guides lovers on the paths of the secret gardens of love. But because he is the complete world, it is also he who allows the lover to escape.

Hermes' world is a complete world; he is everywhere. Just as with love, also with death. So it is Hermes who guides people toward their death, and it is also Hermes who will guide people from their death back to life, as in the example of Eurydice. In the famous story of Orpheus and Eurydice, it is Hermes who guides Eurydice back to life from the underworld, but when Orpheus looks back to see if she is really there, of course, he loses her, and it is Hermes who takes her hand and leads her back to the underworld.

Athena is the goddess of the force that accomplishes things. Exactly parallel with Hermes, each time an action is realized, where we would say, "Oh, I have done this, I have done that," the Greeks would say, "Athena accomplished that." It is Athena who fuels the flame of the courage of the warriors. Every time before they go into battle, the Greeks feel the *presence* of Athena. Even before she has done or accomplished anything, they feel her presence. She acts just through her presence. So she is the one who inspires courage and bravery, but this bravery is always linked to clear seeing. Whenever there is a moment of bravery linked to clarity, the Greeks would see the presence of Athena. It is not that she helps you find intelligence or helps you make sense of something. Rather, to experience her presence is to find, already, sense and intelligence. Just by her being present, sense and intelligence are already present.

Last, Aphrodite, or Venus, the image of eternal beauty, is saluted with jubilation by the whole world. She is born from the sea, and thus, she is also the goddess of navigation. With the same shining splendor with which she fills the whole world, she also fills the ocean. When the sea is completely calm, at that moment when the sea shines like a jewel, that is Aphrodite. The magic of nature, flowers, spring—that is Aphrodite. It is the force that fills all beings, even the wildest animals. Even the most vicious animals can be tender; that tenderness is Aphrodite. So just as the other gods present a whole world, Aphrodite also presents a whole world. And if you had to describe the quality of the world of Aphrodite, it would be the sparkle that attracts and gains our heart. Everything can burst into flames by love. It is the joy of being close. It is beauty and smiling gentleness that attract. It is the enchantment of beholding. It is not pushing in order to grasp. So it is not that Aphrodite is "me" and pushes me to go out and grasp, but it is the beauty of the world that comes to me. Everything that is seductive, everything that is beautiful, everything that is attractive—it could be an action, a saying, an object, anything, as long as it has these qualities—then the Greeks would say that it gains these qualities from Aphrodite.

From these three examples, we see that, although the Greeks represented their gods and goddesses in statues and told stories of their exploits on Mount Olympus, this was not how they experienced them in action in life. The gods and goddesses were felt as the carriers of particular energies and intelligences—good or bad fortune; bravery and clarity; or attractiveness, tenderness, and love—and experienced very directly and forcefully at particular moments. The moment at which a deity appears, an *epiphany,* is described thus by Nobel prize poet Czeslaw Milosz:

> Epiphany is an unveiling of reality. What in Greek was called *epiphaneia* meant the appearance, the arrival, of a divinity among mortals, or its recognition under a familiar shape of man or woman. Epiphany thus interrupts the everyday flow of time and enters as one privileged moment when we intuitively grasp a deeper, more essential reality hidden in things or persons.

We frequently find that, like the Greek gods, the gods of other cultures can also be seen—or rather, felt—as patterns of energy entering into the lives of the people in very specific ways. For example, often particular gods are associated with particular animals precisely because the patterns of behavior of those animals mimic on a small scale the universal energy patterns of their related gods—an example of the medieval alchemical principle of "as above, so below." Now, let's look at how the drala principle manifests in some other cultures.

The Loas of Vodun

The vodun tradition, better known as "Voodoo," was brought to the Americas by people of Africa encaptured for the slave trade. It came from African tribal traditions—notably, the Ebo and Yoruba, whose culture was as sophisticated as the "great civilizations" with which we are familiar and equal to them in power and beauty. According to art historian Robert Farris Thompson:

> The Yoruba are one of the most urban of traditional civilizations of black Africa. Yoruba urbanism is ancient, dating to the Middle Ages, when their holy city, Ife-Ife, where the Yoruba believe the world began, was flourishing with an artistic force that later provoked the astonishment of the West. At a time, between the tenth and twelfth centuries, when nothing of comparable quality was being produced in Europe, the master sculptors of Ife-Ife were shaping splendid art, as exemplified in a terra-cotta head. In the elegant conception of the head, perhaps representing a person of status or a most important spirit, can be seen the signs of spiritual alertness (the searching eyes) and self-discipline and discretion (the sealed lips), which suggest, in Yoruba symbolic terms the confidence of the people's monarchic tradition and the complexity and poise of their way of life.

Douchan Gersi spent many years studying with shamans of the Haitian Voodoo tradition and records his experiences in *Faces in the Smoke*. In Voodoo, the dralas are known as *loas*. According to Gersi:

The invisible world is all around us, among us, behind the cosmic mirror. This world is like a reflection of our visible world. The inhabitants have the same needs and passions as we do. It is populated by the souls of the deceased and by an infinite number of loas, who are the original inhabitants of this world. Sometimes called spirits or angels, loas are energies or entities that have been made divine. They are divided into different families, groups and sub-groups. Some have great power.

The most powerful loas, derived from the Yoruba, are connected with the elements of nature. There is the father-protector of main entries, thresholds, and doorways; the energy of fecundity, symbolized by a snake; the ruler of crossroads; the energy of war, symbolized by a piece of iron; the energy of thunder and lightning; the energy of passion and sex; the energy of the sea, symbolized by a boat; and guardians of the deceased, chief of whom is known as the Brave.

According to Farris Thomson, the Yoruba religion presents a limitless horizon of vivid moral beings, that are generous yet intimidating. They are messengers and embodiments of the "power-to-make-things-happen." The supreme deity is called Olorun, master of the skies. Olorun is neither male nor female but a vital force, the supreme quintessence of the power-to-make-things-happen. This was morally neutral power, power to give and to take away, to kill and to give life, *according to the purpose and the nature of its bearer.* Olorun bestowed this power-to-make-things-happen upon humans through particular animals, such as the royal python and the wood-pecker, whose various natures reflect this range of powers.

The loas of Haiti, according to Gersi, are available to humans to act as guides in the visible world and intermediaries with the invisible. Loas generally are neither good nor evil in themselves and can be used for good or evil. But Gersi emphasizes, "Voodoo is a religion in search of the sacred: it uses the cosmic force only in a positive way, and loas are never used for evil purposes."

Voodoo was long banned by the Catholic church and so given the bad name that it has for most of us. But as Gersi says, "Theologians have begun to consider Voodoo as more sacred and solemn than they had previously thought. More than a religion, Voodoo is a mysticism, a culture, a philosophy, a way of life. And because it is a living and dynamic religion, which, instead of being dogmatic and moral—as most western religions are—is based on initiatory and metaphysical principles, it is impossible to describe Voodoo in everyday language. One can only experience it."

The Kami of Japan

In the Shinto tradition of Japan, the creative function of the world is realized not by one creator god but by the many *kami* harmoniously cooperating as they carry out their responsibilities. According to Seigow Matsuoka, "*Kami* has no physical body; its body and essence exist as a vacuum, a place entirely void of matter. But 'void' does not mean nothing is there. . . . In the beginning the kami was thought to visit, to dwell temporarily in the mountains and the sea. The line of the mountains and hills against the sky, the horizon over the water, these were the kami proscenium arches. Here the kami were accustomed to enter and exist."

Kami are the guardian spirits of the land, occupations, and

skills. There are kami associated with natural objects such as the sun, mountains, rivers, trees, and rocks; natural phenomena, such as wind and thunder; the qualities of growth, fertility, and production; some animals; and ancestral spirits. Each kami has its particular characteristics and mission and is considered the protector of some definite object or phenomenon. For example, one is concerned with the distribution of water, another with the manufacture of medicine, and still another with the healing process. They are protectors in the sense that the real heart and authenticity of something cannot be found unless the kami are respected properly.

Most older Japanese, whether their actual religious worship is Buddhist or Christian or Shinto or none at all, respect the kami. They feel their presence and understand the need to communicate with them *in order to maintain the proper flow of energy in their world.* Even a businessman building a bank at a particular location will perform the appropriate ceremonies to pay respects to the kami of that place before beginning construction. More ceremonies will be performed throughout the building process to gather the energy and power of the kami.

Sokyo Ono writes, "The Japanese people themselves do not have a clear idea regarding kami. They are aware of kami intuitively at the depth of their consciousness and communicate with the kami directly without having formed the kami idea conceptually or theologically. Therefore it is impossible to make explicit and clear that which fundamentally by its very nature is vague."

And Joseph Campbell tells the story of being in Japan for a conference on religion when he overheard another American delegate, a social philosopher from New York, say to a Shinto priest, "We've been now to a good many ceremonies and seen quite a few of your shrines, but I don't get your ideology, I don't get your theology." The Japanese paused as though in deep thought and then slowly shook his head, saying, "I think we don't have ideology, we don't have theology . . . we dance."

The Dralas of Shambhala

Like the Native American spirits, the Greek gods and goddesses, the loas, and the kami, the *dralas* of Shambhala are natural phenomena, not connected with a particular religious doctrine but available to everyone who is open to them. The Shambhala understanding of dralas derives from the indigenous Bon tradition, which existed in Tibet before the arrival of Buddhism in the ninth century. The Buddhist philosophy and psychology do not preclude the existence of dralas. As Tulku Thondup Rinpoche says, "In Tibetan tantric (esoteric) Buddhism there are methods of training, particular ritual ceremonies such as [invoking] gods or spirits, which originated from or were influenced by Bon. . . . In Buddhism we believe that there are numerous systems of living beings besides the ones that we see. What prevents us from seeing them is our lack of common karma and the limited power of our physical eyes."

Each time Buddhism entered a new country, it accepted and acknowledged the local gods, making no attempt to suppress them, while providing a larger spiritual and psychological context for understanding these deities. For example, ever since its introduction to Japan, Buddhism has existed side by side with the indigenous Shinto tradition and the *kami*. Dogen Zenji, founder of the Soto school of Zen Buddhism, wrote, "They consider the mind to be thought and perceptions and do not believe it when they are told that the mind is plants and trees."

Like the kami, the dralas are expressions of the interdependent cocreation in which everything takes part. Dralas, humans, trees, rocks—all exist only within the interconnected, ever-changing, mutually cocreating web of existence. No drala exist as objective entities, outside agents of salvation or grace, like the popular conception of God. There is no one "creator" drala.

Steve Wall and Harvey Arden put this well in their book *Wisdom Keepers: Meetings with Native American Spiritual Elders:*

> Terms now commonly used such as God, Creator, Great Spirit are not adequate names for Sakoiatisan, Wakan Tanka, Taiowa and Kitche Manitou. That is the failure of the English language, not of the idea. God is a term that connotes an anthropomorphic being who dwells outside of humans and nature. Creator is a term that also assigns a male gender to the First Cause. . . . These supernatural beings—who could create worlds and other forms of life—could be male or female. Taiowa and Wakan Tanka are not male deities. These names represent the sum total of all things . . . even spirit has its limitations in English. The English term Great Spirit attempts to define what is incomprehensible. . . . We must understand that these terms God, Creator, Great Spirit—have been used [by the Wisdomkeepers] to convey the concept that all things are interrelated and an equal part of the whole: that we are like drops of rain which will one day return to the ocean, that we are like candles lit by the fire of the sun, forever part of it.

We in the modern world have lost our traditional connection with the dralas, and thus we are losing our life-giving connection with our living world. Kenchen Thrangu Rinpoche, who was a close colleague and friend of Chögyam Trungpa, spoke at Gampo Abbey, the Tibetan Buddhist monastery in Nova Scotia, of why Trungpa felt it was important to reintroduce the modern world to the dralas. In a talk to students at the abbey, Thrangu Rinpoche says:

> Trungpa Rinpoche once said to me that, although there was great development and appearance of wealth in the Western world, through a lot of the manufacturing, mining of the earth, and so forth, that had gone on, much of the vitality of the land had been harmed, had deteriorated, and because of that the drala had departed. As a method for restoring the vitality, for healing a wounded situation, he had given the practice of drala, so that people could bring brilliance and dignity to their physical world and body; potency to their speech; and courage, or strength of heart, to their minds, so that both from the point of view of [spiritual] activity and from the point of view of worldly activity people could experience brilliance and dignity. The oral instructions he gave regarding this are extremely important. Please don't forget them.

Chögyam Trungpa was recognized and trained in Tibet as a *terton,* a person who has the ability to discover *terma,* which are teachings left in the safekeeping of protector dralas by great teachers of the past. They are discovered or revealed, somewhat like taking dictation (rather than authored), by great teachers like Chögyam Trungpa, who have been thoroughly trained to do so. Tulku Thondup Rinpoche describes the terma tradition in *Hidden Teachings of Tibet:* "The tradition has two aspects. First, appropriate teachings can be discovered by realized beings, or they will appear for them from the sky, mountains, lakes, trees, and beings, spontaneously according to their wishes and mental abilities. Second, [realized beings] can conceal teachings in books and other forms and entrust them to gods . . . to protect and hand over to the right person at the proper time."

The terton process is a form of shamanism that probably derived from the ancient Bon tradition of Tibet. However, it was adopted into the Buddhist tradition by Padmasambhava, the great saint who introduced Buddhism to Tibet in the ninth century AD. Thereafter, the terma tradition became a way for a fresh perspective, and fresh teachings appropriate to the time, to enter into the stream of Tibetan Buddhist teachings and enliven the more systematic teachings passed down from teacher to student in the usual way in the formal monastic schools.

Shortly before his year-long retreat in 1977, Chögyam Trungpa had discovered the first Shambhala texts as terma, and it was based on these Shambhala terma that Chögyam Trungpa taught the Shambhala path of sacred warriorship after his retreat. His Holiness Dilgo Khyentse Rinpoche, one of Chögyam Trungpa's first teachers and himself recognized as one of the great tertons of Tibet, later confirmed the Shambhala texts as genuine terma.

Ruth-Inge Heinze, an anthropologist at the University of California, Berkeley, has been researching living shamans and shamanistic rituals for the past thirty years. In *Shamans of the Twentieth Century,* Heinze shows that this opening up of the shamanistic community is beginning to happen in traditional shamanistic societies—such as Indonesia, Thailand, and China—as well as in North America:

> Shamans continue to play a vital role and fulfill special needs of their community which otherwise are not met. I have to add here that, in the twentieth century, "community" does not necessarily mean people living together in the same geographical area. . . .
>
> Becoming more closely involved with one shaman, however, does not necessarily lead to the formation of a new cult. Such open-ended relationships escape the effects of rigidifying codification world religions are suffering from.

According to Heinze, "the services of shamans are needed when the relationship between man and the universe has weakened or has been interrupted. Shamans stay close to the 'source.' They are called to be the mediators between the sacred and the secular."

In his ability, as a terton, to journey between the mundane world, the earth dimension, and the more subtle dimension of the dralas, Chögyam Trungpa showed the characteristics of a shaman as well as being a great teacher and leader in the Buddhist tradition. However, there are some differences between Chögyam Trungpa's shamanism and the shamanism of older, more local cultures. Generally, in the past, shamans have arisen within a particular tribal culture and provide teachings and healing within that tribal family. Chögyam Trungpa, on the other hand, opened up the teachings and powerful warrior practices and ceremonies of Shambhala for anyone who cared to journey on that path. He was proud of the fact that his family name was Mukpo, the same tribe in Tibet from which the great warrior Gesar came, and he would often say to Shambhala students, "You are *all* the Mukpo family." By this, he did not mean to be exclusive, nor that students should reject their own family heritage, but that the Shambhala teachings are open to the whole world, whatever one's racial background or family creed. Whoever wants to practice these teachings is welcomed into the great Mukpo clan and introduced to the Mukpo dralas and the dralas of the ancestral Shambhala lineage of warriors. These dralas of Shambhala have the particular power to protect and help propagate the teachings of spiritual warriorship: there are dralas of unconditioned basic goodness; dralas of fundamental gentleness and tenderness that is free from self-centered concerns; and dralas of bravery and confidence, and the daring needed to propagate human society based on these principles. There are, as well, ancestral dralas—great human beings who continue to communicate as dralas after death—as well as dralas empowering human activities.

Connecting with Dralas Brings Harmony to Individual Lives and to Society

Dorothy Maclean of Findhorn speaks of the crux of how and why renewed connection with drala energy is vital. She speaks of angels in the same way we are speaking of dralas:

> To learn to talk with angels is really learning to talk with ourselves and with each other in new and profoundly deeper ways. It is learning how to communicate with our universe more openly and how to be more in tune with our role as co-creators and partici-

pate in its evolution. Modern communication has developed marvelously and very quickly in the physical, technological mode, but deeper and more subtle forms of communication remain untapped. For the future of our world and ourselves, we must now begin to use those deeper forms. . . . It requires a joyful enlargement of our view of reality, a readiness to be open to ourselves and our environment, and a conscious movement to embrace our own wholeness.

When we open our hearts to the vast, profound, and strange universe, to the earth and to the heavens, to the dralas, to other animals, and to our fellow humans, we bring about true harmony. Harmony in human activity is seeing how things are and acting according to that vision.

Harmony should not be confused with total bliss or quiescent peace. The word tends to be taken this way nowadays because we are so used to discord and war that we can understand harmony only in opposition to them. Harmony is *the correct functioning of everything according to its nature.* There is tremendous harmony in a hurricane and in the eruption of a volcano and in the exploding of a star. There is harmony in the thunder and in rainstorms that nourish crops. There is harmony in an angry roar, if that is what is called for. Harmony is awake, passionate, powerful, and spotless. It is to preserve and cultivate harmony in this sense that the dralas are invoked.

Being in harmony is health. Harmony begins within oneself, within the harmony of body and mind, and extends to create harmony with others, within the community, between communities, and with the cosmos. All of these harmonies are necessary for wholeness and health. When the harmony is broken, disease (dis-ease, dis-harmony) arises, and healing is needed. Connecting with the dralas can help us in healing, but this is really a secondary outcome of invoking dralas. We need to be healed only when we feel diseased. The important point is not to become diseased in the first place, and this is where the connection with dralas is vital. Traditional peoples relate with their dralas through dance and song and ritual in order to maintain health.

The dralas have the power to bring peace and harmony because they transcend the very idea of enmity and therefore are completely free from aggression. When we touch that energy, we feel the world to be alive, authentic, and precious. Feeling drala energy provokes us to care for our world. If the world is alive, and you are a part of that living world, you would no more wish to violate it than you would wish to violate another human or other living being. The dralas support and protect the natural order and the dynamic harmony of the cosmos. When you connect with them, you can feel this greater harmony. You can find your own place in that natural order and put your own energy into supporting that greater harmony.

CHAPTER 17

Power Arises in the Gaps

W E DO NOT HAVE TO BE great warriors or special people to invite the dralas into our world, but we do need to have the proper attitude and intention. We can connect with the dralas only from a mind and heart that are gentle and profoundly relaxed. We cannot think and reason our way into that connection. We need to let go of our fixed ideas about ourselves and our history, about how the world is. We can let go and relax body and mind together, let go and relax, relax, relax . . . until we have nothing on our mind. When you have learned in mindfulness and awareness practice to connect mind, body, and heart together, you can be completely present in the moment. Then your wholehearted activity, your passion, can raise your windhorse energy to actually connect with the energy of drala.

This is the principle of resonance that applies to all forms of energy: when you pluck a string on a guitar, the strings on a nearby guitar will resonate with the note you play on the first one. The positive energy of our care and attention attracts the positive energy of the dralas. The energy radiates out like a lighthouse beacon, attracting further energy from the dralas. It is like turning the dial on a radio and getting static until you actually hit the specific wavelength, when the station clicks in. When alike energy patterns connect and tune in together in this way, living in the world becomes a responsive, back-and-forth dance.

The radio static is like our struggle, our resistance, and our unwillingness to relax. The wisdom and love and energy of the dralas cannot get to the surface world, the earthly dimension, so there is no sense of harmony and depth. That moment when the radio station clicks in is like the moment of opening to first thought, *nowness,* a sudden glimpse of wakefulness. Only in the gap of *nowness*—between thoughts, between things, or between events—can the dralas enter.

The Dralas Enter through Gaps in Time

Dralas enter our world at the moment of *now* through gaps— empty spaces between our thoughts, gaps in time, or shifts in perception caused by sacred spaces and objects. These are gaps or spaces in between what we usually consider as ordinary. A small opening in a rock can have an intense living quality; a moment of silence is often called "pregnant" for good reason. The Japanese word *ma,* with its multilayered meanings, conveys this sense of a gap in which the dralas may dwell. Arata Isozaki writes, "[M]a is the natural distance between two or more things existing in a continuity, as well as the natural pause or interval between two or more phenomena occurring continuously." The same word, *ma,* can also mean "a place where life is lived" or "the way of sensing the moment of movement." Richard Pilgrim, writing on "Ma: A Cultural Paradigm," points out that the original Chinese character for *ma* was a combination of the character for gate or doorway and that for moon. He comments, "It is as though the very word itself invites one to experience the moonlight as it filters through the gate."

Whatever creates a gap in our thoughts—seeing a sacred space or a powerful object, suddenly recognizing connection, a sharp intuition, an auspicious coincidence, a moment of transition between the patterns of your life—if we are present to these places and moments, we may encounter dralas there. When something sudden happens in your life, it cuts through your habitual daydreams, and if you pay attention, it wakes you up. It might be just a flash of color abruptly calling your attention in the sunshine; it might be the sudden sound of a siren a block away; it might be a brief moment of silence in a roomful of chattering people. Or it could be a forceful turn of events in your life—losing a job or finding a job that you did not expect; hearing of the death of a friend; a tree falling on your house; someone insulting you out of the blue; a check arriving in the mail—anything.

Simple experiences like this may not seem to have much to do with dralas, but they do create a gap in our mind through which drala energy can enter. When we feel a longing that goes altogether against any rational reasoning, we can decide to have the courage to follow our longing. When we feel a slight tug—maybe to take a walk down a particular street, perhaps to talk to a stranger, or possibly to take a day off work to sit and gaze gently out of the window—we should be alert to how things unfold. We should follow these long-ings. It is precisely that intuitive insight, that sense of know-ing without knowing how we know, that is the inner ear with which we can hear the dralas. We can hear the dralas if we are willing to slow way down and listen.

When we pay attention to patterns or cycles in time, we can often feel dralas. Some days have particular qualities we recognize. Have you ever felt on a day when *everything* seems to go wrong that "this is just one of those days"? Sometimes, we have a feeling that this day is a good day to get things done or that it is a good day to wait and do nothing. Anthropologist Alton Becker told a story about being in Java when a friend of his, who was a very reckless driver, ran over a small child playing on the village street. The child was not killed, but Becker's friend was devastated. He noted the day on his calendar and told Becker, "Never again will I drive on this day." Becker said, "You mean this date of the year?" His friend replied, "No, this day." Javanese understand the cyclical nature of time and the sense that days have qualities that repeat and can be felt.

Gaps in time, strange interruptions to our habitual unconscious sense of the flow of time, are often felt as meaningful coincidence. When we slow down and pay attention to what is happening now, then we begin to see meaningful coincidences in our life—strange, unexpected connections between events. Coincidences shock us when we pay attention to them. They create a momentary gap in our minds, through which we can feel the presence of dralas, for dralas ride on the vehicle of meaningful or auspicious coincidence. The Tibetan word meaning "auspicious coincidence" is *tendrel,* and *tendrel* also means a link in the chain of cause and effect. It conveys the idea that what appears to be coincidence actually has interconnected causes: that is why such coincidences intuitively feel meaningful to us even though we do not know how they came about.

All coincidence is meaningful, though we cannot possibly see all the many causes of everything that happens to us. Some coincidences are so clearly meaningful that they strike an uncanny chord in us. The meaning of the word *coincidence* is actually a "falling together" on time. Dralas are connected with being on time, on the moment of nowness. When we

are on time, not chasing ahead or lagging in the rear, everything seems to fall together. For a moment, we do see the
larger picture, the web of many cooperating causes and effects, in which our lives are immersed. Meaningful coincidences are messages from the external dralas, messages from
the outer world, as we discussed in chapter 2. Meaningful
coincidences join external reality—an actual event in the
outer world—with our inner awareness and aspirations. Confirmation from the outer world is important for us to see
that the coincidence is not merely wishful thinking; it is an
"objective check," if you like.

A few years ago, Karen had a dream that suggested she
should work with healing. She had no idea what to make of
this. Sometime later (after a series of coincidences), she decided to look into studying *shiatsu*. This is a Japanese technique that facilitates the patient's exchange of ki (chi) with
the environment and so helps the body heal itself. She says:

> I had been exploring this possibility for some time,
> calling various schools and talking to people. I was
> especially thinking about going to Boston for a while
> to study but was having a very hard time deciding. In
> the middle of this confusion and questioning, I went
> to the local Shambhala Center for the first time in a
> few weeks to take care of some business. There I ran
> into an old friend who was visiting from Germany
> and who was showing another visitor around. This
> was a Japanese woman who had never been to Hali-
> fax before and who was only there for a couple of
> days. My friend introduced me to this visitor, who
> lived in Boston and who, I then discovered, was the
> founder and main teacher of the Boston School of
> Shiatsu, the same school I had been considering. I told

her of my interest, and she asked me if I "felt the energy in my hands." I made an immediate, strong connection with her, and two weeks later, I found myself in Boston as her student.

When you listen to people's stories of strange coincidences that changed the course of their lives, you will often hear the sounds of the dralas at play in the fields of coincidence. The dralas may simply be felt as a deeper wisdom, some guidance coming from beyond the cocoon mind. If you look back over your own life, you may find that the dralas have been at work, riding on coincidence, long before you heard about them. As we pay more attention to the details of our lives, these coincidences appear to happen more often. It may be that we are noticing what has always been happening to us, or it may be that our care and attention are beginning to attract meaningful energy—the energy of dralas.

When we pay attention to such coincidences, we begin to feel the magical quality of the most ordinary happenings in our lives, things we have taken for granted as "just" cause and effect. We can begin to see how extraordinary it is, though also very ordinary, that flowers appear in the spring because we planted bulbs in the fall; that water boils when we turn on the stove; that the screech of a crow wakes us from a daydream. We begin to understand how ordinary it is that an old friend calls the day after we dream of him; or we have a strong sense that someone we have just met will be very important to us—and later this proves to be true.

The Dralas Are Attracted to Sacred Places and Objects We Care For

As well as a sense of time, or coincidence, the sense of place is extremely important in opening to drala energy. Some dralas are connected with space and the elements and are attracted to particular places. Some places seem to have more power than others. There are magnetic spots, or power spots, sacred places, on the earth where the drala energy can be felt almost as if it were tangible. Sacred places have the power to evoke energy in us that can change our perception.

Paul Devereux has spent thirty years investigating sacred places and sites of sacred monuments, such as the Avebury circle in England. Devereux explains that the ancient peoples who built the stone monuments, like indigenous peoples today, see the earth in two ways: they see the ordinary physical earth, the only one "civilized" people see, and simultaneously they see the "spirit earth," or the earth as the dwelling place for dralas.

Devereux found confirmation of this twofold perception of place in work with many present-day indigenous peoples— the Australian Aboriginals, the Kalahari !Kung, the Kogi, and many others. He quotes anthropologist Paul Wirz, who, working with the Marind-anim of New Guinea, saw that power spots, the places of *Dema* or drala, had the ability to transform perception: "In most cases such spots have a striking outward appearance in consequence of some strange or unexpected aspect. In them occur unusual land formations, chasms, uplands, swamps with sand banks or gravel deposits fresh or salt. Curious noises may be heard in them. . . . Occasionally people catch sight of strange apparitions, the *Dema* themselves, rising out of the earth, though mostly such visions are but fleeting and uncertain."

The physical and "spirit" earth, then, are two aspects of the same earth. We, too, can see the earth with new eyes if we are willing to open and to care enough. A majestic outcropping of rock, the small group of ancient trees standing on a patch of high ground, a quiet pool in the middle of a forest fed by a series of waterfalls—all can be places for the dralas to arrive.

When you are open, you can discover these places and take care of them. There are such power spots wherever you look. If you raise windhorse and then look at a hillside on the opposite side of the valley, your eye will naturally gravitate to particular spots where the energy of the hill is concentrated. It is as if the landscape had nerves running through it and these spots were the nerve centers. Sometimes, people can actually hear the hum of the earth around such spots. Karen was once on retreat in a very quiet, remote valley in southern Colorado where there was no electricity for miles. She kept hearing an unaccountable, vibratory sound, almost mechanical-sounding. Later, she discovered the local people heard it, too, but no one could find the source. A Tibetan lama had told them it was the "hum of the universe."

Animals naturally find the power spots of a place: cows in a field tend to congregate around them, deer sleep on them, birds land on certain trees. Many of these places have very healthy vegetation, sometimes lots of wildflowers. Ancient monasteries, churches, and castles were often built on these places. Such spots can be places of healing and power, exuding tremendous energy. They are places where we can invoke the dralas. We should literally find our spot and sit on it. It could be a good place to build a house, to sit and be healed, or just to sit.

Invoking Drala

In addition to discovering drala through gaps in time and space, we can also *invite* or *invoke* the dralas into our lives.

We can create gaps intentionally. There are many ways of doing this. The dralas need a definite connection through which to arrive in our world. Treating our own bodies with care and affection attracts dralas. How we dress, clean, and nourish our bodies affects our state of mind and our wind-horse. We don't have to wear expensive clothes or eat extravagantly, but we can dress and eat with an attitude of respect and appreciation for our bodies. This includes a certain quality of formality. We lose our windhorse when we become completely sloppy and casual. Special scarves, lapel pins, or hats attract dralas—anything we wear around our head and shoulders that uplifts us and raises our windhorse.

Generalized dralas don't exist. There are specific dralas: dralas of fountains, dralas of wind, dralas of gardens—lots of them. So you need a specific drala-catcher to invoke them. It could be a flower arrangement, a painting, or a rock. Any specific object with authentic richness and quality can act as a drala-catcher. When you put energy into something, the energy stays there. It is captured in the object: in your work of art, in the meal you cook, in the perennial flower bed you cultivate. This energy radiates out and attracts drala energy. Everything in the world is sacred, but by cherishing objects, we bring out and nourish their sacredness so that it can be seen and felt. When an old wood carving is left in the corner of an attic collecting dust and mildew, it seems like nothing: you might as well light a fire with it. But if you take it out and polish it and place it in an appropriate spot—one with space around it so it can be seen properly—you might discover that it brings power as well as beauty to your home.

Dralas need space to arrive into. The dralas are attracted to an environment that is uplifted and clean—you could even say elegant—and spotless. Such an environment is harmonious, free from confusion, and has had care and attention put into it. There's a feeling of freshness and space. If we refine and cultivate our environment, we invite drala energy into it. You can have a one-room cabin in the woods or a mansion—it doesn't matter—but wherever you live, you can take care of it. You can keep it clean and uncluttered, maybe adorn it with fresh flowers, as if to welcome an honored guest. You could create a special space in your home—a special room or simply a small corner of your apartment. You could place a flower arrangement there and a calligraphy or picture. This can be your sacred place to practice in. If you take care of that place, simply going there can create a feeling of gap, first thought, and bring freshness into your daily life.

We can create specially reserved, protected spots in the natural environment for the dralas to come to. In Japan, for example, as Matsuoka writes:

> The kami makes an appearance, then vanishes. Rather than not know at all where the kami might make its temporary appearances our ancestors took to demarcating an "area of kami" [*kekkai*] by enclosing a particular space with a twisted rope thus sanctifying it in preparation for the visit of kami. There might be nothing within the *kekkai* or perhaps just one tree or rock. . . .
> The *kebai* (spiritual atmosphere) of kami's coming and going was to pervade the structure of homes, the structure of tea houses, literature, arts, and entertainment. . . . [T]his is what we call *ma* . . . the magnetic field from which the *chi* of kami subtly emanates. . . . Minute particles of kami, as it were, fill that *ma*.

In Japan, the countryside is filled with small shrines to the kami, placed at such power spots. Every garden and home has at least one shrine marking the power spot of the garden. The shrine is not elaborate—it can be nothing more than a rope or a group of rocks marking off an area—or it can be a small wooden dwelling with an opening for fresh flowers. And of course, it is not only in Japan that you can see these shrines to the deities of nature. You see such shrines in any country where the power of materialism has not completely conquered the hearts of the people—from the cairns, or piles of stones, in Tibet to the shrines to local saints in Costa Rica. In Jeremy's boyhood hometown, a suburb of London, England, there was an elm tree said to be six hundred years old. This was the May tree, around which villagers had danced centuries ago, at springtime, to invite fertility to their fields. Even as all the houses and developments had grown up around the old elm tree, the local council had preserved this tree with a small, cared-for area of grass and bushes around it, a circle of stones, and a plaque telling its history.

You also could build a simple shrine of rocks in your garden, if you have one. If you do not have a garden, find a secret spot in nearby woods and build a drala shrine there. When you care about something, you *take* care of it; when you care about someone, you *take* care of him or her. Your continued care for the objects, places, and people in your life maintains the drala energy and keeps it contained. Otherwise, it seeps out, and the connection is lost. If you treat your world kindly and gently with affection and appreciation, that makes a lot of room for the dralas to enter and remain.

CHAPTER 18

Arousing Windhorse
through Contemplative Art

*I*T IS POSSIBLE TO OPEN to the inspiration of the dralas
at any time in a moment of first thought, a moment of
gap in our habitual mind. We described in the previous chapter how awareness of gaps in space and time can bring us
abruptly to first thought. And we've talked at length about
mindfulness, awareness, and windhorse practice as tools to
open our mind and heart. When we practice mindfulness,
awareness, and windhorse in daily life, our life takes on an
artful quality as we begin to pay attention to uplifting our
world and bring some elegance and grace into it. This is what
attracts the dralas into our world.

As a bridge to applying our practice to ordinary daily activities, it is helpful to practice an art form—a "contemplative
art." Practicing an art form in a contemplative way is a powerful means to raise windhorse and to draw down drala energy. Any skill can be practiced as a contemplative art if we
practice it wholeheartedly—painting, writing, canoeing,
horseback riding, gardening, calligraphy, playing an instrument, cooking, mountain climbing, belly dancing, any kind
of craft, even scientific research—anything we can learn and

practice with precision and loving attention to detail in a quiet way. Whatever it is, passionate and complete involvement engages the heart and mind and body in one activity. We are contained, not dribbling away our energy or entertaining ourselves in halfhearted frivolity. Practicing these art forms springs from longing to see things as they are, longing to connect ourselves to the order and harmony of the natural world, and longing to communicate this harmony to others.

When you work with the particular form by paying attention to the minute details involved, your perceptions are sensitized and this intensifies the presence of the world. You see more vividly and deeply and from that clarity you can execute your "work of art." You empty yourself of the small mind and perform the action so completely that you lose self-consciousness. There is a precise awareness undisturbed by inner chatter. Then you can tap into the larger, more creative mind in which you do not feel separate from your materials and your art. Everything "clicks" and your action feels unified and effortless. When you persevere in practicing the forms, then you can actually connect with them so thoroughly that sometimes you feel as if *you* did nothing—the form of your work just came through you.

True creativity—that is, creativity in which something genuinely fresh enters the human realm—comes from connection with dralas. Contemplative art gives us a vehicle to practice this tuning in to a larger awareness. It provides a channel to focus on—a way to intensify our energy on one point. If we don't have one focal point our energy gets scattered and it is very hard to connect with the dralas. A creative act is an act of inspiration, which literally means being "breathed into" by the gods, as Robert Grudin, teacher of writing at the University of Oregon, writes:

The word "inspiration" originally meant a breath of divinity or transfusion of soul received from the gods by some deserving individual. The word now denotes the experience of a sudden insight that cuts across categories or otherwise leaps over the normal steps of reasoning. Though both these definitions are helpful it is the ancient one, with its religious overtones, that seems to hold more psychological truth. To be inspired is to surrender one's mind to a new force, heedless and powerful. Experiencing inspiration is like leaving the world of effort and abandoning oneself to an irresistible flow, like a canoeist drawn into the main channel of a rapids, or a body surfer who catches a fine wave just below the crest.

Contemplative Art Is Learning How to Live

Contemplative art is not just learning how to make art. It is learning how to live. It is bringing energy to the world and making it sacred. It is a matter of tuning ourselves in to the natural energy of the world. There is only one energy. There is only one pulse. We can all partake of it if we connect to it.

There is a ritual quality to any contemplative art or any action done contemplatively. We can experience the sacredness of life when we regard each act as a ritual act. When we stay with the boredom of ordinary things instead of looking for constant entertainment, we discover real joy that comes to us from the act itself rather than from the hopes and expectations we project onto it. Even the seemingly trivial aspects of life—the clothes you wear and how you wear them, the food you eat, or the mug you drink out of—can contribute to the overall sacredness of your life when you appreciate the inner meaning of ritual. A ritual can be simply paying attention to one's breath repetitively, over and over, perhaps for days and weeks, going through boredom and fear. Thus, there is no separation between sacred and profane; all actions in life become part of the sacred; all acts become sacred rituals and ways to attract the interest and energy of the dralas.

Philip O'Connor, a British vagrant—a "tramp," or as we would say nowadays, a "homeless person"—wrote that in walking endlessly the roads of England he sometimes had an

> incomparable feeling . . . as though one were a prayer winding along the road; the feeling is definitely religious. . . . All hard nodules of concepts are softly coaxed into disbursing their cherished contents. . . . Maybe mental fireworks will gloriously light the mind—but quickly the world will attach the inner light to outer phenomena. . . . The speed of transit between inner state and outer appearance is a feature of tramping. . . . Time stops in such perceptions.

The different experience of time and place when he was alone in the landscape was apparent whenever O'Connor came in contact with townspeople. They would appear "terribly quick, jerky and doll-like, with chatter to suit." O'Connor's insights were clearly the result, in part, of his own extraordinary openness and his confidence in his own way of being and perceiving. The slow, repetitive, and often boring nature of walking, however, probably had a lot to do with preparing him for these insights. These are precisely the qualities of much ritual and ceremony. Even simply walking along the road can be a contemplative discipline that attracts drala energy.

Ikebana: Living Flowers

An example of a contemplative art form is the Japanese art of ikebana. Ikebana is the practice of arranging branches, flowers, water, container, and especially space in order to train one's perceptions and state of mind. In the West, it is often referred to as "flower arranging," but this implies some attitude of decorating or entertaining that has nothing to do with ikebana as a practice to raise windhorse.

The word *ikebana* means "living flowers." The materials, including the rocks, are alive and close to nature. They have their own strength, their own gentleness, their own dignity and elegance. You can communicate with them. Any branch or flower can be used in the arrangement. Nothing is rejected as ugly. It is all workable. The point is to connect with each element and allow it to find its proper place.

As we begin to practice, we first have to organize the environment we are working in and the materials we will be using. We don't just slop in and start throwing things together. Our practice space and our materials are sacred, and we can care for them with that attitude. When our space is clean and uncluttered, our mind is not distracted. Traditionally, the container, branches, and flowers are carefully chosen to be in harmony with the season. The container is clean, the place where the arrangement is to go is prepared, and the flowers and branches are carefully laid out. Once the environment and materials are ready, we need to slow down, pause, sit with mindfulness, and allow ourselves to open to space and uncertainty. We have no idea what to do or what the arrangement will look like.

Then we look at the details of our materials—the flowers, water, container, branches, space—and we see the relationships between the details. For example, when we look at the branch, we notice the thin white bark peeling from it, how it grew from the tree, which side is its front and which is its back, how its leaves grew toward the sun. We notice its strengths and weaknesses, where it feels confused, and where its energy, innermost form, and harmony lie. The arranger does not try to make the branch conform to any idea. Rather, the idea is to prune the branch to allow its essential nature to manifest.

We also we look at the space around the branch. The space is as important as the objects in the space. It provides the accommodation: it allows each branch and flower to stand out on its own but also to be seen in relationship to the other elements.

Next, we are ready to actually make the arrangement. We open our mind further, raise windhorse, and connect with the objects to be arranged without knowing exactly what to do. We let our heart feel the energy and details of each object and see what the object is communicating. It shows you where it belongs, and this becomes clear without your needing to figure it out. When we are open we can get that kind of feedback from our materials even with an object that we don't consider "living." We can feel richness and life in the vase, as well as in the branch, as well as in ourselves. A circular process of energy happens—when we give out our interest and energy, something comes back. If we pay attention to the energy we don't have to add anything or crank up anything. There is some kind of spark. We find that we can execute each action, placing a branch or flower suddenly, spontaneously, and free from ideas of how it should be. If we manage to do this, the finished arrangement feels inspired and harmonious. People feel energized looking at it and the environment feels uplifted.

Finally, we have to finish our action properly. If we just walk out and leave a mess, there is no room for our mind to rest and no way to ride on the energy. We have to clean up after ourselves. We have to wash and put away our equipment, throw away the clutter. The finished arrangement is set in a place of honor with a clear background and space around it. Then we can let go of whether we think it is good or bad and let it be as it is.

The completed arrangement actually reflects the state of mind of the arranger. It reflects back how much she was able to open, feel the sacredness of the world, and connect with larger energy. People viewing the arrangement can feel this. If the arrangement is inspired, they may feel their mind stop and open and they will feel the energy of windhorse in the environment. If the arranger has concocted the arrangement from a confused state of mind, the viewer will feel that confusion in the arrangement as well. One student tells how in her very first arrangement she left a large hole in the middle of the arrangement. Her teacher came up and looked at it and exclaimed, "Oh you left the middle empty—that's compassion." The openness at the center of the arrangement reflected the open heart of the student. In contrast a cramped, small, overcrowded arrangement can reflect hesitation or lack of generosity.

This description of the practice of ikebana illustrates the principles involved in practicing any art form in a contemplative way:

1. *Preparation:* Choose and prepare the materials to be used and arrange the space you'll be working in, pause and sit with your uncertain, blank mind without thought of how to proceed.
2. *Appreciation:* Extend your perceptions into the space with

curiosity and inquisitiveness, and with a light, playful touch, appreciate the details of whatever you're working with.

3. *Execution:* Open your mind and heart, raise your wind-horse and execute your art form, without self-consciousness or judgment.

4. *Ending properly:* Finish by letting go of your result and then cleaning up properly.

These four stages of executing a contemplative art exemplify the four qualities of authentic presence (meekness, perkiness, outrageousness, and inscrutability) described in chapter 14. They can carry over very simply into everything you do in your life, including washing the dishes and cleaning the house, caring for your clothes, cooking and eating, having an argument, or making love. In this way all your actions become an expression of "contemplative art," and a manifestation of authentic presence.

The whole process of practicing contemplative art is very much the same as raising windhorse: the sense of openness and uncertainty, the feeling of sadness and joy as we contemplate our materials, the sense of a larger pool of creative energy available to us, cutting our feeling of doubt and poverty, and the sudden spark of insight that allows us to expand and extend ourselves into our materials and out to others.

Dralas Have Inspired Many Accomplished Artists

Many truly accomplished artists—painters, musicians, poets, and writers—have said that at times they feel as if their work were created by an energy coming from beyond their ordinary state of being. Some say this energy feels almost like an entity using them as an instrument. Sometimes they refer to these energies that are almost entities (we could say dralas) as "divine" or "God" or "spirits," depending on their particular belief system.

For example, composer Johannes Brahms refused for years to talk about how he composed and only gave in to questions when he felt near death. Then he said:

> All right then! I shall relate to you and our young friend here how I establish communication with the creator—for all inspired ideas come from God.
>
> If I feel the urge to do some work, I turn to my creator. . . . Immediately afterward, I feel vibrations penetrating me. They are the spirit that moves the soul energies within, and in this condition of ecstasy I comprehend clearly what remains dark during my normal state of mind. These vibrations take the form of certain mental images after I have expressed that I want to be inspired to compose something that will uplift and advance humanity—something of lasting value. The finished work is revealed to me bar by bar when I find myself in this rare, inspired state.
>
> I have to be in a semi-trance to get such result—a condition when the conscious mind is in temporary abeyance, and the subconscious mind is in control.

Richard Strauss described how, "while the ideas were flowing in upon me, the entire musical, measure by measure, it seemed to me that I was dictated to by two wholly different Omnipotent Entities. . . . I was definitely conscious of being aided by more than an earthly Power, and it was responsive to my determined suggestions."

Puccini said that the music of his opera *Madame Butterfly* "was dictated to me by God; I was merely instrumental in putting it on paper and communicating it to the public."

Poet Amy Lowell said, "Let us admit at once that a poet is something like a radio aerial—he is capable of receiving messages on waves of some sort; but he is more than an aerial, for he possesses the capacity of transmuting these messages into those patterns of words we call poems. . . . I do not hear a voice, but I do hear words pronounced, only the pronouncing is toneless. The words seem to be pronounced in my head, but with nobody speaking them."

Novelist Thomas Wolfe wrote, "I cannot really say the book was written. It was something that took hold of me and possessed me. . . . It was exactly as if this great black storm cloud had opened up and, amid flashes of lightning, was pouring from its depth a torrential and ungovernable flood. And I was borne along with it."

The English poet William Blake wrote the poem *Milton* "from immediate dictation, twelve or twenty or thirty lines at a time, without premeditation, and even against my will."

Philosopher Friedrich Nietzsche wrote, "One can hardly reject completely the idea that one is the mere incarnation, or mouthpiece, or medium of some almighty power. . . . There is the feeling that one is utterly out of hand, with the most distinct consciousness of an infinitude of shuddering thrills that pass through one from head to foot . . . Everything occurs quite without volition, as if in an eruption of freedom, independence, power and divinity."

Artists seem to be more willing than scientists to articulate their experiences of dralalike energy and their feelings that true creativity comes from letting go of self-centered ambitions and opening to a greater world. Yet some great scientists and mathematicians have also described their creative process as involving a connection with patterns of energy and inspiration beyond their mundane experience.

The German mathematician Johann Friedrich Karl Gauss, who is considered one of the very greatest of mathematicians, struggled to prove a theorem for two years. "Finally two days ago," he wrote, "I succeeded, not on account of my painful efforts, but by the grace of God. Like a sudden flash of lightning, the riddle happened to be solved. I myself cannot say the conducting thread which connected what I previously knew with what made my success possible."

At the conference "Humans in Nature," held at The Naropa Institute in 1991, the eminent physicist George Sudarshan said that at the point of a substantial discovery, one feels not elation but weak knees, awe mingled with fascination. During these creative moments, Sudarshan said, one does not feel authorship but rather a sudden connection of mind and body. We do not create—we discover, we tune in. Suddenly, we are in a witnessing mode. This can happen in many daily-life situations, Sudarshan added, where there is a sudden conjunction of oneself and one's environment.

The people quoted above all had the ability to tune in to powerful energy and to let this energy flow through them and inform them. They had passion for what they did and they did it wholeheartedly. In addition to this they all had something very important in common: discipline. All of them had trained thoroughly in their field so that they had a tool or a way to focus the energy. They no longer had the awkwardness and self-consciousness associated with learning a skill. They had thoroughly mastered their form and so could relax and let go with it. This confident relaxation opened them to drala energy.

We have suggested in these last two chapters a few of the countless ways to invite drala energy to enter your life. The dralas also come into existence in our world and make themselves known to us when we call on them with heartfelt longing, motivated by genuine caring for ourselves and others. We can call on them and invoke their response and help. They will not *save* us from ourselves—that is up to us—but they can help us and are willing to help. Ed McGaa writes, "Spirit people from the spirit world are called on in the *Yuwipi*, spirit-calling ceremony. They have a higher realm much freer from the constraints of time and space than that in which we dwell. Therefore they can be of help to us if properly beseeched."

The dralas will gather round with their energy and help you to build your connections with other warriors and with the sacred world when you listen to your intuitive insights and to auspicious coincidence, when you pay attention to the elements and care for the earth, and when you regard every act as a gesture of contemplative art, and care for every object as a sacred object. They will gather in whatever you undertake when you do it with passion, wholeheartedness, and concern for others' well-being. Finally, they will gather whenever you raise windhorse, whether you are alone or in a group. To make these genuine connections is the way to begin to build an enlightened society, which is the fruition of the Shambhala teachings of sacred warriorship.

CHAPTER 19

Establishing Enlightened Society

ONNECTING WITH THE ENERGY of the dralas means
nothing if we keep the discovery to ourselves. We must
bring that energy to earth and help other people. We can
manifest windhorse in the good old day-to-day world of
friends and society. The purpose of the Shambhala teachings
is not merely to provide another path of personal spiritual
development. The purpose is to provide the means by which
we can begin, together, to build a community of warriors. We
all need the company of fellow travelers on a spiritual path.
We need a genuine human society.

Can we imagine a society where people trust each other
and are trustworthy; where no one is defensive because people are genuinely who they are and they trust themselves;
where people are not made to feel neurotic if they are sad;
where they can relax and do not feel the need for protection
from each other; where people help each other and care about
each other through all their ups and downs; where they take
care of the world and environment; where everyone can be
cheerful and delighted, listening to trees and dralas, dancing
with their energy? Does it sound like Shangri-la? This does
not have to be a utopian fantasy. It has been done before and
we can do it now, but we have to help each other.

Chögyam Trungpa reintroduced the modern world to dralas for the express purpose of helping to create a good society—an enlightened society—on earth again, in the context of the modern world and modern understanding. He constantly encouraged his students to pay attention to the state of the world and to the desperate need for a society founded on basic goodness, where people know how to nourish basic goodness, where they care for each other and act genuinely toward each other.

Given the state of the world today, enlightened society may seem far out of reach. But with the help of the dralas, we can touch into enlightened energy and bring it onto earth. Establishing an enlightened society is very much a question of relating with the real earth upon which we dwell, opening to it with bravery and tenderness, and caring for it. As Chögyam Trungpa wrote:

> Too often, people think that solving the world's problems is based on conquering the earth, rather than on touching the earth, touching the ground. That is one definition of the setting-sun mentality: trying to conquer the earth so that you can ward off reality. There are all kinds of deodorant sprays to keep you from smelling the real world, and all kinds of processed food to keep you from tasting raw ingredients. Shambhala vision is not trying to create a fantasy world where no one has to see blood or experience a nightmare. Shambhala vision is based on living on this earth, the real earth that grows crops, the earth that nurtures your existence. You can learn to live on this earth: how to camp, how to pitch a tent, how to ride a horse, milk a cow, build a fire. Even though you

may be living in a city in the twentieth century, you can learn to experience the sacredness, the *nowness* of reality. That is the basis for creating an enlightened society.

Authentic Action

Enlightened society does not come about by accident or by simpleminded magic. It is built step-by-step when our action is authentic. Authentic action is based on responding to situations, not on reacting to them. A reaction is mindless and automatic, and it always produces the same situation as the one you are reacting to. If you react to aggression, you will only produce more aggression. When you see a situation clearly and feel sympathy for it at the same time, you can be responsive to it and bring to it what it really needs. If it needs to be pacified, you can pacify it; if it needs to be enriched, you can enrich it; if it needs to be stopped, you can stop it.

To act in the world genuinely and responsively, we have to let go of continually manipulating our experience and elaborating what is really very simple. Instead of taking everything out of proportion, we can simply touch our gentleness, see what needs to be done, do it in a straightforward way, and let go. Seeing what needs to be cultivated and what needs to be stopped is very different from scheming to manipulate a particular situation to your own benefit. It is not at all the same as making judgments of things as "good" or "bad." It is much more subtle than that, like knowing when to say "yes" and when to say "no" to a child. You can know when to say "yes" or "no" to a child only if you care for her enough to feel how *she* feels and see what will benefit *her*.

A genuinely responsive action can have the quality of a contemplative art, as we described in the previous chapter:

1. *Preparation, meekness:* An action always needs to begin with listening, looking, and feeling the ground of the situation. Taking an attitude of humbleness at the beginning provides space for others to express their needs and fears as well as their positive contributions. Before acting, we can take a genuine interest in what is actually going on.

2. *Appreciation, perkiness:* Not being trapped in doubt and hesitation, we can approach the situation with a fresh attitude. No matter how grim it might appear to be, a breath of fresh air can bring some cheerfulness to it. Then, and only then, can we act without personal bias or misunderstanding.

3. *Execution, outrageousness:* If we are not caught up in our own or in other people's expectations and fears, we can be aware of moments of openness or gaps in the situation. We can step in without hesitation and without worrying about whether we are making a mistake. Therefore, it is possible to act in a way that transforms the energy of the situation rather than imposes energy on top of it.

4. *Ending, inscrutability:* Finally, the action must end without any expectation about the outcome. Any doubt and wandering mind that might creep in at the last moment can be cut, as well as any attachment to what we would like the outcome of our action to be and any self-congratulation that might come from a seemingly successful result.

Let us consider an example of how these four stages of contemplative action might apply in a specific situation. Perhaps you are in a group making an important decision that will affect the whole group and each member of it. The first stage, which lays the groundwork, is listening, listening, and listening. Listening to your own thoughts and to your heart before you speak, so that you know what you really want to say; listening attentively with open mind and heart to what others are saying; and encouraging others to listen to their own hearts and to others in the same way. Listening is perhaps the most important aspect of working together in a group. If this groundwork is not laid, true group decision is impossible. For example, the meeting might begin by going around the group with everyone expressing their first thoughts on the topic, with no commentary by others until the entire group has spoken. A more penetrating exercise that is very revealing is for each person to repeat what she thought she heard the previous speaker say before expressing her own view. This *really* makes you listen!

The next stage is to take a more active role in finding out what people really mean and want. Be genuinely curious, ask for more explanation or information if you do not understand what someone is saying, and encourage others to do the same. Listen behind the words to try to hear the feeling of what is being said. Pay attention to the body language. If two people have a strong conflict, try to find out what is behind the conflict: is it really a disagreement over the decision on the table, or is it a carryover from a past conflict between them? In these ways, you can encourage lively, inquisitive, and cheerful dialogue in the whole group.

Don't allow yourself to be caught up in taking sides on the issue or hoping that the decision will go the way you at first wanted. Do try to be aware of the group's larger vision, so that the final decision is made from this point of view rather than from weariness and confusion of conflicting ideas, as so often happens. You can always be ready to go beyond the bounds of the discussion to bring a fresh point of view or to resolve an impasse. At a certain point, you may begin to have a sense of the group mind and to see what is the best decision for the group as a whole. Because the groundwork of listening and inquisitiveness has been laid, you can offer that vision with clarity and confidence. Even though it may not be to everyone's liking, since you have tuned in to the group wisdom and waited for the right moment of opening, people will pay attention and pick up on this vision. Then let the final discussion unfold, not trying to manipulate the final outcome or jumping in and claiming credit for it at the last moment, so that it is truly a group decision and the group recognizes this.

Any genuinely beneficial action—personal or social—can come only from appreciating sacredness and basic goodness. Though it may be well-meaning, social action only makes situations worse when it stems from guilt, depression, or aggression. As the Dalai Lama has said on many occasions, "First practice not harming others, then perhaps you can help others." We can only bring others to an appreciation of their own basic goodness and the sacredness of our home, the earth, if our own actions stem from this appreciation. Genuine social action can come only from the personal discipline of being gentle and fearless, letting go of self-centered ambition, and helping others from a joyful and genuine heart.

What Is an Enlightened Society?

An enlightened society is not merely a group of individuals who just happen to be practicing together. Of course, some form of spiritual practice is essential in an enlightened society, and in a modern society, many different practices and traditions can coexist. However, to nourish basic goodness and provide opportunities for people to awaken to their goodness, the enlightened society itself has to be structured according to the principles of warriorship. The structure of society begins with one-to-one relationships. Its primary relationships are modeled in the family, however one defines this, and small community. In the personal relationships of the home, family, and friendships, we can practice creating an enlightened society. We have to begin here if it is to be genuine. The family provides a practical and immediate realm to practice sacredness in community. When sharing and working with others in a gentle and fearless way, the most mundane activities are sacred—even cleaning the toilet bowl. We can always be working to extend our feeling of family, and we could feel ourselves as part of a larger family—the world tribe of warriors—which includes our ancestors, our neighbors, and future generations.

The way to establish an enlightened society is not complicated or difficult to understand. We don't have to fight and compete, criticize each other, make the best deals, slaughter the competition, spy on them, and cut them off. We don't need to *worry* about ourselves—no matter what our personal history. We can wake up here and now, work together, and care for *others*. We can develop *maitri,* loving-kindness, for ourselves and others and allow each other space to make mistakes. The dralas are ready to help us establish enlightened human society again. Yet to do so, we cannot go back to a prescientific era. Even if we could, it would make no sense. We cannot forget what we have learned, our scientific discoveries and our technology. Enlightened society must be possible even within that context. We can only go forward in the vision of the *great eastern sun* rather than let ourselves slip into the darkness of the *setting sun.*

People can be decent and trustworthy when they recognize

basic goodness in each other. Being decent citizens of enlightened society comes from our practice and from our tender heart. Our decency is as literal as paying our debts on time, as much as we can, and trying not to disappoint our friends who have been kind to us. It is in relaxing in our discipline and having a natural sense of humor. It is practicing good speech—speaking gently and refraining from empty chatter or back-stabbing gossip. There is no benefit to be gained from slandering others. We can respect others in our society, starting with our parents, who gave us life, and our elders, who showed us how to go forward with vision and bravery. We can appreciate everyone who ever taught us anything—including insane leaders who teach us how important it is to be sane.

When there is respect for wisdom, leadership is natural in a good human society. People who practice together the disciplines of mindfulness and awareness, gentleness and fearlessness, and raising windhorse know who their leaders are. A leader with authentic presence raises people up—encourages them to follow the path of warriorship. When there is genuine leadership, based on the sanity and practice of the people, then the political setup respects a natural hierarchy. Nor does authoritarian rule arise, based on confusion and greed and keeping people down, because people are willing to be fearless as well as gentle.

The natural hierarchy of an enlightened society is like a flower reaching from the solid support of earth to the open space of heaven, in contrast to a lid that keeps people squashed down. We pay attention to the natural hierarchy of the sun and the sea and the moon, the flowers and the birds, the rocks and the earth, the dust bits and the garbage bits. If we slow down, are inquisitive, and let ourselves feel, then we can make our society a work of art.

Many of the conventional manners in modern society originated as ritual ways for people to show respect for each other or as gestures of peace—for example, the simple practice of shaking hands when you meet a friend. In Oriental societies, bowing to each other serves a similar function: by bending one's head and shoulders toward another person, one is offering one's dignity and windhorse to them as a gesture of trust and friendship. All of us practice ritual in everyday life in even the simplest interactions with one another. These daily rituals have tremendous subtlety to them, as Herbert Fingarette explains in *Confucius: The Secular as Sacred:*

> I see you on the street; I smile, walk toward you, put out my hand to shake yours. And behold—without any command, stratagem, force, special tricks or tools, without any effort on my part to make you do so, you spontaneously turn toward me, return my smile, raise your hand toward mine. We shake hands—not by my pulling your hand up and down or your pulling mine, but by spontaneous and perfect cooperative action. Normally we do not notice the subtlety and amazing complexity of this coordinated "ritual" act. This subtlety and complexity become very evident, however, if one has had to learn the ceremony from a book of instructions, or if one is a foreigner from a non handshaking country.
>
> Nor, normally, do we notice that this "ritual" has "life" to it, that we are "present" to each other, at least to some minimal extent. . . . This mutual respect is not the same as a conscious feeling of mutual respect;

when I am *aware* of a respect for you, I am much more likely to be piously fatuous or perhaps self-consciously embarrassed. . . . No, the authenticity of the mutual respect does not require that I consciously feel respect or focus my attention on my respect for you; it is fully expressed in the correct "live" and spontaneous performance of the *act*.

Such simple everyday rituals carry centuries of wisdom about how to bring peace into relationships. The raw wildness of being human has been tamed over thousands of years by our ancestors, both men and women, who in their wisdom developed rituals for all aspects of human intercourse. It is only because of this wisdom of our ancestors, combined with our own trust in basic goodness and appreciation of nowness, that there is any human society at all.

Today, the etiquette of simple decency or manners is often disdained as an expression of repression and lack of freedom, and people try to do away with it and become completely casual. When windhorse and the connection with dralas is lost, such mannered ways of behaving can be hollow and petty. They become just another form of externally imposed morality or authoritarian rule that in the end buries genuine goodness alive.

In the West, with the separation between the secular and the sacred, social norms of behavior and ceremonies have lost their heartfelt magical ritual quality and have become hollow shells. Ceremony has become empty-hearted theatrics. The result is further and further depression. Yet when we raise windhorse, we can feel the heart of our traditional ways. When we rediscover the heart in simple codes of behavior and group ceremonies, they become part of the celebration of life and of each other's humanity rather than rules and theatrics that are imposed on us through fear or ignorance.

Ritual and Ceremony in an Enlightened Society

Ritual and ceremony play a profound role in all human communities, even a community of two. Ruth-Inge Heinze points out that "Christians believe that, during the Holy Communion, Christ manifests in the host. Hindus know that, during rituals, their priests call the gods and these gods will manifest in the temple's statues. Other ethnic groups have rituals to evoke nature spirits [residing in stones, trees, mountains;] they may also evoke deified ancestors or the 'nameless' Divine, the life force per se." Yet Heinze also warns:

> In the twentieth century, we cannot revive the heritage of the paleolithic. Nobody can bring back the past. Our environment, the society we live in, even the climate, kept changing and so have forms of [ritual]. Like a snake shedding its skin, [ritual] has kept renewing itself, from the inside out. Imitators of ancient traditions, therefore, deceive themselves when they "religiously" repeat old patterns. Not familiar with the belief system on which "old" rituals have been built, their "blind" imitation obstructs the process of ritual development. In other words, different times give birth to different rituals.

Dolores LaChapelle, director of the Way of the Mountain Learning Center in Colorado, leads ceremonies and rituals to renew our connection with earth. Ritual, she says, "gives us new insight into truth. It is not something out there to be searched for, or worked towards, or fought for. Rather truth appears out of the interactions of all those present—human and non human—during the time of the Festival itself. The more one enters into the play of the Festival, the deeper one penetrates into the truth."

Ceremonies and rituals provide a gap in the normal flow of daily life for an entire group—a kind of group gap. They are nothing like the shows that are put on for tourists—and often for anthropologists. Rituals sometimes can continue without break for days, can involve fasting and sleeplessness and endless repetition of spoken phrases, drumming, chanting, and dancing. Ceremonies are also the observance of natural order, and their purpose is to align humans with natural events in order to contact dralas. As the ancient Taoists say, nature creates ceremonies and humans observe them.

Rituals bind human beings together, with each other, with the natural world, and with the dralas. You can generally feel the power of the dralas more easily when you invoke them in a group for the well-being of all. Group rituals, ceremonies, and festival celebrations invoke dralas for an entire society. Through group ceremonies that invite the dralas to join in, a society maintains wisdom, compassion, and power, as well as internal harmony and a connection with the nonhuman worlds on which they depend—the worlds of animals and plants, of mountains and lakes, and of dralas.

In Indonesia, the Javanese portray, as well as invoke, the interaction and collaboration between their dralas and humans in their shadow theater, the *wayang*. *Wayang* plays are performed, usually at night, primarily for the local "gods," ancestors, and all manner of spirits and demons; the human audience is just passing through. A *wayang* play portrays the Javanese view of reality. Within it, as in reality, many worlds and times—of the dralas of raw nature, of the ancestral heroes, of the ancient gods, and of human clowns—simultaneously coincide and interweave.

The performance of the play is itself considered a meeting, a meaningful coincidence of dralas and humans. It is in these coincidences that the subtlety of the *wayang* lies. According to anthropologist Alton Becker, the *wayang* places the present in the context of the past and the small human world in the context of the energies and power of nature and the cosmos:

> *Wayang* teaches men about their widest, most complete context, and it is itself the most effective way to learn about context. . . . Shadow theater, like any live art, presents a vision of the world and one's place in it which is whole and hale, where meaning is possible. The integration of communication (art) is, hence, as essential to a sane community as clean air, good food and medicine to cure errors. In all its multiplicity of meaning a well performed *wayang* is a vision of sanity.

Rituals often bring together energy patterns and meanings operating at different levels, such as plant, animal, and deity—a reflection of the principle "as above, so below." An example of this principle is the snake dance, described by Trudy Sable in her study of the Mi'kmaq people's traditional ways of transmitting knowledge to their children. In the snake dance, a line of dancers, often children, snakes around the dance floor with their hands on each other's shoulders or waists. The dance is accompanied by the sound of chanting and the rattling of a horn filled with pebbles. At one point, the leader stops, and the line spirals in around him to form a tight coil and then reverses and spirals out again. The line moves across to the other side of the dance floor, and the spiraling in and out is repeated.

The form of the dance is like the form of a medicinal plant called the *meteteskewey*. This, too, curves in a spiral and has seeds that rattle, like a rattlesnake. The medicine extracted from the *meteteskewey* can also be poison if it is not gathered at the proper time and used in the proper way. So the plant has a protector who needs to be properly honored. The protector of the plant is a serpent, or snake, the *jipika'm*. There are legends and stories about all these elements—the plant, the medicine, the turning of the seasons, and the protector serpent.

Sable suggests that the dance brings together three levels of meaning. On the external level, the rattling of the horn, filled with pebbles, mimics or reflects the rattling or tapping sound of the plant. And the chant that accompanies the dance seems to mimic the beat of the rattling leaves or stalk—*metetesk, metetesk, metetesk*—onomatopoetically. This plant, in turn, would be powerful medicine for the people if properly respected. Sable writes:

> On another level, the dance and chant most likely was a part of becoming, awakening, honoring, and possibly testing the energy of the *jipika'm,* the essence of the medicinal plant. The plant itself most likely mirrored the features of the *jipika'm* in both appearance and the sound it made. The sound and rhythm of the dance embodied the essence or nature of the *jipika'm,* which was inseparable from the medicine.
>
> The third level of the dance may have to do with "turning over" the seasons, and also be connected in

some way with the stars. At this level the dance would be performed to mark or effect the changing of the seasons. . . . There are two particular legends which talk about the turning over of the seasons, in connection with medicines.

Ritual brings group energy together to expand the atmosphere and transport the participants to drala time. It raises the windhorse of the group together so that those who are having trouble connecting can come along. It raises the awareness of the participants so that their perceptions are clarified and they can see sacredness in that moment. The powerful atmosphere of group windhorse attracts the dralas, and on it, they can descend.

Smoke is very frequently used to invoke the dralas during group rituals. For example, in Native American traditions, sweet grass is burned and brushed over participants with a sacred feather in a purification ceremony called "smudging." The sacred pipe is smoked and passed around the circle in a ritual that confirms the peaceful connectedness of the people in the circle to each other and to all beings.

In similar ceremonies using smoke to invoke the dralas, Shambhala and Tibetan Buddhist programs often open with the traditional Tibetan *lhasang* ceremony. *Lhasang* literally means "calling the gods." Dried juniper branches are burned on glowing charcoal. As the thick, sweet-smelling white smoke rises up, Shambhala groups chant a long invocation calling on the dralas. At the end of the chant, the participants circumambulate the smoke in a clockwise direction, chanting continuously the Tibetan victory cry: *"Ki, Ki, So, So: Lha Gyelo; Tak, Seng, Kyung, Druk: dYar Kye!" Ki* dispels negative energies, while *So* invites harmony and calls on the dralas.

Lha Gyelo means "victory to the gods," or dralas. *Tak, Seng, Kyung, Druk* means "Tiger, Lion, Garuda, Dragon"—these four animals symbolize the qualities of authentic presence that we described in chapter 12. And finally *dYar Kye!* is a joyful cry celebrating accomplishment. As the Shambhala warriors walk round and round the smoking juniper, chanting and carrying pennants representing the four animals, they pass through the smoke anything that they wish to purify and energize with drala energy. The smoke passes over them as well, and they breathe it in. One can feel the group windhorse rising and a potent energy gathering, descending on the smoke.

Enlightened Society Is Preexistent

An enlightened society is not a utopia, by any means. It is not a dreamland where everyone is already perfect. An enlightened society is one where people are willing to practice, to let go of their fear, to be genuine and kind to each other. There have been enlightened societies, though never utopias, many times before, all over the world, at various periods in history, in large civilizations and small tribal groups. Certainly, such societies had not only their own color and style, determined by the culture and beliefs of the times, but also their corruption and ego-centered forces. But each does, or did, recognize the fundamental goodness of humans and sought to nourish this goodness and to promote decency, dignity, elegance, and bravery in its people.

Sakyong Jampal Dradül, Chögyam Trungpa's son and successor, commented to a group of Shambhala students:

> When we think about enlightened society we often
> feel that we have to create something. I think it is

important to realize that nothing is created; everything already exists. The enlightenment of society is pre-existent. It is a matter of tuning in to the situation. You could go to countries that are based on similar principles of compassion and teachings on how to create enlightened society, but there is still corruption and abuse, so I don't think we can imitate any examples of that kind. Rather, we are trying to communicate with one another's dignity. So enlightenment and enlightened society are self-existing. If that realization comes about, then everything is possible.

Enlightened society wouldn't mean having cars that don't touch the ground or anything like that. Enlightened society is very much right here in this room, among ourselves. If we actually acknowledge basic goodness and tender heart, if we can acknowledge our fear or whatever we may feel, then there is some kind of common ground to work with. That is what we mean by enlightened society.

By trusting basic goodness, we can bring some joy and laughter, caring and tears to the world. We can conduct ourselves with dignity and wholesomeness. We can stop polluting the world with our neurosis. We can stop making war. *We* can do this. We don't have to worry about others doing it. Good society comes from this.

We start from square one and take a little baby step, and then another, and then suddenly we find ourselves leaping giant steps. When we plant a tender seed, we nurture and nourish it, water it and care for it. It sprouts tender shoots, uncertain and doubtful—and maybe afraid of being trampled on or eaten by the cat. But before we know it, it has grown into a lovely, blossoming bush—very quickly. The start is slow, but then it takes off with vigor and energy. We can start our enlightened society slowly, with patience, but we have to remember that time is running out. We have so little time to create our enlightened society. We cannot waste time in cocoon fascination. Time passes quickly. We thought it took so long for our baby to learn to walk, but oh, my, she's already leaving home. When we are very young, we think we have all the time in the world, but when we reach middle age, we know we don't.

Yet time is also endless. When we renounce the setting-sun world, we discover we already have an enlightened society, and suddenly, we *do* have all the time in the world. The time is *now*. We can go along *now* with the energy of the great, big, glorious sacred world, strange and full of magic. When we look around, we'll see that we don't have to struggle or create anything: our world is already enlightened. As Sakyong Jampal Dradül said, "If that realization comes about, then everything is possible."

Appendix

Training in the Sacred Path of Shambhala warriorship has been offered to the public since 1977. The training is offered in more than seventy Shambhala centers, in twenty-one countries in North and South America, Europe, Japan, New Zealand, and Australia. The programs take place in weekend and other formats and consist of talks, individual private interviews, group discussions, and instruction and practice of mindfulness-awareness, raising windhorse, and executing the stroke of primordial confidence.

For further details, please write, phone, fax, or E-mail:

Shambhala Training International
1084 Tower Road
Halifax, Nova Scotia
Canada B3H 2Y5

PHONE: (902) 423-3266
FAX: (902) 423-2750
E-MAIL: kikisoso@shambhala.org

References and Recommended Further Reading

General

Trungpa, Chögyam. *Shambhala: The Sacred Path of the Warrior.* Boston: Shambhala Publications, 1988. The original work on the Shambhala teachings; contains material relevant to every chapter in this book.

Basic Goodness

Carse, James P. *Breakfast at the Victory: The Mysticism of Ordinary Experience.* New York: HarperCollins, 1994.

Patterson, Freeman. *Photography and the Art of Seeing.* Toronto: Van Nostrand Reinhold, 1979.

Trungpa, Chögyam. *Born in Tibet.* Boulder, Colo.: Shambhala Publications, 1977.

Tulku Rinpoche, Ugyen. *Repeating the Words of the Buddha.* Kathmandu: Rangjung Yeshe, 1992.

Trust

Dossey, Larry. *Meaning and Medicine.* New York: Bantam, 1992.

Seng-ts'an. "On Trust in the Heart." In *Buddhist Texts through the Ages,* translated and edited by Edward Conze, I. B. Homer, David Snellgrove, and Arthur Waley. New York: Harper and Row, 1954.

Opening to Intuitive Wisdom

Black Elk, Wallace, and William S. Lyon. *Black Elk: The Sacred Ways of a Lakota*. New York: HarperCollins, 1991.

Cleary, J. C., trans. and ed. *Worldly Wisdom: Confucian Teachings of the Ming Dynasty*. Boston: Shambhala Publications, 1991.

Dong, Paul, and Aristide H. Esser. *Chi Gong: The Ancient Chinese Way to Health*. New York: Paragon, 1990.

Franck, Frederick. *Zen Seeing, Zen Drawing*. New York: Bantam, 1993.

Hayward, Jeremy, and Francisco Varela, eds. *Gentle Bridges: Conversations with the Dalai Lama on the Sciences of Mind*. Boston: Shambhala Publications, 1992.

Jahn, Robert, and Brenda Dunne. *Margins of Reality: The Role of Consciousness in the Physical World*. New York: Harcourt Brace Jovanovich, 1987.

Liu I-Ming. *Awakening to the Tao*. Translated by Thomas Cleary. Boston: Shambhala Publications, 1988.

Radin, Dean. *The Conscious Universe: The Scientific Proof of Psychic Phenomena*. New York: Harper Edge, 1997.

Sagarn, Keith, ed. *D. H. Lawrence and New Mexico*. Salt Lake City: Gibbs Smith, 1982. Thanks to Bill Gordon for this quote.

Suzuki, Shunryu. *Zen Mind, Beginner's Mind*. New York: Weatherbill, 1973.

Cocoon

Assagioli, Roberto. *Psychosynthesis*. London: Turnstone Press, 1975.

Gurdjieff, G. I. *Views from the Real World*. New York: Dutton, 1973.

Guterson, David. "No Place Like Home." *Harper's,* November 1992.

Langer, Ellen J. *Mindfulness*. Reading, Mass.: Addison-Wesley, 1989.

Moore, James. *Gurdjieff: The Anatomy of a Myth*. Shaftesbury, Dorset: Element, 1991.

Ouspensky, P. D. *In Search of the Miraculous: Fragments of an Unknown Teaching*. New York: Routledge and Kegan Paul, 1950.

Rowan, John. *Subpersonalities*. London: Routledge, 1990.

Sliker, Gretchen. *Multiple Mind: Healing the Split in Psyche and World*. Boston: Shambhala Publications, 1992.

Mindfulness and Awareness

Borysenko, Joan. *Minding the Body, Mending the Mind*. New York: Bantam, 1987.

Boyd, Doug. *Rolling Thunder*. New York: Delta, 1974.

Devereux, Paul. *Re-visioning the Earth: A Guide to Opening the Healing Channels between Mind and Nature*. New York: Fireside, 1996.

Kabat-Zinn, Jon. *Full Catastrophe Living*. New York: Delacorte, 1990.

Goldstein, Joseph, and Jack Kornfield. *Seeking the Heart of Wisdom*. Boston: Shambhala Publications, 1987.

Sogyal Rinpoche. *The Tibetan Book of Living and Dying*. New York: HarperCollins, 1992.

Thich Nhat Hanh. *Peace Is Every Step*. New York: Bantam, 1991.

Trungpa, Chögyam. *The Heart of the Buddha*. Boston: Shambhala Publications, 1991.

Walker, Susan, ed. *Speaking of Silence*. New York: Paulist Press, 1987.

Fear and Fearlessness

Epstein, Mark. *Thoughts without a Thinker*. New York: Basic Books, 1995.

Goldman, Daniel. *Vital Lies, Simple Truths: The Psychology of Self-Deception*. New York: Touchstone, 1985.

Katz, Nathan. *Buddhist and Western Psychology*. Boulder, Colo.: Prajna Press, 1953. For Chögyam Trungpa's quote on original sin.

Kornfield, Jack *A Path with Heart*. New York: Bantam, 1993.

Genuine Heart

Chodron, Pema. *The Wisdom of No Escape and the Path of Loving Kindness*. Boston: Shambhala Publications, 1991.

272   *References*

Fryba, Mirko. *The Art of Happiness: Teachings of Buddhist Psychology.* Boston: Shambhala Publications, 1989.

May, Gerald G. *The Awakened Heart: Opening Yourself to the Love You Need.* New York: HarperCollins, 1991.

Wegela, Karen Kissel. *How to Be a Help Instead of a Nuisance.* Boston: Shambhala Publications, 1996.

Welwood, John. *Journey of the Heart.* New York: HarperCollins, 1990.

Williamson, Marianne. *A Return to Love: Reflections on the Principles of a Course in Miracles.* New York: HarperCollins, 1992.

Windhorse

Csikszentmihalyi, Mihaly. *Flow: The Psychology of Optimal Experience.* New York: Harper and Row, 1990.

Gold, Peter. *The Circle of the Spirit: Navajo and Tibetan Sacred Wisdom.* Rochester, Vt.: Inner Traditions International, 1994.

McNeley, J. K. *Holy Wind in Navaho Philosophy.* Tucson: University of Arizona Press, 1981.

Rheingold, Howard. *They Have a Word for It.* Los Angeles: Tarcher, 1988. For the quote on baraka.

Authentic Presence

Angelou, Maya. *I Know Why the Caged Bird Sings.* New York: Bantam, 1971.

Cheng, François. *Empty and Full: The Language of Chinese Painting.* Boston: Shambhala Publications, 1994.

Coe, Stella Mathieu. *Ikebana.* Woodstock, N.Y.: Overlook Press, 1984.

Feuerstein, Georg. Introduction to *The Divine Madman,* by Keith Dowman. Clearlake, Calif.: Dawn Horse Press, 1990.

Forward, Nancy Wake. *White Mouse.* Melbourne: Macmillan Australia, 1982.

Herrigel, Eugen. *Zen in the Art of Archery.* New York: Vintage, 1971.

La Borde, Roger. "Gerald Red Elk." *Vajradhatu Sun,* December 1984.

Stevens, John. *The Sword of No-Sword.* Boston: Shambhala Publications, 1984.

Zim, Joshua. "Letter to Rinpoche." *Vajradhatu Sun,* December 1985/January 1986.

Patterns of Living Energy

Abram, David. *The Spell of the Sensuous: Perception and Language in a More-Than-Human World.* New York: Pantheon, 1996.

Armstrong, Karen. *A History of God.* New York: Ballantine, 1994.

Berman, Morris. *The Reenchantment of the World.* Ithaca, N.Y.: Cornell University Press, 1981.

Davis-Floyd, Robbie, and Sven Arvidson. *Intuition: The Inside Story.* New York: Routledge, 1997.

Hayward, Jeremy. *Letters to Vanessa: On Love, Science, and Awareness in an Enchanted World.* Boston: Shambhala Publications, 1997.

Hayward, Jeremy, and Francisco Varela, eds. *Gentle Bridges: Conversations with the Dalai Lama on the Sciences of Mind.* Boston: Shambhala Publications, 1992.

Huxley, Aldous. *The Perennial Philosophy.* New York: Harper and Row, 1944.

Masson, Jeffrey Moussaieff. *When Elephants Weep: The Emotional Life of Animals.* New York: Delacorte, 1995.

Matsuwa, don José, quoted in Joan Halifax, *Shamanic Voices.* New York: Arkana, 1979.

McGaa, Ed, Eagle Man. *Mother Earth Spirituality.* New York: HarperCollins, 1989.

Moyers, Bill. *Healing and the Mind.* New York: Doubleday, 1993.

Nollman, Jim. *Dolphin Dreamtime.* New York: Bantam, 1990.

Smith, Huston. *Forgotten Truth: The Common Vision of the World's Religions.* New York: HarperCollins, 1992.

Trungpa, Chögyam. *Journey without Goal: The Tantric Wisdom of the Buddha.* Boulder, Colo.: Prajna Press, 1981.

van der Post, Laurens. *The Lost World of the Kalahari.* New York: Harcourt Brace Jovanovich, 1956.

Wilber, Ken. *Sex, Ecology, Spirituality: The Spirit of Evolution.* Boston: Shambhala Publications, 1995.

Wilber, Ken, Jack Engler, and Daniel P. Brown. *Transformations of Consciousness.* Boston: Shambhala Publications, 1986.

Gods of All Ages and Cultures

Bloom, Harold. *Omens of the Millennium: The Gnosis of Angels, Dreams, and Resurrection.* New York: Riverhead, 1996.

Gersi, Douchan. *Faces in the Smoke.* Los Angeles: Tarcher, 1991.

Gold, Peter. *The Circle of the Spirit: Navajo and Tibetan Sacred Wisdom.* Rochester, Vt.: Inner Traditions International, 1994.

Halifax, Joan. *Shamanic Voices.* New York: Arkana, 1979.

Heinze, Ruth-Inge. *Shamans of the Twentieth Century.* New York: Irvington, 1991.

Irwin, Lee. *The Dream Seekers: Native American Visionary Traditions of the Great Plains.* Norman: Oklahoma University Press, 1994.

Maclean, Dorothy. *To Hear the Angels Sing.* Hudson, N.Y.: Lindisfarne Press, 1990.

Malidoma, Patrice Some. *Of Water and the Spirit: Ritual, Magic, and Initiation in the Life of an African Shaman.* New York: Putnam, 1993.

Maybury-Lewis, David. *Millennium: Tribal Wisdom and the Modern World.* New York: Viking, 1992.

Midal, Fabrice, personal communication. Thanks to Fabrice for the material on the Greek gods.

Ono, Sokyo. *Shinto: The Kami Way.* Rutland, Vt.: Tuttle, 1962.

Parisen, Maria. *Angels and Mortals: Their Co-Creative Power.* Wheaton, Ill.: Quest Books, 1990.

Samuel, Geoffrey. *Civilized Shamans: Buddhism in Tibetan Societies.* Washington: Smithsonian Institution Press, 1993.

Thompson, Robert Farris. *Flash of the Spirit: African and Afro-American Art and Philosophy.* New York: Vintage, 1984.

Thondup Rinpoche, Tulku. *Hidden Teachings of Tibet.* London: Wisdom, 1986.

Wall, Steve, and Harvey Arden. *Wisdom Keepers: Meetings with Native American Spiritual Elders.* Hillsboro, Oreg.: Beyond Words, 1990.

Dralas in Time and Place

Devereux, Paul. *Symbolic Landscapes: The Dreamtime Earth and Avebury's Open Secrets*. Glastonbury, England: Gothic Image Publications, 1992.

Isozaki, Arata. "Ma: Space-Time in Japan." *Japan Today*, no. 36.

Koestler, Arthur. *The Roots of Coincidence*. New York: Vintage, 1972.

Lawlor, Robert. *Voices of the First Day*. Rochester, Vt.: Inner Traditions, 1991.

Matsuoka, Seigow. "Aspects of Kami." *Japan Today*, no. 12.

Peat, F. David. *Synchronicity: The Bridge between Matter and Mind*. New York: Bantam, 1987.

Pilgrim, Richard, B. "Ma: A Cultural Paradigm." *Chanoyu Quarterly*, no. 46.

Dralas in Creativity, Art, and Ritual

Coe, Stella Mathieu. *Ikebana*. Woodstock, N.Y.: Overlook Press, 1984.

Fingarette, Herbert. *Confucius: The Secular as Sacred*. New York: Harper and Row, 1972.

Ghiselin, Brewster. *The Creative Process*. New York: Mentor, 1952.

Grudin, Robert. *The Grace of Great Things*. New York: Ticknor and Fields, 1990.

Harman, Willis, and Howard Rheingold. *Higher Creativity*. Los Angeles: Tarcher, 1984.

LaChapelle, Dolores. *Sacred Land, Sacred Sex*. Silverton, Colo.: Finn Hill Arts, 1988.

Mathieu, W. A. *The Listening Book*. Boston: Shambhala Publications, 1991.

Sardello, Robert. *Facing the World with Soul: The Reimagination of Modern Life*. New York: HarperPerennial, 1994.

CREDITS

Frontispiece, page ii: Drala calligraphy by Chögyam Trungpa, from the collection of Jeremy and Karen Hayward. Used by gracious permission of Diana J. Mukpo.

Page 106: "Escape," by D. H. Lawrence, from *The Complete Poems of D. H. Lawrence* by D. H. Lawrence. Edited by V. DeSola Pinto and F. W. Roberts. Copyright © 1964, 1971 by Angelo Ravagli and C. M. Weekley, Executors of the Estate of Frieda Lawrence Ravagli. Used by permission of Viking Penguin, a division of Penguin Books USA Inc.

Page 129: "Thursday," by William Carlos Williams, from *William Carlos Williams: Collected Poems 1909–1939*, vol. 1. Copyright 1938 by New Directions Publishing Corp. Reprinted by permission of New Directions Publishing Corp.

Pages 154 and 192: Poems by Rumi, from *Open Secret: Versions of Rumi*. Translated by John Moyne and Coleman Barks. Copyright 1984. Used by permission of Threshold Books, RD 4, Box 600, Putney, VT 05346.

INDEX

About the Authors

Jeremy Hayward received a Ph.D. in physics at Trinity College, Cambridge University, in 1965. This was followed by research in molecular biology at Massachusetts Institute of Technology and Tufts Medical School. During the research period, he also worked with a group practicing the Gurdjieff teachings on consciousness and its possible evolution in ordinary life. In 1970, Jeremy met the visionary Chögyam Trungpa, one of the most outstanding and renowned teachers to bring Tibetan Buddhism to America. Jeremy became a close friend of Chögyam Trungpa and one of his foremost students. He helped Trungpa to establish The Naropa Institute in Boulder, Colorado, where he served as vice president from 1975 to 1984, and remained a trustee until 1996. After Trungpa began to bring forth the spiritual teachings of Shambhala warriorship, in 1976, Jeremy worked closely with him to develop Shambhala Training, a nonreligious spiritual path for ordinary life. He is now education director of Shambhala Training International.

Karen Hayward studied theater at the University of Denver and spent several years in repertory theater. She was also a close friend and student of Chögyam Trungpa from 1972 until his death in 1987, and has taught in the Shambhala Training program since its beginning. She was the first director of the Kalapa Ikebana school of flower arranging, which was founded by Chögyam Trungpa. She helped establish The Naropa Institute in 1974, creating the department for student services and meditation instruction. Presently she is working with mind-body energy as a Shiatsu therapist.